PREPARING EDUCATORS TO
INVOLVE FAMILIES

PREPARING EDUCATORS TO
INVOLVE FAMILIES

From Theory to Practice

Heather B. Weiss
Harvard Graduate School of Education, Harvard Family Research Project

Holly Kreider
Harvard Graduate School of Education, Harvard Family Research Project

M. Elena Lopez
Harvard Graduate School of Education, Harvard Family Research Project

Celina M. Chatman
University of Chicago, Center for Human Potential and Public Policy, Harris Graduate School of Public Policy Studies

Editors

SAGE Publications
Thousand Oaks ■ London ■ New Delhi

For information:

Sage Publications, Inc.
2455 Teller Road
Thousand Oaks, California 91320
E-mail: order@sagepub.com

Sage Publications Ltd.
1 Oliver's Yard
55 City Road
London EC1Y 1SP
United Kingdom

Sage Publications India Pvt. Ltd.
B-42, Panchsheel Enclave
Post Box 4109
New Delhi 110 017 India

Printed in the United States of America

Library of Congress Cataloging-in-Publication data

Preparing educators to involve families : from theory to practice / edited by Heather B. Weiss . . . [et al.] (Harvard Family Research Project).
    p. cm.
Includes bibliographical references and index.
ISBN 1-4129-0909-0 (cloth) — ISBN 1-4129-0910-4 (pbk.)
    1. Education, Elementary—Parent participation. 2. Elementary school teachers—Training of. 3. Home and school. 4. Child development. I. Weiss, Heather Bastow. II. Harvard Family Research Project.
LB1048.5.P74 2005
372.119'2—dc22
                                    2004025362

This book is printed on acid-free paper.

05   06   07   08   09   10   9   8   7   6   5   4   3   2   1

Acquiring Editor:	Diane McDaniel
Editorial Assistant:	Marta Peimer
Production Editor:	Sanford Robinson
Typesetter:	C&M Digitals (P) Ltd.
Copy Editor:	Terese Platten, Freelance Editorial Services
Indexer:	Teri Greenberg
Cover Designer:	Edgar Abarca

Contents

Preface

This book is a collaboration of several members of the John D. and Catherine T. MacArthur Foundation's Research Network on Successful Pathways through Middle Childhood. The book features teaching cases based on a wealth of research data from key Network studies, as well as the theoretical perspectives of several Network members to provide insight into the cases. The Network was established to examine influences on children's outcomes during their elementary school years, to explore ways to increase the likelihood of successful outcomes, and to use research findings to inform policy and practice. Studies conducted under the auspices of the Network focus on several major areas of research, including continuity across the life span, psychological processes, diversity, intervention, and context. Important developmental contexts under investigation include schools, family, community, and culture, as well as children's individual differences.

Through a collaborative Network effort, this book is able to represent many of these themes and contexts of child development during the elementary school years. In addition, the leading role of the Harvard Family Research Project (HFRP) enables this book to home in on the crucial educational topic of family involvement. Specifically, many of the cases in this book come from the School Transition Study (STS), a Network study codirected by Heather Weiss at HFRP and Deborah Stipek at Stanford. The STS is a longitudinal mixed-method study of diverse low-income children's development from kindergarten through the fifth grade that followed approximately 400 children in three geographic sites across the United States. The involvement of families in their children's learning is a main area of investigation. A case study component with in-depth qualitative data on a subsample of 23 children and their primary caregivers, teachers, and schools during first and second grade yielded rich data from which to construct teaching cases on dilemmas of practice between families and schools.

HFRP also brought to this endeavor a research background in teacher preparation for family involvement. In 1997, HFRP reviewed state teacher certification requirements and found that only 22 states' requirements mentioned family involvement. HFRP then surveyed 60 teacher education programs in these 22 states and found that family involvement training was often limited in its content focus, teaching methods, and delivery (Shartrand, Weiss, Kreider, & Lopez, 1997). In addition, the survey revealed the need for increased faculty research on family involvement and teaching tools for course development.

Subsequent research by others has substantiated the need for greater preparation of preservice teachers to involve families in children's education (Broussard, 2000; Epstein, Sanders, & Clark, 1999; Evans-Schilling, 1999; Foster & Loven, 1992; Tichenor, 1998; Winkelman, 1999). Research has also highlighted the potential for course experiences in family involvement to offer prospective teachers the knowledge, skills, and confidence to partner with families more effectively (Morris & Taylor, 1998). This volume is one attempt to help equip teachers with the skills they need and seek through their coursework.

In short, this book intersects two important research pathways, that of HFRP and its research on preparing educators in family involvement, and that of the MacArthur Network and its research on successful development in middle childhood. This book also represents the key intersection of research, theory, and practice, a linkage that has not been well-considered in previous education casebooks. Finally, this book is fortunate to appear alongside other powerful applied books emerging from Network research, including books that thoughtfully examine methodological and contextual issues in developmental research and that can serve as additional resources to readers wishing to learn more about development in the elementary school years (see Cooper, Garcia Coll, Bartko, Davis, & Chatman, in press; Huston & Ripke, forthcoming; Weisner, 2005).

We would like to thank the John D. and Catherine T. MacArthur Foundation for generously supporting the development of this book as part of its Research Network on Successful Pathways through Middle Childhood. We also would like to thank the DeWitt Wallace-Reader's Digest Fund, as part of its School/Family Partnerships Initiative, and Kraft Foods, an operating company of the Philip Morris Companies, both of which partially funded the development of individual teaching cases from the School Transition Study.

We would like to thank Margaret Caspe and Angela Shartrand for their invaluable editing support on teaching cases, discussion questions, and theoretical approaches; Cassandra Wolos for thorough bibliographic research and copyediting; Jacquelynne Eccles for expert feedback on the conceptualization of the book; Eleanor Drago-Severson and Ellen Mayer for advice on book publishing; and Diane McDaniel, Margo Crouppen, and Marta Peimer at Sage Publications for editorial guidance. We would like to thank Lee Shumow, Sandra Christenson, Helen M. Marks, Leo R. Sandy, and Constance Flood for reviewing our prospectus, and Joel Nitzberg, Helen M. Marks, Amy J. Malkus, Judith Mayton, and Ithel Jones for reviewing our draft manuscript. Finally, we thank study participants from the many studies reflected in this volume for sharing their experiences, feelings, and struggles in bridging children's worlds of home and school.

References

Broussard, A. C. (2000). Preparing teachers to work with families: A national survey of teacher education programs. *Equity and Excellence in Education, 33,* 41–49.

Cooper, C. R., García Coll, C. T., Bartko, W. T., Davis, H. M., & Chatman, C. (in press). *Developmental pathways through middle childhood: Rethinking context and diversity as resources.* Mahwah, NJ: Erlbaum.

Epstein, J. L., Sanders, M. G., & Clark, L. A. (1999). *Preparing educators for school-family-community partnerships.* Baltimore, MD: Center for Research on the Education of Students Placed At Risk.

Evans-Schilling, D. (1999). Preparing educational leaders to work effectively with families: The parent power project. In M. S. Ammon (Ed.), *Joining hands: Preparing teachers to make meaningful home-school connections* (pp. 101–121). Sacramento, CA: California Department of Education.

Foster, J., & Loven, R. (1992). The need and directions for parent involvement in the 90's: Undergraduate perspectives and expectations. *Action in Teacher Education, 14*(3), 13–18.

Huston, A. C., & Ripke, M. N. (Eds.) (forthcoming). *Middle childhood: Contexts of development.* New York: Cambridge University Press.

Morris, V. G., & Taylor, S. I. (1998). Alleviating barriers to family involvement in education: The role of teacher education. *Teaching and Teacher Education, 14*(2), 219–231.

Shartrand, A., Weiss, H., Kreider, H., & Lopez, M. E. (1997). *New skills for new schools: Preparing teachers in family involvement.* Washington, DC: U.S. Department of Education.

Tichenor, M. S. (1998). Preservice teachers' attitudes toward parent involvement: Implications for teacher education. *Teacher Educator, 33*(4), 248–259.

Weisner, T. S. (Ed.) (2005). *Discovering successful pathways in children's development: Mixed methods in the study of childhood and family life.* Chicago: University of Chicago Press.

Winkelman, P. (1999). Family involvement in education: The apprehensions of student teachers. In M. S. Ammon (Ed.), *Joining hands: Preparing teachers to make meaningful home-school connections* (pp. 79–100). Sacramento, CA: California Department of Education.

Introduction:
Preparing Educators
in Family Involvement

Inés didn't know what to do. Her daughter Nina sat under the kitchen table crying, refusing to continue with her homework. Inés was exasperated. Nina had been working on her homework assignment for the past three hours and was beside herself. "I don't like it, I don't know what to do," she cried.

In the beginning of the year, Nina had been placed in a bilingual first-grade classroom. Inés went to the school and talked with the principal to request an all-English setting. Inés felt it was good for her daughter to be in an all-English classroom so that Nina could avoid the struggle with English that her mother faced. She felt that for her daughter to become a professional in America, she had to be fluent in English. Inés herself enrolled in English classes at the community high school and, at the advice of her close friends from church, only spoke to her daughter in English. Inés was grateful that the principal permitted the switch but then faced the problem of not being able to help her daughter with homework.

At the parent-teacher conference in the beginning of the year, Inés was afraid to tell the teacher, Ms. Chesin, about her difficulties helping Nina with homework and understanding what was sent home. Nina translated throughout most of the meeting. When Inés asked the teacher for more direction on how to help, Ms. Chesin encouraged Inés to read with her daughter in Spanish at home.

With the spring parent-teacher conference coming up in the next few weeks, Inés was prepared to ask again for help with the homework, but she also anticipated Ms. Chesin recommending a bilingual placement. She wondered if she had made the wrong decision by choosing a monolingual classroom for her daughter. Would Nina be better served in a bilingual classroom? How could Inés know?

The case of Inés points to some of the many facets of family involvement in education, including homework help, advocating for one's child, and navigating the choices of the school system. By **family involvement**, we mean the activities that families engage in to support their children's learning, whether at home, at school, or in the community. As the story of Inés illustrates, family involvement has multiple dimensions, including parental aspirations, parenting behaviors, and school relationships. Inés had high hopes for her daughter's success through going to school and learning English. She offered herself as a model for her daughter by taking English classes. She advocated her daughter's classroom placement with the principal and participated in parent-teacher conferences. Yet she questioned the outcome of her involvement and struggled to help with her child's homework. Like Inés, many parents want to be involved in their children's learning, but find it challenging because they lack information on which to base their decisions, confidence to approach teachers, and practical skills to help their children.

Many teachers want to help parents, too, but lack the skills and school supports that facilitate meaningful conversations with parents. Today's teachers meet increasingly diverse students and families, with different languages and ways of thinking about learning; they find parents who work and have little time to come to school; and those serving poor communities encounter families who are overwhelmed with the strains of poverty and the lack of supports in their neighborhoods. Teachers, however, who actively contact the families of low-achieving students do make a difference in improving their performance over time (Westat & Policy Study Associates, 2001). Through outreach, families can provide their children with the home supports that align with school expectations. By understanding families, teachers can align their instruction with the knowledge and resources that families possess or what is referred to as family "funds of knowledge." To prepare for home-school relationships, including solving the complicated issues such as those in Inés' case, educators can benefit from preservice training and continuing professional development in family involvement.

Teachers need new skills to develop strong partnerships with families. Their repertoire of skills should include being able to do the following:

- Relate to parents—and families—in ways that build trust and encourage participation
- Communicate with parents the new standards that are affecting all schools and all children
- Learn about parent involvement from parents' perspective and not solely from the school's official policies
- Communicate with and engage families who come from different socioeconomic and cultural backgrounds than their own

About This Casebook

We created this casebook as a teaching tool to encourage the integration of family involvement in the preparation of teachers and school administrators. A vast literature on family involvement confirms that when families are involved in children's learning, no matter what their income or background, they have a positive influence on student social and academic outcomes (Henderson & Mapp, 2002). Despite the importance of family-school partnerships, teacher education programs frequently do not cover family involvement in their curriculum (Epstein, Sanders, & Clark, 1999; Shartrand, Weiss, Kreider, & Lopez, 1997). New teachers, in particular, feel that they lack adequate preparation in working with families (Public Education Network, 2003).

In developing this casebook for educators, we focused on connecting theory and research to practice in family involvement. We adopted Ecological Systems Theory as an overarching framework for thinking about the multiple contexts of children's lives and for considering how families, schools, and communities can best support child development. Within this framework, seven theoretical perspectives serve as "lenses" through which to analyze family involvement practice. We also chose to use cases to capture the complexity of the relationships of families, schools, and communities and paid particular attention to developing cases that focus on dilemmas of practice—difficult and ambiguous situations in which educators and parents must negotiate their differences. The cases reflect the lives of children in the elementary school years and their families.

ECOLOGICAL SYSTEMS THEORY

Ecological Systems Theory highlights the importance of context in children's development (Bronfenbrenner, 1979, 1986a; Bronfenbrenner & Crouter, 1982). Context is understood in terms of various systems[1] that influence the child's development either directly (e.g., through daily routines and interactions that occur in the child's immediate context) or indirectly (i.e., through more distal factors that impact those routines and interactions). A primary tenet of Ecological Systems Theory is that every level of the ecological system is interconnected and thus can influence all other subsystems. These influences are reciprocal rather than unidirectional. Thus, routines and interactions in the child's classroom affect what happens in the child's home and vice versa. Ecological Systems Theory has the capacity to explain how issues such as social and economic policies (considered distant from a child's everyday experience) affect what happens in the child's immediate contexts. It is a theory that is powerful precisely because it portrays the complexity of these multiple levels and helps explain the mechanisms through which children and their families are influenced.

Ecological Systems Theory is represented visually as a set of concentric circles surrounding the child (See Figure FM.1). Immediate contexts in which the child interacts comprise the microsystem. Adults that nurture and teach children, peers and siblings who play and socialize with them, and settings such as day care, home, and school constitute the **microsystem**. The **mesosystem** is the next level of Ecological Systems Theory and involves interactions and relationships between and among individuals and settings that comprise the microsystem. For example, mesosystem interactions include those between parents and teachers (individuals) and among microsystem settings (e.g., child care centers, afterschool programs, and/or schools). In this way, the mesosystem represents the degree of connection, coordination, and continuity across a child's microsystems.

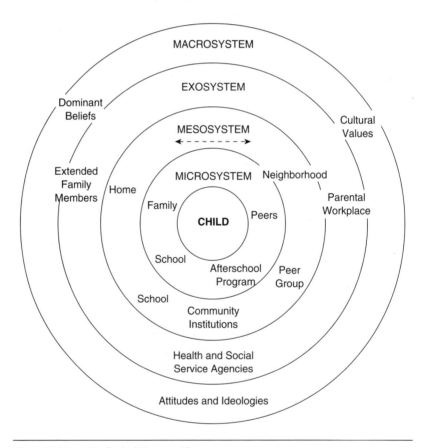

Figure FM.1   Ecological Systems Theory

SOURCE: Adapted with permission from Zigler, E. F., & Stevenson, M. F. (Eds.) (1993). *Children in a Changing World: Development and Social Issues* (p. 10). Pacific Grove, CA: Brooks/Cole.

The **exosystem** of the Ecological Systems Theory is comprised of the contexts that influence the child indirectly. Thus, the exosystem exerts its influence on the child via its impact on individuals and institutions in the child's microsystem. For example, parents' workplaces may institute new work schedules that interfere with parents' ability to read to their children each night, which then affects the children's literacy achievement. The **macrosystem** operates at the broadest level of influence and is comprised of political systems, social policy, culture, economic trends, and so forth. Macrosystems determine to a great extent the resources, opportunities, and constraints present in the lives of children and families. For example, welfare reform (initiated at the national level) has exerted control over parents' access to economic support and has changed the conditions under which parents receive that support and the ways that they provide and care for their children. Cultural practices and belief systems affect what parents and teachers prioritize and value and how they organize their daily routines to achieve their goals.

The **chronosystem** represents the element of time, both in the individual's life trajectory (e.g., infancy, childhood, adolescence, adulthood, etc.) and historical context (See also Bronfenbrenner, 1986b). This volume focuses on the developmental period of middle childhood, and at a time in which economic factors and technological developments profoundly shape the contexts and settings in which children live. For example, economic and cultural changes in society over the past 50 years have led to a dramatic increase in dual-income families, which in turn has affected children's daily routines and experiences through nonparental care. Furthermore, the rise of computer use and other visual media have had a profound impact on how children spend leisure time, learn cultural norms and values, and gather information. It is easy to lose sight of how important these changes have been to children's daily life experiences and to fail to consider how they influence their development.

THE CASES: FAMILY INVOLVEMENT DILEMMAS

We created this casebook to address some of the difficulties that schools face in establishing communication and meaningful relationships with low-income families whose racial, ethnic, cultural, and linguistic backgrounds differ from those of school staff. The cases present situations requiring problem solving that sharpen teachers' critical thinking skills and also expose them to perspectives of parents, students, and other family members that they may not learn about through a teacher's daily routine. According to Dennis Shirley, professor at Boston College, teachers must know how to "think critically quickly, creatively, and responsively" (Harvard Family Research Project, 2003). Such skills are best learned through reflection and problem solving in the classroom and in field settings. This volume supports skill development by offering teachers, through the use of cases for discussion-based learning, a broad understanding of the constraints on and opportunities for engaging families in children's education. Supplementing this book, we at the Harvard Family Research Project also host the Family Involvement Network of Educators (FINE; www.finenetwork.org), an online resource that provides up-to-date research, bibliographies, and additional teaching cases on family involvement in education.

The 12 cases in this book focus on contemporary educational issues that defy easy answers but instead encourage creative inquiry and reflection. They illustrate dilemmas of practice that occur when teachers, principals, and other school personnel construct (or fail to construct) relationships with families. Parents and teachers find themselves in ambiguous situations in which they must make choices among alternative courses of action. Their situations invite users of this casebook to discuss these alternatives and propose resolutions. Specifically, the dilemmas in this casebook center on key issues in family involvement, such as how families and schools construct their roles in children's learning, how economic and time poverty interfere with involvement wishes, and cultural differences that arise between families and schools.

Despite a common desire to see children make strides in their learning, parents and teachers often hold different viewpoints about the roles of families and schools. They experience what Sara Lawrence-Lightfoot (1978, p. 26) has described as the ambiguities that grow out of "overlapping worlds with fuzzy boundaries." Some of the contested areas of family and school control that are highlighted in this casebook include defining academic progress, advocating student safety, and negotiating afterschool time for children. We hope that a careful examination of these situations leads readers to focus on the right questions, those that go beyond the blaming of either parents or teachers for the failure of involvement and instead emphasize the relationship between meaningful involvement opportunities afforded by schools and parental agency.

The dilemmas in this casebook reflect, in particular, what happens in schools and communities that are resource poor, where teachers often do not reflect the communities they serve and where low-income parents struggle with making a living and meeting school expectations of involvement at home and in school. Several cases focus on what Chin and Newman (2002) have described as "time poverty," referring to the competing demands on the time of working poor families to earn a living (often by putting in long work hours and taking irregular shifts), and to support and monitor their children's learning. These cases invite analysis that moves from the microcosm of interpersonal relations to the macrocosm of social issues that impact children's learning.

Race, culture, and class divisions provide the context for most of the cases in this volume and present another dimension to dilemmas of practice.

Teachers' and school administrators' perceptions of parents' socioeconomic backgrounds influence how they interact with parents, and whether or not they support or reject parent strategies of involvement (Bloom, 2001; Lareau & Horvat, 1999). All too often, school personnel treat poor parents from a deficit perspective, which becomes a barrier to family involvement. The larger school climate, however, influences the home-school relationship. When schools nurture a strong sense of community where respectful relationships exist among teachers, school leaders, and parents, class and cultural differences do not necessarily become barriers to meaningful family involvement (Bryk & Schneider, 2002; Lewis & Forman, 2002). By presenting real world situations, the cases in this book invite readers to examine the multiple perspectives of actors in their specific class, culture, and institutional contexts.

About Family Involvement in Education

Family involvement in education refers to the beliefs, attitudes, and activities of parents and other family members to support children's learning. Although such involvement usually focuses on parents, it also includes grandparents, siblings, and extended family members who have significant responsibility in a child's upbringing. Family involvement covers a broad range of constructs, including parental aspirations and expectations, parenting behaviors, and participation in school activities. Some consistent findings about family involvement *processes* suggest their significance for children's learning and development.

- Parent *values and expectations* are associated with children's motivation to learn as well as their academic achievement (Fan & Chen, 2001; Scott-Jones, 1995). Beneficial values can take the form of high but realistic educational aspirations and expectations, a focus on effort rather than ability, and the value placed on specific subject matter.
- Parent *behaviors* around learning activities such as reading, conversations about school-related matters, and visiting the public library are correlated with improvements in children's reading comprehension (Anderson, 2000; Lee & Croninger, 1994).
- Parent *participation in school*—in the form of attending conferences and class events and volunteering—also supports student achievement. Such involvement is associated with students' earning high grades, enjoying school, avoiding grade repetition, suspension and expulsion, and participating in extracurricular activities (Nord, Brimhall, & West, 1997).
- Parent *leadership* in decision-making bodies and through community organizing brings about school policy changes and delivers new resources to under-resourced schools (Shirley, 1997). These changes create the school conditions that enhance student achievement (Gold, Simon, & Brown, 2002).

Far from being straightforward, the relationship between family involvement and student achievement is complex and varies with a host of factors such as the type and circumstances of involvement. For example, one large survey of children from kindergarten through third grade found that family involvement in the home strongly predicted children's achievement in math and reading, and that the quality of parent-teacher interactions was positively related to children's socioemotional adjustment (Izzo, Weissberg, Kasprow, & Fendrich, 1999). The frequency of parent-teacher contacts, however, did not have the same beneficial outcomes for children and could indicate that a parent is responding to a child who is not doing well in school. The research nonetheless points to the importance of the home environment and suggests that schools can improve their efforts to communicate with parents about their children's academic progress and to promote constructive parent-teacher relations.

Family involvement must be understood as dynamic: Differences in how and when family involvement matters for children's school success develop over time. Some longitudinal research studies suggest that earlier involvement leads to stronger effects than later involvement. In a study of low-performing Title I students in elementary and middle grades, higher parent involvement increased student achievement in both reading and math, but younger children made the most improvement (Shaver & Walls, 1998). A study of an early intervention program in the Chicago public schools also reported that parents' school involvement while their children attended preschool and kindergarten had benefits for children at age 14, including higher reading achievement, lower rates of grade retention, and fewer years in special education (Miedel & Reynolds, 1999). Through their participation in the early intervention program, parents may have developed the commitment to remain involved in their children's education and to monitor their school progress over time. However, family involvement tends to decline as children move through the upper grades. This is unfortunate because family involvement continues to have a positive effect on student achievement in middle and high school (Keith & Keith, 1993; Patrikakou, 2004). The benefits of early and continuous family involvement carry implications for schools and communities to strengthen their approaches to promote family involvement from prekindergarten to twelfth grade.

A CHILD DEVELOPMENT PERSPECTIVE

Family involvement is important to understand in terms of child development. This casebook focuses on family involvement in the educational experiences of elementary school children (roughly ages 6 to 12 years). Originally thought of as a period of relative stagnation during which children simply refine all the skills they acquired in early childhood and prepare for adolescence (Eccles, 1999), researchers can now identify changes in cognition, social relationships, and identity commonly associated with the elementary school years or **middle childhood** (Sameroff & Haith, 1996), many of which have relevance for family-school relationships.

During the elementary years, children use more sophisticated strategies in their reasoning about their world and develop reading and math skills, self-awareness, self-reflection and evaluation, and perspective-taking (Canobi, Reeve, & Pattison, 2003; Harter, 1988, 1999; Morris, Bloodgood, Lomax, & Perney, 2003).

Children enter formal schooling at about this time in many cultures and start to spend a significant portion of their lives away from their families and outside of their homes (Eccles, 1999; Erikson, 1968). They experience new interactions with significant adults such as teachers and other school personnel and with a wide range of peers and diverse types of families. They take on new social roles and are exposed to feedback from new people about their competencies in various activities. Often, they are presented with frequent opportunities for self-comparison with their peers. The extent to which these comparisons are consistently favorable or unfavorable may begin to shape children's sense of competency and esteem (Pomerantz, Ruble, Frey, & Greulich, 1995).

With entry into formal schooling, children must grapple with increasing demands that they maintain control over their behavior (e.g., adhere to rules, be well-behaved; Entwisle & Alexander, 1998; Goldsmith, Aksan, Essex, Smider, & Vandell, 2001). At the same time, they are beginning to be afforded more freedom and autonomy from their parents and other adults. To meet adults' expectations while exercising more choice, children must learn to monitor their own behavior, judge adults' perceptions of them and of others and make adjustments based on both of these sources of information. These developmental tasks extend to children's roles in family-school relationships. One study noted that elementary school children often take an active role in shaping when and how their parents are involved in their schooling, driven in part by their growing desire for autonomy (Edwards & Alldred, 2000).

During this time, children begin to formulate notions about who they are, what they are good or not good at, and what they are capable or incapable of. This information will come from many sources other than their families, such as teachers and other adults in the schools, coaches, other parents, friends, and peers (Eccles, 1999). Children are faced then with the task of making sense of this information, integrating it with past knowledge of the self, and speculating about prospects for the future. In this critical period of cognitive and behavioral development, identity formation, social comparisons, and the integration of knowledge from multiple sources, it is critical that families and schools work together to optimize children's positive experiences in their early schooling.

APPROACHES TO FAMILY INVOLVEMENT IN EDUCATION

No one best approach represents how families and schools can work together. Several educators have proposed frameworks and strategies that schools and communities can apply and adapt to their localities. Following are some of the more commonly used frameworks that guide school and community practice.

1. A family-school partnership

Joyce Epstein contends that students achieve greater success if families, schools, and communities operate as overlapping spheres of influence in a child's life, interacting frequently and sharing common goals (Epstein, 1995). By emphasizing their overlap, Epstein provides schools with a vision of what they can strive to be: family-like schools. These schools recognize each child's individuality and treat each child as special. Likewise, school-like families recognize children as students and reinforce the importance of school, homework, and other activities that build on student success.

Epstein specifies six types of family and community involvement in education that schools can support. Type 1, *parenting*, encourages families to create home environments that support success in school. Type 2, *communicating*, helps families and schools share information. Type 3, *volunteering*, brings parents into school buildings. Type 4, *learning at home*, supports parents as they assist their children with schoolwork. Type 5, *decision making*, invites parents to participate in schools' policy development. Type 6, *community collaboration*, seeks to integrate community resources into school programs to enrich student learning and provide nonacademic support.

According to Epstein, children are likely to achieve both academic and nonacademic success when a partnership of support exists between families, schools, and communities. The six types of family involvement promote students' improved organizational abilities, motivation, communication skills, classroom performance, respect for parents, and awareness of the future.

2. A comprehensive school improvement model

James Comer's program begins with the premise that children's healthy development is a crucial factor in their learning (Comer, Haynes, & Joyner, 1996). Children learn well when adults in their lives create a healthy climate for their development. Conditions in many poor, urban schools, though, are not conducive to healthy child development and learning. In these schools, personnel do not fully understand the development of disadvantaged children and develop low expectations of them.

Based on Comer's research, the school development program restructures schools so that adults in a child's life—parents, school personnel, community members—interact positively and create a caring and predictable environment conducive to child development and learning. A school planning and management team, a parent team, and a student and staff support team provide mechanisms through which to promote these interactions.

Parent involvement is considered to be the cornerstone of the program. Parents bridge the gap between home and school and bring an understanding of the social development needs and strengths of children to the daily activities and decision-making process in schools. (Haynes et al., 1996).

The school development program creates the following three mechanisms for social interactions that support child development and learning:

1. The school planning and management team, consisting of the principal and representative teachers, parents, and other school staff, develops and monitors a comprehensive school plan for the academic, school climate, and staff development goals of the school.

2. The parent team involves parents at three different levels of participation. At the first level, the majority of parents support the school by attending parent-teacher conferences, reinforcing learning at home, and participating in social activities. At the second level, some parents serve in the school as volunteers and paid aides to support learning activities. At the third level, parents who are selected by other parents serve on a school planning and management team.

3. The student and staff support team, consisting of the school psychologist, guidance counselor, school nurse, and other staff with child development and mental health experience, consults with teachers and the school planning and management team on child development and behavior issues.

Because parents are crucial to the success of the program, schools need to improve their outreach and involvement strategies. Successful schools build trust, plan well, empower parents, and monitor activities continuously to improve responsiveness to parents (Haynes et al., 1996).

3. Funds of knowledge

"Funds of knowledge," initially conceptualized by Luis Moll and his colleagues, refers to the knowledge and skills that households have accumulated over time to ensure household functioning and well-being (Moll, Amanti, Neff, & Gonzalez, 1992). A household's cultural and cognitive resources have great potential for classroom instruction, a viewpoint often missing in school relationships with immigrant and working-class households. For example, by learning about the occupations and daily routines of households, a teacher or network of teachers can develop classroom projects connected to the lives of children and their families. Children participate as active learners as they use their social contacts outside the classroom to gain new knowledge. Parents also participate in the classroom as experts who share intimate knowledge about a topic.

The funds of knowledge approach proposes that to increase the effectiveness of schools, the resources, experiences, and knowledge residing in the family and community must be placed in the foreground of children's school and educational experiences. It reframes family-school relationships to make communication, interactions, and curriculum development a two-way process. Teachers learn from parents and family networks and vice versa. Through dialogue, parents and teachers serve as resources for one another as they come to understand problems and solutions from multiple points of view (Civil & Quintos, 2002).

The funds of knowledge approach rejects one-way attempts to replicate and transmit school values and activities to the home, regardless of the cultural relevance these values and activities have for the families and communities they try to influence. It is particularly relevant for transforming practices in schools that serve minority, immigrant, and poor children, whose school performance lags behind white, middle-class students. The approach suggests that disadvantaged children can succeed in school if classrooms are reorganized to give them the same advantage that middle-class children always seemed to have had—instruction that puts their knowledge and experiences at the heart of learning (Roseberry, McIntyre, & Gonzalez, 2001).

4. Empowerment approaches

Empowerment approaches have evolved from family involvement research and practice among low-income communities. Schools often display deficit-oriented and stereotypical attitudes toward low-income families. When families feel disrespected and intimidated, they choose to distance themselves from schools. Empowerment approaches address this problem by instilling parents with the confidence to advocate for better schools and better outcomes for children.

One type of empowerment approach focuses on the *individual* and works to impart to parents new knowledge, skills, and opportunities to effect change in communicating and relating to school personnel. For example, the Boston-based Right Question Project provides a simple methodology of framing questions that parents can use in teacher conferences and parent meetings (Coffman, 2000). Parents can also be supported in developing leadership skills to monitor school reform. For example, the Commonwealth Institute for Parent Leadership trains parents to understand Kentucky's education standards and to initiate school projects that enrich students' learning and promote family involvement (Hernandez, 2000).

A second approach to empowerment focuses on the *collective* action of parents. It is in and through communities that low- to moderate-income and ethnically diverse families can create the public space to address school concerns. Through one-on-one conversations, group dialogue, and reflection, parents and other residents develop a strong sense of community and learn how to use their collective power to advocate for school change (Delgado-Gaitan, 2001; Gold et al., 2002; Shirley, 1997; Warren, 2002). All too often schools individualize systemic problems. For example, a student might be faulted for poor performance, when in reality the problem also lies in the lack of qualified teachers and instructional materials. Community organizing counters this individualizing trend by bringing people into relationships with one another so that they can identify and act on systemic problems—overcrowding, deteriorating school facilities, lack of teacher quality, poor school performance, and inadequate funding.

EDUCATIONAL CONTEXT OF FAMILY INVOLVEMENT

Family involvement is important in relation to the educational issues of our time—the achievement gap and the focus on performance standards and accountability. The achievement gap between more- and less-advantaged students is perhaps the most pressing educational issue for a democratic society. School reform efforts that focus only on school practices have not made a significant dent in closing the achievement gap. High quality academic instruction in conjunction with the values and preparation afforded by the home, and the community learning opportunities that reinforce the work of schools—that is, a child's social ecology—make up the context in which to impact educational inequality. In *The Black-White Test Score Gap*, Phillips and colleagues reported that traditional measures of education and economic inequality did not explain much of the gap among five- and six-year-old children (Phillips, Brooks-Gunn, Duncan, Klebanov, & Crane, 1998). Parenting practices, however, had a sizeable effect on children's test scores. Additionally, the key predictors of the achievement gap include the home learning environment, the home-school connection, and the community (Barton, 2003). The interface among home, school, and community as contexts of learning are apparent in the cases in this volume, such as "Staying on the Path Toward College" (Case 7), "Afterschool for Cindy" (Case 8), "Piecing It Together" (Case 9), "What Words Don't Say" (Case 10), "Raising Children Alone" (Case 11), and "Learning in the Shadow of Violence" (Case 12).

We are also in a time in which education policies emphasize standards and accountability. State and district systems sometimes lose sight of the importance of family involvement in terms of being a critical part of student achievement when worried about teacher quality and falling test scores. However, families play an important role in advocating for high performing schools and have been instrumental in supporting the creation of small schools and afterschool programs as measures to improve student achievement in underperforming schools (Shirley, 1997; Gold, Simon & Brown, 2002). In Chicago, where local school councils must have a majority of parent members, elementary schools that improved reading achievement over a seven-year period had effective councils (Moore, 1998). The family-school connection in relation to school policies is captured in the cases "Lunchtime at Sunnydale Elementary School" (Case 4), "Defining 'Fine'" (Case 5), "Bilingual Voices and Parent Classroom Choices" (Case 6).

How to Use the Casebook

This casebook is organized to connect several theoretical perspectives within Ecological Systems Theory to the analysis of the cases. It presents four sections of theoretical approaches and corresponding cases: microsystem, mesosystem, exosytem, and macrosytem. Readers can use the cases to help them understand the theories and also apply the theories to analyze issues in the cases. For example, in "Motivation to Learn," Deborah Stipek focuses attention on interactions and events that occur most frequently within the child's microsystem, such as direct interactions between children and the adults who teach and parent them in the primary contexts of school and home. In the case "Tomasito Is Too Big to Hold Hands," readers can consider how Tomasito's teacher and family members can nurture intrinsic motivation. The case also invites the application of theoretical perspectives from other sections, such as Thomas Weisner's description of middle childhood as an ecocultural project in which developmental pathways are determined by cultural activities that are organized into a child's daily routines. Thus, although the sections provide structure, the cases, by their richness and complexity, lend themselves to analyses from multiple theoretical perspectives.

Data Sources for the Cases

The data sources for the cases are based on research conducted by members of the MacArthur Network on Successful Pathways through Middle Childhood, and as such focus on children whose ages range from 6–12 years:

- *Study:* California Childhoods: Institutions, Contexts, and Pathways of Development
  Related cases: Lunchtime at Sunnydale Elementary School; Staying on a Path Toward College

- *Study:* Children of Immigrants and Ethnic Identity Development
  Related case: Learning in the Shadow of Violence

- *Study:* New Hope Child and Family Study
  Related cases: Raising Children Alone; Piecing It Together

- *Study:* School Engagement Study
  Related case: My Favorite Subject Is Lunch

- *Study:* School Transition Study
  Related Cases: Tomasito Is Too Big to Hold Hands; A Special Education Plan for Anabela; Defining "Fine"; Bilingual Voices and Parent Classroom Choices; What Words Don't Say; Afterschool for Cindy

The various studies draw from different sources—representing a range of quantitative and qualitative data from child, family, and school participants as well as from observations and independent assessments. Although each of these datasets captured key family involvement dilemmas in middle childhood, it should be noted that in some instances the cases in this volume have been partially fictionalized to convey the action, dialogue, and multiple perspectives conducive to effective teaching tools. Names and identifying information have also been changed to insure confidentiality to study participants.

All of the cases are formatted to help the reader navigate the text. A list of characters precedes each case to orient the reader to the key actors in the situation. An initial set of questions help readers link the teaching cases back to relevant theories presented earlier in the book. The learning objectives and a set of broader discussion questions follow each case to help guide case-based analysis and discussion.

The matrix presented in Table FM.1 can help guide the selection of cases for use in a course or workshop. It briefly describes the central educational and family involvement topic of each case, as well as specific theories that align well with each case and can lend insight into the case issues presented. As described earlier, we suggest a flexible approach whereby readers combine different theories and cases, recognizing that there is no simple formula for resolving issues between families and schools, and that multiple and unexpected perspectives can yield greater understanding. In fact, we encourage readers to bring personal and professional experiences as well as other theories not included into this volume to bear as they analyze and problem solve the cases. Finally, we provide a set of recommended readings that can supplement each case and the relevant theories in this volume. These additional readings focus on family involvement research and program models closely related to the case issue at hand.

Table FM.1 A Guide to the Cases and Theoretical Approaches in this Book

Case	Title	Gender	Grade	Race/Ethnicity	Topic	Theoretical Approaches
1	Tomasito Is Too Big to Hold Hands: The Developing Child and the Home-School Relationship	M	2nd grade	Mexican American (immigrant parents)	A child's growing desire for autonomy from his parents impacts their involvement.	• Motivation to Learn • Developmental-Contextual
2	A Special Education Plan for Anabela: Does Supporting Her Needs Mean Holding Her Back?	F	2nd grade	Mexican American	A school team considers how to engage a family in a child's special education referral, placement, and grade retention.	• Motivation to Learn • Developmental-Contextual
3	My Favorite Subject Is Lunch: Motivating a Disengaged Student	M	4th grade	African-American	Teachers and family members grapple with strategies to motivate a student disengaged from learning.	• Motivation to Learn • Developmental-Contextual
4	Lunchtime at Sunnydale Elementary School: What Do First Graders Need?	F	1st grade	Mexican American (immigrant grandmother)	Differences in values and expectations arise between families and school staff regarding a school's role in children's development.	• Social Executive Functioning • Community Support
5	Defining "Fine": Communicating Academic Progress to Parents	M	1st grade	Caucasian	A school struggles to inform parents about and engage them in academic issues in the context of standards-based reform.	• Social Executive Functioning • Community Support
6	Bilingual Voices and Parent Classroom Choices: Family Involvement in Language and Literacy	F	1st grade	Mexican American (immigrant mother)	A Spanish-speaking mother wonders how to support her daughter's learning and reconcile her bilingual placement beliefs with those of the teacher.	• Social Executive Functioning • Community Support

Case	Title	Gender	Grade	Race/Ethnicity	Topic	Theoretical Approaches
7	Staying on the Path Toward College: One Boy at the Crossroads	M	6th grade	Mexican American (immigrant parents)	Competing school, family, and peer influences shape a Latino youth's choice about preparing for college.	• Social Executive Functioning • Community Support
8	Afterschool for Cindy: Family, School, and Community Roles in Out-Of-School Time	F	2nd grade	Caucasian	A teacher and a guidance counselor consider their roles and limitations in linking a family and child to community programs.	• School-based Family Support
9	Piecing It Together: Linking Systems to Support a Student and Family	M	6th-8th grade	African American	Fragmentation of a school, community, and family system lead to a student who is at risk of academic failure being overlooked.	• School-based Family Support
10	What Words Don't Say: Talking About Racism	M	1st grade	African American and Native American	A teacher and mother fail to recognize and speak up about the effects of racism and classism on one student's school experience, respectively.	• Ecocultural Understanding • Ethnic and Racial Minority Parenting
11	Raising Children Alone: Poverty, Welfare Reform, and Family Involvement	F	3rd grade	African American	A mother making the transition from welfare to work faces barriers to family involvement, including issues of child care, employment, and teacher contact.	• Ecocultural Understanding • Ethnic and Racial Minority Parenting
12	Learning in the Shadow of Violence: Community, Culture, and Family Involvement	F	4rd grade	Cambodian (refugee parents)	One family's traumatic homeland experience and current neighborhood context influence parenting and family involvement.	• Ecocultural Understanding • Ethnic and Racial Diversity

HOW TO USE THE CASE METHOD

The case discussion method of teaching is an active learning approach that helps students arrive at understandings through practical experience. As such, it involves a considerable investment of time and thought (Garvin, 1991). Using the case discussion method well takes considerable preparation on the part of students and instructors. In our own graduate-level course on family-school partnerships, we expect students to read a case carefully in advance of the case discussion and often provide them with study questions to guide their reading. With some cases, we ask them to write an individual or team-based analytic memo based on the case and prepare their own set of discussion questions to bring to a class discussion. Each of these preparatory steps is meant to engage students deeply with the readings. Instructors must also prepare. In our course, we think carefully about the placement of each case in the course, moving from lesser to greater complexity in terms of the dilemmas presented. We also supplement cases with other readings reflecting research and theoretical approaches that are relevant to the case issues presented. Finally, we prepare a short set of key discussion questions to guide the case discussion based on our identified learning objectives for the session.

In addition to preparation, instructors must make choices about how to facilitate a case discussion. Case discussions are typically facilitated in a sequence of description and problem definition; analysis of the main characters, actions, and events in the story (including contributing factors and conflicting viewpoints); prescription of possible solutions to the dilemma; and evaluation of the consequences and consideration of alternative courses of action (Boehrer, 1995). The discussion questions accompanying each case in this book follow a similar progression. Adapted from facilitators' guides featured in Miller and Kantrov's education casebook (1998a), each case is paired with learning objectives and a series of discussion questions that move from description of the situation and exploration of contributing factors to articulating possible next steps, replaying the case, and looking at the bigger picture. Depending on an instructor's learning objectives, a few or many of these discussion questions may be appropriate for facilitating a case discussion.

Successful case discussions may include a number of other tactics, such as follow-up questions that probe, challenge, and sum up earlier remarks. Other activities, such as reflective writing and small group discussions can also introduce variety and match diverse styles of learning (Miller & Kantrov, 1998b). Although there is no one best approach to facilitating a case discussion, we hope these general ideas are helpful in planning and facilitating a discussion that yields critical thinking skills and the artistic sensibility so needed among today's educators (Garvin, 1991).

Note

1. The word "system" here refers to various forms of social, cultural, economic, or political organization or practices. In ecological theory, each system represents a different level of organization. Broad social and economic systems occur at national and global levels, while school and family systems occur at the local and regional levels.

References

Anderson, S. A. (2000). How parental involvement makes a difference in reading achievement. *Reading Improvement, 37*(2), 61–86.

Barton, P. E. (2003). *Parsing the achievement gap: Baselines for tracking progress.* Princeton, NJ: Policy Information Center, Educational Testing Service. Retrieved May 13, 2003, from http://www.ets.org/research/pic/parsing.pdf

Bloom, L. R. (2001). "I'm poor, I'm single, I'm a mom, and I deserve respect": Advocating in schools as/with mothers in poverty. *Educational Studies, 32*(3), 300–316.

Boehrer, J. (1995). *How to teach a case.* Cambridge, MA: John F. Kennedy School of Government, Harvard University.

Bronfenbrenner, U. (1979). Contexts of child rearing: Problems and prospects. *American Psychologist, 34*(10), 844–850.

Bronfenbrenner, U. (1986a). Ecology of the family as a context for human development: Research perspectives. *Developmental Psychology, 22*(6), 723–742.

Bronfenbrenner, U. (1986b). Recent advances in research on the ecology of human development. In R. K. Silbereisen, K. Eyferth, & G. Rudinger (Eds.), *Development as action in context: Problem behavior and normal youth development* (pp. 287–309). Heidelberg, Germany and New York: Springer-Verlag.

Bronfenbrenner, U., & Crouter, A. C. (1982). Work and family through time and space. In S. B. Kamerman, & C. D. Hayes (Eds.), *Families that work: Children in a changing world* (pp. 39–83). Washington, DC: National Academy Press.

Bryk, A. S., & Schneider, B. L. (2002). *Trust in schools: A core resource for improvement* (The Rose Series in Sociology). New York: Russell Sage Foundation.

Canobi, K. H., Reeve, R. A., & Pattison, P. E. (2003). Patterns of knowledge in children's addition. *Developmental Psychology, 39*(3), 521–534.

Chin, M. M., & Newman, K. S. (2002). *High stakes: Time poverty, testing, and the children of the working poor.* New York: Foundation for Child Development.

Civil, M., & Quintos, B. (2002, April). *Uncovering mothers' perceptions about the teaching and learning of mathematics.* Paper presented at the meeting of the American Educational Research Association, New Orleans, LA.

Coffman, J. (2000). *The right question project: Capacity building to achieve large-scale sustainable impact.* Retrieved September 16, 2003, from http://www.gse.harvard.edu/hfrp/projects/fine/resources/case_study/abstract.html#cs3

Comer, J. P., Haynes, N. M., & Joyner, E. T. (1996). The school development program. In J. P. Comer, N. M. Haynes, E. T. Joyner, & M. Ben-Avie, (Eds.), *Rallying the whole village: The Comer process for reforming education* (pp. 1–26). New York: Teachers College Press.

Delgado-Gaitan, C. (2001). *The power of community: Mobilizing for family and schooling.* Lanham, MD: Rowman & Littlefield.

Eccles, J. (1999). The development of children ages 6 to 14. *Future of Children, 9*(2), 30–44. Retrieved September 18, 2003, from http://www.futureofchildren.org/ information2826/information_show.htm?doc_id=71891

Edwards, R., & Alldred, P. (2000). A typology of parental involvement in education centering on children and young people: Negotiating familialisation, institutionalisation, and individualisation. *British Journal of Sociology of Education, 21*(3), 435–455.

Entwisle, D. R., & Alexander, K. L. (1998). Facilitating the transition to first grade: The nature of transition and research on factors affecting it. *Elementary School Journal, 98*(4), 351–364.

Epstein, J. (1995). School/family/community partnerships: Caring for the children we share. *Phi Delta Kappan, 76,* 701–712.

Epstein, J. L., Sanders, M. G., & Clark, L. A. (1999). *Preparing educators for school-family-community partnerships.* Baltimore, MD: Center for Research on the Education of Students Placed At Risk.

Erikson, E. H. (1968). *Identity: Youth and crisis.* New York: W. W. Norton.

Fan, X., & Chen, M. (2001). Parental involvement and students' academic achievement: A meta-analysis. *Educational Psychology Review, 13*(1), 1–22.

Garvin, D. A. (1991). Barriers and gateways to learning. In C. R. Christensen, D. A. Garvin, & A. Sweet (Eds.), *Education for judgment: The artistry of discussion leadership* (pp. 3–13). Boston: Harvard Business School Press.

Gold, E., Simon, E., & Brown, C. (2002). *Strong neighborhoods, strong schools: The indicators project on education organizing.* Chicago: Cross City Campaign for Urban School Reform.

Goldsmith, H. H., Aksan, N., Essex, M., Smider, N. A., & Vandell, D. L. (2001). Temperament and socioemotional adjustment to kindergarten: A multi-informant perspective. In T. D. Wachs & G. A. Kohnstamm (Eds.), *Temperament in context* (pp. 103–138). Mahwah, NJ: Erlbaum.

Harter, S.(1988). Developmental processes in the construction of the self. In T. D. Yawkey & J. E. Johnson (Eds.), *Integrative processes and socialization: Early to middle childhood* (pp. 45–78). Hillsdale, NJ: Erlbaum.

Harter, S. (1999). *The construction of the self: A developmental perspective.* New York: The Guilford Press.

Harvard Family Research Project (2003). Program Spotlight. *FINE Forum E-newsletter (7).* Retrieved August 26, 2004, from http://www.gse.harvard.edu/hfrp/projects/ fine/fineforum/forum7/spotlight.html

Haynes, N. M., Ben-Avie, M., Squires, D. A., Howley, P., Negron, E. N., & Corbin, J. N. (1996). It takes a whole village: The SDP school. In J. P. Comer, N. M. Haynes, E. T. Joyner, & M. Ben-Avie (Eds.), *Rallying the whole village: The Comer process for reforming education* (pp. 42–71). New York: Teachers College Press.

Henderson, A. T., & Mapp, K. L. (2002). *A new wave of evidence: The impact of family, school, community connections on student achievement.* Austin, TX: Southwest Educational Development Laboratory.

Hernandez, L. (2000). *The Prichard committee for academic excellence: Building capacity for public engagement in education reform.* Retrieved May 11, 2004, from http:// www.gse.harvard.edu/hfrp/projects/fine/resources/case_study/abstract.html#cs5

Izzo, C. V., Weissberg, R. P., Kasprow, W. J., & Fendrich, M. (1999). A longitudinal assessment of teacher perceptions of parent involvement in children's education and school performance. *American Journal of Community Psychology, 27,* 817–839.

Keith, T. Z., & Keith, P. B. (1993). Does parental involvement affect eighth-grade student achievement? Structural analysis of national data. *School Psychology Review, 22*(3), 474–496.

Lareau, A., & Horvat, E. M. (1999). Moments of social inclusion and exclusion: Race, class, and cultural capital in family-school relationships. *Sociology of Education, 72,* 37–53.

Lawrence-Lightfoot, S. (1978). *Worlds apart: Relationships between families and schools.* New York: Basic Books.

Lee, V., & Croninger, R. (1994). The relative importance of home and school in the development of literacy skills for middle-grade students. *American Journal of Education, 102,* 286–329.

Lewis, A. E., & Forman, T. A. (2002). Contestation or collaboration: A comparative study of home-school relations. *Anthropology and Education Quarterly, 33,* 60–89.

Miedel, W. T., & Reynolds, A. J. (1999). Parent involvement in early intervention for disadvantaged children: Does it matter? *Journal of School Psychology, 37*(4), 379–402.

Miller, B., & Kantrov, I. (1998a). *Casebook on school reform.* Portsmouth, NH: Heinemann.

Miller, B., & Kantrov, I. (1998b). *A guide to facilitating cases in education.* Portsmouth, NH: Heinemann.

Moll, L. C., Amanti, C., Neff, D., & González, N. (1992). Funds of knowledge for teaching: Using a qualitative approach to connect home and classrooms. *Theory Into Practice, 31,* 131–141.

Moore, D. (1998). *What makes these schools stand out: Chicago elementary schools with a seven-year trend of improved reading achievement.* Chicago: Designs for Change. Retrieved August 18, 2004, from http://www.designsforchange.org/pubs.html

Morris, D., Bloodgood, J. W., Lomax, R. G., & Perney, J. (2003). Developmental steps in learning to read: A longitudinal study in kindergarten and first grade. *Reading Research Quarterly, 38*(3), 302–328.

Nord, C., Brimhall, D., & West, J. (1997). *Fathers' involvement in their children's schools.* Washington, DC: National Center for Education Statistics, U.S. Department of Education.

Patrikakou, E. N. (2004). *Adolescence: Are parents relevant to high school students' achievement?* Cambridge, MA: Harvard Family Research Project. Retrieved October 12, 2004, from http://www.gse.harvard.edu/hfrp/projects/fine/resources/digest/index.html

Phillips, M., Brooks-Gunn, J., Duncan, G., Klebanov, P., & Crane, J. (1998). Family background, parenting practices, and the black-white test score gap. In C. Jencks, & M. Phillips (Eds.), *The Black-white test score gap.* Washington, DC: Brookings Institution Press.

Pomerantz, E. M., Ruble, D. N., Frey, K. S., & Greulich, F. (1995). Meeting goals and confronting conflict: Children's changing perceptions of social comparison. *Child Development, 66,* 723–738.

Public Education Network. (2003). *The voice of the new teacher.* Washington, DC: Author. Available online at: http://www.publiceducation.org/PENreports.asp

Roseberry, A., McIntyre, E., & Gonzalez, N. (2001). Connecting students' cultures to instruction. In A. Roseberry, E. McIntyre, & N. Gonzalez (Eds.), *Classroom diversity: Connecting curriculum to students' lives* (pp. 1–13). Portsmouth, NH: Heinemann.

Sameroff, A. J., & Haith, M. M. (Eds.) (1996). *The five to seven year shift: The age of reason and responsibility.* The University of Chicago Press.

Scott-Jones, D. (1995). Parent-child interactions and school achievement. In B. Ryan, G. Adams, T. Gullotta, R. Weissberg, & L. Hampton (Eds.), *The family-school connection: Theory, research and practice.* Thousand Oaks, CA: Sage.

Shartrand, A., Weiss, H., Kreider, H., & Lopez, M. E. (1997). *New skills for new schools: Preparing teachers in family involvement.* Washington, DC: U.S. Department of Education.

Shaver, A. V., & Walls, R. T. (1998). Effect of Title I parent involvement on student reading and mathematics achievement. *Journal of Research and Development in Education, 31*(2), 90–97.

Shirley, D. (1997). *Community organizing for urban school reform.* Austin: University of Texas Press.

Warren, M. (2002). *Dry bones rattling: Community building to revitalize American democracy.* Princeton, NJ: Princeton University Press.

Westat and Policy Studies Associates. (2001). *The longitudinal evaluation of school change and performance (LESCP) in Title I schools.* Rockville, MD and Washington D.C.: Author.

Section 1

The Microsystem

In the introduction to this volume, we presented an overview of Ecological Systems Theory, the overarching paradigm within which we have organized the teaching cases and theoretical lenses contained herein. In Section 1, we focus specifically on the **microsystem**, or the immediate contexts in which the developing child interacts with important others. Adults that nurture and teach children, peers and siblings who play and socialize with them, and settings such as day care, home, and school constitute the microsystem.

Ecological Systems Theory posits that, within contexts that contain the developing child, processes occurring in the child's daily routines and activities can have substantial influence on the child's development. Though not explicitly stated in the original theory, it is certainly implied (and later amended to reflect the same) that children can also influence the actors within these contexts. Children bring to situations their own individual characteristics, such as temperament, cognitive skills, and social skills that can directly influence their interactions with other persons. Similarly, other individuals, such as teachers and parents, bring to situations their own individual characteristics, which together with these individuals' reactions to individual children can influence their interactions. As a result, the contexts in which these interactions occur must always be considered in understanding children's development.

Although the theoretical lenses in this volume are not necessarily based in Ecological Systems Theory, inherent to most is some emphasis on one or more levels of the embedded contexts to which the theory refers. For example, some of these theoretical approaches focus on interactions between developing children and their families, while others focus on how parents' work demands influence their capacity to be involved in their children's education. We have presented the theoretical lenses in this volume in such a way that they serve as illustrative examples of micro, meso, exo, and macrosystemic approaches to interpreting and analyzing family educational involvement.

In this section, we include Deborah Stipek's "Motivation to Learn" and Penny Hauser-Cram and colleagues' "Children With Disabilities: A Developmental-Contextual Perspective" as examples of theoretical approaches at the microsystem level. Stipek focuses on internal and external factors related to children's academic motivation. In her review of motivation theory and research, she describes the ways in which parents' and teachers' interactions with children at home and at school—both of which are microlevel contexts—can contribute to or undermine children's academic motivation. Hauser-Cram and colleagues focus on the reciprocal relations among children's self-regulation skills, children's intellectual development, and parent well-being. She emphasizes the family context, wherein children's positive relationships with their parents contribute to positive growth in both social and cognitive skills.

We encourage readers to consider these theoretical perspectives in interpreting and analyzing the three cases contained in this section of the book. For example, in "Tomasito Is Too Big to Hold Hands," Tomasito is fortunate to be in a loving family environment that likely facilitates his academic performance, as would be suggested by Hauser-Cram and her colleagues. Although Tomasito is not doing so well in math, his teacher's greatest concern is communicating this to his family. In "My Favorite Subject Is Lunch," the three Cs—competence, control, and connection—to which Stipek refers in her review of learning motivation are all evident in Anthony's attitudes about school. Finally, in "A Special Education Plan for Anabela," one can explore the many ways in which Anabela's interactions with her parents might contribute to her educational experiences. Because these three cases all focus on interactions between developing children and their parents or teachers, at home and at school, they well represent processes at the microsystem level that can contribute to children's development.

Although we have grouped the theoretical lenses and cases in this section as examples of microsystem approaches, we challenge readers to apply these lenses to cases appearing in other sections of this volume as well. As you read the cases throughout this volume, you might consider, for example, how the children themselves are acting as agents in their own educational experiences, including the extent to which their families are involved in those experiences. Both Stipek and Hauser-Cram and colleagues conceptualize children as exerting influence on the micro-level contexts in which their development occurs. Both describe children as having bidirectional influences on family functioning, for example. Because almost all of the cases in this volume focus on children's academic engagement and performance, to some degree, considerations of children's academic motivation will almost always have relevance. Similarly, because all of the cases include perspectives from adults, such as parents and teachers, who interact with the children, by definition the microsystem is always at play.

1

Theoretical Perspectives on the Microsystem

I n this chapter, Deborah Stipek and Penny Hauser-Cram and her colleagues describe how children's interactions in the family and classroom contexts relate to their social and cognitive development and their educational experiences. These interactions are important considerations in understanding family educational involvement, as Stipek and Hauser-Cram and colleagues demonstrate below. As Stipek argues, children's motivation to learn can be greatly influenced by both teachers' and parents' praise or criticism. Hauser-Cram and colleagues describe how children's social-emotional regulation can contribute to parents' stress levels, and how parents' interactions with their children can contribute to the children's social and cognitive growth. Although we present these theoretical perspectives as tools that may be used to interpret and analyze the cases in the next chapter, they may also be useful in interpreting other situations as well.

Motivation to Learn

by Deborah Stipek

C hildren do not learn unless they exert effort on academic tasks. At a minimum, they need to pay attention to and complete tasks. Ideally, they enjoy learning, seek challenging tasks, and take pride in their accomplishments. Researchers have found many advantages for children who enjoy learning compared with those who do schoolwork because they feel they must or who work to achieve extrinsic rewards (e.g., high grades) or avoid punishment (e.g., low grades). For example, children who enjoy learning for its own sake seem to learn at more conceptual levels, seek intellectual challenges more frequently, and persist longer during difficult tasks than children who focus on external rewards and punishments (Stipek & Seal, 2001).

Teachers and parents are the two most important influences on children's achievement-related beliefs and behavior. Messages about learning and achievement are conveyed through children's interactions with parents and teachers during school-related conversations and tasks. Thus, promoting children's **motivation to learn**, that is, their enjoyment of and investment in learning, should be a joint venture in which parents and teachers play complementary roles.

Teachers can help support and promote children's motivation to learn directly, through effective classroom practice, and indirectly, through conveying information to parents. Teachers must have a solid understanding of motivation theory so they are able to develop effective educational practices and provide parents with strategies to support children's motivation to learn.

Theoretical Frameworks for Understanding Children's Motivation to Learn

Theories of motivation emphasize differently the roles of external factors (e.g., rewards and punishments) and internal factors (e.g., thoughts, expectations, intrinsic rewards) on children's educational achievement (Stipek, 2002), as Figure 1.1 illustrates. Historically, **reinforcement theory**, which emphasizes the role of external rewards and punishments, has provided powerful tools for influencing children's behavior (Stipek, 2002). Both teachers and parents use external motivators at times. Praise, high grades, and special privileges are common rewards used to encourage desirable behaviors, while criticism, loss of privileges, low grades, and disapproval are common punishments used to deter undesirable ones. Although these external motivators are sometimes necessary and often effective in the short run, researchers have found that they are not effective in producing long-term behavior change or in building children's internal motivation (Kazdin, 1988; Kazdin & Bootzin, 1972; O'Leary & Drabman, 1971).

Social cognitive theory, by contrast, views children as active interpreters of the world, who do more than simply respond to rewards and punishments (Stipek, 2002). Social cognitive theorists propose that children's beliefs, values, expectations, emotions, and other unobservable thoughts and feelings play a central role in achievement motivation and behavior. For example, social cognitive theorists suggest that children's expectations about rewards or punishments (e.g., whether they believe they will be rewarded in a particular setting or situation) determine behavior more than actual past experiences with external motivators. In theory, this should result in more long-term behavior change because the individual is no longer dependent on the presence of external motivators (Mace & Kratochwill, 1988; Shapiro & Cole, 1994).

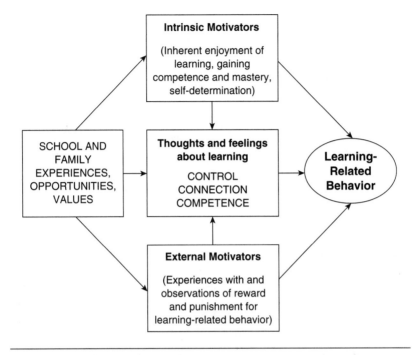

Figure 1.1   Theories of Motivation

Intrinsic motivation theory provides a different perspective of children's achievement related behaviors. This theory posits that individuals often find learning new information and skills inherently enjoyable and do not need external rewards or praise for engaging in such behaviors. In fact, researchers have discovered that providing external rewards for such activities can actually undermine interest in that activity by shifting children's attention away from the intrinsic value to the reward itself (Lepper, 1973). Thus, when the reward is removed children may cease engaging in the behavior that they had previously enjoyed for its own sake.

The Three C's: Competence, Control, and Connection

Clearly, finding ways to optimize and sustain children's intrinsic motivation is critical. Psychological research has helped discover three achievement-related thoughts and feelings (i.e., cognitions) that affect children's motivation to learn: their perceptions of their competence, their feelings of control, and their feelings of social connectedness. These cognitions are discussed in more detail in the following paragraphs.

Perceptions of competence. Feelings of competence, especially of new competencies and accompanying expectations for success, are highly motivating (Bandura, 1977). Feelings of competence contribute to children's desire to engage in academic work and encourage children to seek challenges and persist in the face of difficulty. Feelings of *in*competence and an expectation of failure encourage children to give up and withdraw from academic work. Some children put more energy into trying to avoid looking incompetent (e.g., pretending to understand when they don't; "forgetting" their homework because they don't think it is correct, even if they did it; giving excuses for poor performance) than they put into trying to succeed. Children feel a sense of competence only when they engage in learning activities that are challenging (so they see their skills and understanding developing) but manageable (effort really does lead to success). Success on easy work does not produce the feelings of competence that energize students to do more, and work that is too difficult engenders discouragement and helplessness.

Feelings of control. Children enjoy academic work more when they feel that they are doing it because they *want* to, not just because they *have* to. Feelings of control or autonomy are undermined by close monitoring, salient external consequences (e.g., "you better get to work or you'll get an F"; "if you read this book, you'll get a certificate for a MacDonald's burger"), and a lack of choice. A feeling of choice, even among different academic tasks, contributes to feelings of control.

Feelings of connectedness. Children do not enjoy learning if they feel disrespected and emotionally disconnected. This applies to any learning context. A close, caring relationship with the teacher and being respected and valued by peers fosters higher levels of engagement and learning in the classroom. Children who have close relationships with parents and feel that their perceptions and beliefs are respected are more likely to exert effort and to take academic risks than children who perceive their parents as controlling and unsupportive.

Conclusion

Parents and teachers are the most important influences on children's learning. Learning occurs best when children enjoy it and exert effort in the process of learning. Both parents and teachers can play complementary roles to support and promote learning. They commonly offer extrinsic motivations, such as rewards and punishments; but more importantly, they can optimize a child's intrinsic motivation to learn. A passion for learning is nurtured when teachers and parents provide challenging but manageable tasks that build a child's competence. They can offer choices in academic tasks and thereby support children's feelings of control over their learning. Finally, they can develop a caring and respectful learning context in which children feel a sense of connectedness with adults and peers.

Implications for Educators

Teachers and parents can support or undermine children's perceptions of their competence, their feeling of autonomy and their feeling of being secure and well supported. Teachers can provide parents with tools and strategies that encourage children's internal motivation and complement teachers' work in the classroom.

Cultivate positive and supportive interactions around learning. It is important for children to feel accepted and supported by their parents in their educational endeavors both inside and outside of school. Teachers can support parents to develop children's sense of responsibility for schoolwork. Helping children develop and commit to a homework routines and encouraging them to stick to the routine allows the children to feel greater self-determination and reduces the likelihood of negative interactions with parents.

Teachers can help parents support their children's passion for learning in all its forms. They can suggest that parents encourage children's growing interests and passions without undermining their feelings of self-determination. Helping children access additional information about a topic of interest, for example, allows them to maintain a sense of independence and control. However, pressuring or forcing children to engage in learning activities can be counter-productive, even if it is about a topic they are interested in.

Maximize children's feelings of competence. Teachers can work with parents in ways that help children develop and sustain feelings of competence, which is inherently motivating. Sometimes children do not work hard in school or do not complete homework because they don't believe they can do it. The first task for teachers, then, is to consult with parents to determine how children are feeling about their abilities. It is not easy for teachers to make this determination on their own because children are not always forthright. Some are reluctant to reveal that they don't understand the work, while others use this as an excuse when they simply don't want to do the work. Parents can often provide additional insight about the real cause of a child's reluctance to complete tasks that can help the teacher decide on an appropriate course of action.

Stress learning and effort over performance. Teachers can remind parents to emphasize children's learning over their grades for a number of reasons. First, an emphasis on grades and other forms of external evaluation has been found to undermine students' interest in a topic (Ryan & Grolnick, 1986). By contrast, an emphasis on learning focuses children on their developing competence, which is motivating in its own right. Second, deemphasizing external evaluation allows children to feel more autonomous and less controlled. Third, if children are doing poorly relative to the rest of the class, an emphasis on learning and effort can minimize feelings of alienation and incompetence, which undermine children's motivation to learn.

When children are having difficulty with a subject, sometimes parents want an immediate and dramatic improvement in the child's grade. A better approach that teachers can suggest, however, is to emphasize the child's increased effort and gradual, but steady improvement. This enhances the child's feelings of competence and helps to maintain a focus on learning rather than grades. Teachers can facilitate this attitude by informing parents of the child's progress in ways that highlight the child's hard work and gains in understanding. Teachers can also provide suggestions to parents for encouraging children's progress in ways that are realistic and most likely to produce long-term improvement.

Use rewards and praise thoughtfully. Rewards can be motivating in the short run, but they can undermine intrinsic motivation and make it less likely that a behavior will occur when the reward is withdrawn. Teachers can explain to parents that rewards and even praise can often feel controlling to children. Thus, when offering a reward, parents can frame it in terms of a choice the child can make freely based on natural consequences (e.g., you can finish your homework now or later, but if you finish it before dinner we will have time to play). In the same vein, praise that makes children feel manipulated should be avoided, using instead language that emphasizes the child's own autonomy and self-determination.

Inform parents about innovative classroom practices. It is important that teachers explain clearly to parents any innovative classroom practices that are intended to promote children's internal motivation. This is particularly true, for example, when teachers utilize nontraditional forms of evaluation. Parents are most accustomed to using scores, class rank, and grades to judge their children's progress and achievement in school. However, motivation theory suggests that such comparative assessments may undermine some children's internal motivation. Thus, if teachers choose to modify their ways of evaluating students, they must also be prepared to explain and justify their reasons for doing so. At a minimum, they must help parents to understand alternative forms of feedback so they can continue to understand their children's progress. Keeping parents informed about such educational practices can prevent misunderstandings and will increase home-school continuity regarding achievement-related messages.

A Developmental-Contextual Perspective

by Penny Hauser-Cram, Marji Erickson Warfield,
Jack P. Shonkoff, Marty Wyngaarden Krauss,
Aline Sayer, and Carole Christofk Upshur

Contemporary psychological research on children with developmental disabilities is beginning to focus on the factors that support development rather than solely describing the ways in which these disabilities may impede development. Our work has focused on skills and characteristics within the child and within the family that are associated with positive development. These relationships are multidirectional: Family members influence children's development and children, in turn, affect the well-being of other family members (Minuchin, 1988). These relationships are also dynamic because changing needs and influences shape the family over time (Lerner, 1991).

From a developmental-contextual perspective, family processes and children's development are mutually interrelated. This theoretical lens considers the bidirectional influences of parents and children upon each other. Research on these relationships provides three important insights for working with children and their families: (1) children promote their own development through processes of self-regulation, (2) family relationships shape child development, and (3) children affect parent well-being and their capacity to engage in children's schooling.

Although this area of research focuses on the relation between the development of children with disabilities and their families, this work is identifying processes that appear to be central to the development of *all* children.

The Research

One of the most fruitful ways to examine children's development is through empirical studies that gather information over time. Such longitudinal studies can help researchers better understand the pathways of child development, examine the degree to which development can be influenced by interventions, and understand how changes in the child and family affect each other. In this chapter, we present findings from the Early Intervention Collaborative Study, a longitudinal study of children with biologically based disabilities and their families (Hauser-Cram, Warfield, Shonkoff, Krauss, Sayer & Upshur, 2001). This research, which followed children from infancy until age ten, has revealed important information about the reciprocal influences of child development and parent well-being over time (Hauser-Cram et al., 2001; Shonkoff, Hauser-Cram, Krauss, & Upshur, 1992).

Children act as agents of their own development. One of the most important ways in which children advance or impede their own development is through **self-regulation**, which is the capacity to regulate one's behavior in accordance with environmental demands. Children who can control their emotions and actions well during intellectual challenges or frustrating situations show developmental advantages over those with poorer self-regulation skills (Bronson, 2000). We found two areas of self-regulation that predicted children's positive developmental change. One manifestation of self-regulation is **mastery motivation**, which is present when a child persists at a problem-posing task even when the task is quite challenging (e.g., matching unusual shapes, completing a complex puzzle, working a multistep tape recorder). Our research found that preschool children with high mastery motivation made greater gains throughout the middle childhood years, especially in cognitive growth. Cognitive growth, in turn, led to positive changes in other areas of development such as social, communication, and daily living skills.

The second aspect of self-regulation is **social-emotional regulation**, which is the ability to manage socially appropriate behavior during frustrating or demanding situations. When children have difficulty regulating their emotions they exhibit behavior problems such as tantrums, defiance, and withdrawal. We found that children who exhibited these behaviors in their early childhood classroom displayed less positive change in cognitive performance through the middle childhood period. Thus, both types of self-regulation (i.e., mastery motivation and social-emotional regulation) contribute to children's cognitive growth.

How does self-regulation relate to children's development at different ages? Preschool-aged children become more goal-oriented and monitor their actions more effectively (Bullock & Lutkenhaus, 1988). They also evaluate the success or failure of their actions more accurately (Stipek, Recchia, & McClintic, 1992). As they persist in their goals, young children learn to correct their actions and as a consequence experience the rewards of successful performance. As children persist, self-correct, and evaluate the results of their efforts they benefit emotionally from developing mastery and benefit cognitively from understanding their errors. In this way children promote their own developmental progress (Bandura, 1997).

Children with better social-emotional self-regulation also are more engaged in growth-promoting activities with their peers, less involved in disputes with others, and can take advantage of the classroom experience in a way that helps them advance cognitively (Hauser-Cram et al., 2001).

Family relationships shape child development. Family relationships, however, also contribute to child outcomes. We found that preschool children whose mothers interacted more positively with them during a teaching task displayed greater growth in cognitive performance, communication, and social skills in later childhood. Likewise, children whose families had more positive relationships with each other experienced more growth in their social skills. Taken together, these findings demonstrate that children's self-regulation and positive family relationships are both important to children's development.

Children affect parent well-being. Having a child with a disability presents parents with new and unexpected challenges. A number of factors affect how parents adapt to their child with a disability, including their coping skills and sources of social support. Parent well-being includes parent satisfaction with and adaptation to the child's temperament and behaviors, and parents' emotional resources and adjustment to the parenting role.

We found that as children grew from infancy to age ten, fathers' and mothers' stress levels increased considerably. Fathers displayed higher levels of stress than mothers did when the child was in the infant and toddler years and had more moderate increases thereafter. Mothers, on the other hand, showed a continuous increase in stress levels over time. Both mothers and fathers experienced higher levels of stress when their children exhibited poor social-emotional self-regulation. However, certain factors reduced parental stress. Specifically, mothers' stress levels were lower when they had strong social support networks, while fathers' stress levels were lower when they had greater problem-focused coping skills.

Conclusion

Our research examined the bidirectional relations among child and parent characteristics and the influences of child and family processes. Children, to some extent, advance their own development through self-regulatory processes. Family processes—mother-child interactions and parent assets (e.g., problem-focused coping skills and social supports)—are also critical components of improved development in children with disabilities and parent well-being. These processes govern the development of children with and without developmental disabilities.

Implications for Educators

Develop family-focused services. When families move from early intervention programs to school-based services, they experience a shift from a family-focused to a child-focused system. In view of the high levels of stress that parents experience as their children grow into and through middle childhood, schools should pay greater attention to the mental health of children and their parents, especially during early and middle childhood (Knitzer, 2000). Neglecting the needs of parents may have long-term consequences for their children, especially as they become adolescents.

Tailor different types of supports for fathers and mothers. Different types of parent assets (e.g., social support for mothers and problem-focused coping skills for fathers) predict changes in parents' well-being over time. School services can help connect mothers with opportunities for social support. Similarly, services that support the problem-focused styles of fathers may serve to improve their well-being over time. Improved parent well-being may enhance parents' involvement in their child's school.

Initiate teacher professional development that focuses on the family system in child development. All those who work with children (with and without disabilities) need to acquire knowledge about the contexts of child development and especially the role of families, so that they can promote children's self-regulatory processes and positive parent-child interactions. Knowledge of the multiple and changing facets of the family system is vital to teacher collaboration with families. Teachers and service providers might benefit from a collection of case examples in which potential collisions between families and practitioners were averted. In addition, it would be beneficial to provide examples in which teachers and other service providers have revised standard practices in ways that support families and benefit children (Hauser-Cram & Howell, 2003).

2

The Cases

The cases appearing in this chapter have been grouped as such because they all focus most clearly on children's interactions in the family and classroom contexts—or the microsystem as described by Ecological Systems Theory. As a way of illustrating how theory can inform interpretation and problem solving using the teaching case method, we have presented in this section (in Chapter 1) two theoretical lenses readers might apply to the cases appearing here. As you study the following cases, you might also consider how theoretical perspectives in subsequent chapters inform your interpretation of the dilemmas presented here.

Case 1: Tomasito Is Too Big to Hold Hands

The Developing Child and the Home-School Relationship[1]

by Ellen Mayer

Characters:

Tomasito, second grader at Morrison Elementary (See Table 2.1)

Linda, Tomasito's teacher

Ria, Tomasito's mother

Tomas, Tomasito's father

Edward, Tomasito's older brother

TOMASITO'S PORTFOLIO

It was early spring, and the final round of parent-teacher conferences was over. Linda Brady, in her sixth year as a classroom teacher, was cleaning up her classroom at the end of the day. She tucked inside Tomasito's second-grade

Table 2.1   Morrison Elementary School

Title 1 Public School

Location	Large Western city, population over 1,000,000
Grades served	Pre-K to 5
Enrollment	N = 298
• Latino/Latina • African American • Caucasian (non-Latino/a) • Asian American	62.7% 12.3% 18.8% 2.4%
School staff (administrators, teachers, aides) ethnicity	N = 43
• Latino/Latina • African American • Caucasian (non-Latino/a) • Asian American	23% 2% 37% 35%
Students eligible for free and reduced-priced lunch	75%
Students performing at least one year below grade level in reading	51–75%
Students performing at least one year below grade level in mathematics	26–50%
Limited or non-English proficient students	45%
Classroom language instruction	Some full and modified bilingual classes; program in flux
School-based services	Parent education program; morning ESL classes for parents, before afterschool care

portfolio his most recent story, about traveling to a distant planet with his school friends. Like the rest of his work, this was excellent. Pausing in her chores, she leafed through his portfolio. A smile spread over her face. His carefully drawn self-portrait: a tall boy, looking very big, standing proudly with his best friends in the background. Copies of his many Good Citizen school awards. Then she came to his math work. For the first time a shiver of concern ran through her—his math test results seemed so erratic. Was it possible that his math learning wasn't that solid? Was he even slipping in math? Yet his homework was always perfect. What was going on with Tomasito?

As you read this case, consider applying the following theoretical lenses to your analysis:

- Developmental-Contextual: How do family processes involving his mother and father influence Tomasito's development? How has his development since kindergarten in turn impacted his mother's well-being? How has it affected her participation at Morrison Elementary?
- Motivation to Learn: How would you characterize Tomasito's sense of connectedness with his parents, older brother, and teacher? How does this relate to his engagement in learning?
- Ecocultural Understanding: What are Tomasito's weekday routines and activities that influence his development? How are these routines meaningful, that is, having moral and cultural value?

Tomasito at School and Home

LINDA BRADY, TOMASITO'S SECOND-GRADE TEACHER

"The most distinctive thing about Tomasito is that he is such a nice, kind, good little boy. I don't think he has ever said anything bad about anybody in his whole life. He helps all the kids and gets along with everyone in the room. I have at least two kids in the room I'd call clinically misbehaving, who demand a lot of my time, so it's a joy to have Tomasito, who's quiet and obedient. He's probably the most popular child in the room. Although he's the oldest in the room, he's very shy. He never speaks in class unless he's called on, which makes him a model student in a way.

"He's also doing well in school academically. Most of my students aren't on grade level, but Tomasito is. He's very conscientious and hard working in all his subjects. My sixth sense, though, is that we need now to look at him closely in math, and I've just been talking with my classroom aide about it. But we haven't been able to figure out what's going on. It's not because of his language skills, since Tomasito is virtually fluent in English. I haven't signaled to Tomasito my concern about his math, since he's trying as hard as he can, and sometimes his self-confidence isn't all that strong.

"At home, I think if I'm right, Tomasito is the oldest child. My sense is that he has a loving, supportive family that takes wonderful care of him—getting him to school everyday on time, clean and well fed. Tomasito's main weaknesses are that he has parents who speak limited English, and my guess is he probably doesn't have an academic role model at home. Other than that I can't really say. He's a pretty reserved little guy and compared to most of his classmates doesn't share anything about his home life with me. All these second graders are pretty good talkers by now, and most of them aren't self-conscious about what they say. When we go around the room on Monday mornings talking about what we did over the weekend, and again on Fridays when the kids can volunteer for Show and Tell, I sometimes learn a good bit about my kids' life outside school. But not from Tomasito—all he ever talks about is playing Nintendo over the weekend, and he's never once participated in Show and Tell.

"Even though he doesn't chit-chat to me, I do have my special teacher radar, and it tells me that somebody at home is following up and making sure Tomasito does his homework. It's always very neat, correct, and thorough. I've never asked Tomasito anything about his homework, partly because I've never been that concerned about him, and because whatever he's doing is looking fine."

RIA, TOMASITO'S MOTHER (TRANSLATED FROM SPANISH)

"Tomasito, my middle child, is my most wonderful son. He is noble—kind and unselfish. Tomasito likes to have friends, and people who have friends have everything, right? My husband Tomás and I think being noble is the most beautiful thing in a human being, and we want Tomasito to be this way for the rest of his life. His teacher says, 'If I had twenty Tomasitos in my class, I wouldn't have any problems.' In meetings with her, the first thing she always says is that Tomasito is respectful, cooperative, and knows the rules. So maybe his personality has helped him win the teacher's approval?

"I call him 'Tomasito two-side' because he can be shy out of the house, but at home he is so talkative and expressive. With Tomasito, EVERYTHING he sees and hears outside of the house, he tells us about. He told us the teacher uses his work as examples for the class. At home, what a mimic he is! But at school he does not always participate. This is because he is reserved, like his father. He is not like me—I have a strong personality, I like socializing with all people. When I went to school I loved participating in all the social activities!

"We are a very happy family. I have vowed not to be harsh and neglectful with my children as my mother was with us in Mexico. We tell our boys that they are *nuestros muñequitos,* our little dolls, the most precious things we have in life. I try to kiss and hug my Tomasito a lot. When I am cleaning shops part-time, my husband takes care of the children; we have never ever used a babysitter. It is important that our sons have love and attention and what pleases them. But sometimes I worry if I am doing all the right things? Should I have rules about watching TV? I like it when experts give me advice. Once his first-grade teacher told me I should let Tomasito read to me everyday, and I appreciated that. I also learn a lot from watching other families and analyzing what they do.

"When Tomasito grows up, most of all, we want him to have a *corazon bueno,* a good heart. Even though we are poor, we want him to finish college, although we don't care if he becomes a professional or intellectual in life. In Mexico, I never went to college. Tomás graduated and works here as a restaurant manager. Tomasito's older brother Edward is really an example to Tomasito. I know I shouldn't compare the boys, but Edward is much smarter than Tomasito.

Edward's teacher says he is always determined to be first in academics. But Tomasito could teach him much about kindness!

"In the last conference, Ms. Brady just said that Tomasito was doing fine in all his school subjects. But Tomás and I share a worry about the math. Sometimes Tomasito just seems confused or he forgets what he has learned. I just don't know why it is so hard for him.

"When Tomasito does his homework, we allow him to do it whenever he wants in the afternoon, but he is supposed to finish it before his father gets home. Tomasito often gets caught up with television, playing Nintendo, or with telling stories and his homework just sits there. Or he is doing his homework, and he gets distracted by his baby brother who is a lively toddler and wants to play. Tomasito needs a lot of help with his math homework. I am not much good at helping. At his school there are special math classes for parents to explain the math teaching, but I haven't been to them. Edward is the one who helps Tomasito with math most of the time. If it is still needed, my husband helps when he comes home from work. Sometimes Tomás has to explain two, three, four times! Edward is so quick, but it seems so much harder for Tomasito to do math. I just discovered that Edward had been doing Tomasito's math homework for him. I came so close to spanking Edward! I said to Edward, 'I told you to help him—not do it for him.' I put a stop to it."

TOMASITO

"My teacher tells me I'm good at school, and I like it when I get a lot of homework stickers for perfect homework. I am the tallest one in my class and really great at math. My friends at school and I share our Mario Nintendo games. But I wish I had Nike shoes like one of my friends—you know, stuff that is in style and not cheap. When I grow up, I want to be a football player like on TV. It's boring just being an eight year old. You can't go to any countries, and I like to travel. I can't drive a car. I can't have a wife.

"When my mom hugs and kisses me I pretty much hate it now. Edward and me like to watch football with our dad. Edward and me do a lot of stuff together. He is great at drawing, and I like to color in the pictures that he makes. I also like to watch him play Mario. He is SO GREAT and gets to really high levels! Sometimes he even helps me when I play it. In our bedroom we share a bed, and we even have our very own VCR. Isn't that an important responsibility?"

LINDA, TOMASITO'S SECOND-GRADE TEACHER

"I was standing in the classroom doorway just before the start of school, when an odd thing happened. Tomasito's mother comes running in, waving a book. It was a classroom library book that Tomasito had borrowed and was due in today. I gathered his mother had just dropped Tomasito off outside, and that he had forgotten the book. Well, I *never* see her in the building like that. And I should add that parents often casually hang out in our building—our school has a nice village-like feel. Anyway, Ria Montero blurted out in her choppy English that Tomasito had been 'careless with the book,' embarrassing him right in front of all his friends. Tomasito darted out from behind me, grabbed the book, and ran back into the classroom. I tried quickly to take advantage of Mrs. Montero being there, and suggested that she come in sometime and chat with me. Who knows, maybe this would help me sort out what is going on with Tomasito and his math. But as soon as I invited her, she scurried away.

"Apart from those formally scheduled things, like parent-teacher conferences, open houses, or awards ceremonies, his parents simply don't set foot inside the school. I'm not making a value judgment, but when we have a class party, poor Tomasito lugs in heavy bags of food all by himself, while his classmates' parents carry in the stuff for their kids. I know that Tomasito gets dropped off at school and picked up by his mother everyday, but all this happens outside at the curb. I have a bunch of parents who come inside for drop off or pick up, and I get to chat with them. I have several parents regularly volunteering in my room, but not Tomasito's parents. I really like it when parents come in. Being able to have those informal chit-chats feels like the best way to build up good relationships with parents. And when you have good relationships, it's just so much easier to really talk about some things.

"It seems to me there are a bunch of reasons why Tomasito's parents don't come in. Mrs. Montero seemed to be just plain nervous being in the building that time with the book. She clearly lacks some self-confidence and is shy, just like her son Tomasito. When she does get in, like for a conference, her limited English isn't a problem. She's able to talk to me, which is good, since we don't have enough interpreters here. It's got to be hard for her to just pop in with her baby. In fact, the school doesn't even have childcare for the formally scheduled meetings like conferences. I don't know whether she works, but I know that the father does. That's the main story around here—working parents just can't find the time to come into the building. I really should send home a reminder note to his parents that they are entitled to come into the building and hang out, observe in the room, volunteer. Since Tomasito is their first child, this is their first experience with second grade, and they just may not understand that they are welcome to be in the classroom.

"Speaking of notes, one thing his parents do is respond to notes. I always send them notes via Tomasito reminding them about when he will be getting Good Citizen awards at the assemblies. And he dutifully brings me back little thank-you messages from them. It's partly thanks to Tomasito that we can communicate like that. Nothing ever gets lost in *that* backpack! Also, when I sent classroom parents notes home recommending the use of flash cards at home for math, Mr. and Mrs. Montero wrote back immediately, 'Thank you, Teacher, for this advice. We have started to use the flash cards with our son.' They certainly took what I said very seriously.

"Well, Mrs. Montero's behavior when she brought in the book surely was odd. There was another odd encounter with them—at the fall open house. Mrs. Montero approached me, asked me how Tomasito was doing in school, and I said very well. Then she proceeded to tell me how Tomasito's handwriting was bad!

Whaa . . . ? I was amazed that his parents seemed to believe that he wasn't doing well academically. That just didn't fit with the Tomasito in my class. I was surprised that they were so critical of his ability. It just made me wonder that maybe they don't appreciate how great their son is."

TOMASITO

"Having your mom come into the school building—that's definitely for BABIES! If your dad comes in, well that's maybe not quite as bad. That's like KIDS' stuff, I guess. Both are pretty bad, though. After mom brought me this book at school, that night I told her NOT to bring me stuff when everyone is at school. Mom brings us to our school every day, but Edward and me now make our mom leave us off and wait for us way over at the curb outside. Before she used to cross us, but now I tell her that the crossing guard is there. I used to hold the crossing guard's hand, but since I'm in second grade I don't. We always ask mom to get us to school early. Then I won't be late, or I won't be one of the last ones to be in the classroom. And I get to have time with my friends. Edward and me also told mom that we want to walk home from school some days. We're big, you know? And I bet she will let us do it!"

TOMÁS, TOMASITO'S FATHER (TRANSLATED FROM SPANISH)

"We have children of different ages, so that really helps us to see that children change and go through different stages as they grow older. In kindergarten, Tomasito was delighted to have his mama come into the classroom. Then that changed in first grade. Now Edward is in fifth grade, and I am volunteering once a week in his classroom, because the teacher really needs help with the older kids. And Edward accepts this.

"My wife told me the other day how mortified Tomasito was to have her come into school unexpectedly to bring him the book. She saw the terrible expression of embarrassment on his face—this made her turn around and leave right away. Later that evening, Tomasito said that his teacher and classmates would think he was not obeying the rules because he was not careful with the classroom library book.

"Poor Ria, she feels sad that not long ago, Tomasito would squeeze her hand tightly while crossing the street and close his eyes. He was little and scared and needed his mama. But now he leaves her in the street, while he goes into school by himself. She thinks maybe he is ashamed of her. She herself would have thought it a wonderful thing if her mother had ever taken her into school. I tell her this is because of his getting older. He does not want his mama being in school with him because this embarrasses him in front of his friends. But I don't think he would want me there, either.

"Still I can see that there are times when he seems pleased that we are in the building. At open house—that's when all the parents and little brothers and sisters come in to see the children's schoolwork—Tomasito seemed very proud to be showing us what he had done. The teacher had told the students how to show their work to the families. Tomasito and Edward had said the week before 'Hey, Mommy—let's go to open house, you know you have to.' And Tomasito does not protest when Ria and the baby go to the big awards ceremonies every month."

RIA, TOMASITO'S MOTHER

"I love being in my sons' school. It feels so safe, even when I go there at night to a meeting. This is a dangerous city, but the school is in a quiet place with houses and families. It's easy to get to, close to our home. The principal is not Latina, but she speaks Spanish and says hello to parents by name when we come in. Ms. Brady wants parents to participate at school, which my husband and I feel is important. Children's *fortuna buena o mala*, good or bad fortune, starts at home, not at school. The teachers are only our helpers, and parents are the ones who are responsible for their upbringing. However, besides their mom, the teachers are the ones who know kids the best.

"But I have a problem in participating with Tomasito's teacher, and with doing things in the school. The problem is that my English is not good, like my husband's, and Ms. Brady doesn't speak Spanish. Tomasito says the classroom helper speaks Spanish, but I am not certain who he is. I can say things to Ms. Brady okay, but I have trouble really understanding her. When I returned the book, I just couldn't understand what Ms. Brady was saying to me—she was talking quickly, and there was lots of noise. I would like to learn English well, so I could volunteer for the teachers and help them in the classroom. Also, if I knew English, I could be a better helper to my children with homework. I would like to be able to volunteer also so I could see how the teachers teach, what the environment is really like. Maybe they need someone to help clean up? And I could bring my baby son with me?

"With Tomasito's teacher, I don't know if it's because I don't understand English well, or who knows, but she *always* says in the meetings that Tomasito is doing things well, that he is improving. But that is all. Also, she talks mostly about his behavior. I used to get very excited about those little certificates. But then they give out so many awards to Tomasito, all for being a good citizen, for following the rules. I wish the teacher would let us know as much about his academic progress as about all those awards. It is true, after all, that Tomasito is not that far ahead in his schoolwork. And I wish she would tell us what to do about his math.

"I do like getting notes. Since my English is not good, this gives me a chance to slowly understand things. And notes, not like phone calls, you can share with your husband, or show it to the child and tell them—'Look, this is what the teacher says.' Most of all, I wish we could just talk together at school. But then Tomasito doesn't like that."

COMMUNICATING ABOUT TOMASITO'S MATH

Linda Brady needs to connect with Tomasito's family to figure out the sources of his math difficulties. Parent-teacher conferences are over for the year. With summer fast approaching, she feels she needs to do something soon to prevent any further slippage over the summer months. What should she do?

DISCUSSION QUESTIONS

Major Issues

The purpose of this case is for educators to consider the child as actively shaping and being shaped by home and school contexts generally, and the home-school relationship in particular. The case is designed to help educators gain a comprehensive and ecological understanding of the child, including the following:

- How the child influences the parent-teacher relationship
- Different ecological contexts shaping the child's development
- Communicating a comprehensive picture of the child to parents

Describing the Situation

- What is Tomasito like?
- How does Linda view Tomasito? What does she see as his strengths and weaknesses? How does this compare to Tomasito's parents' view of him and his academic ability?
- What is the relationship between Linda and Tomasito's parents like?
- What is the central problem in this case?

Exploring Contributing Factors

- How do home and classroom contexts shape Tomasito's development? For example, how do Tomasito's homework routines influence his math learning? To what extent does Linda understand this home context?
- How does Tomasito—his characteristics, preferences, and behaviors— influence the relationship between his family and his teacher? How much information are they able to acquire about the other?
- What expectations do Ria and Tomás have for their children? What function do you think culture plays in the development of these expectations?

Articulating Possible Next Steps

- What should Linda do next?
- How might she better understand and build on Tomasito's active influence in the home-school relationship?
- How might she communicate more complete information about Tomasito to the family?
- What support might she offer to this family around homework?

- What should Ria and Tomás do next?
- How might they better support Tomasito's math learning? For example, how could Tomasito's homework routines be shaped to be more sustainable, meaningful, and congruent?

Replaying the Case

- What might Linda, Ria, or Tomás have done differently at any point in the story?
- For example, what if Ria decided not to leave the classroom in response to Tomasito's embarrassment? What if Linda did not jump to a conclusion about why Ria left suddenly, but asked Ria about it directly? How might this have changed the evolution of the case?

Looking at the Bigger Picture

- What assumptions does Linda make about Tomasito's family based on his culture? What assumptions suggest cultural bias? How might these assumptions get in the way of her expectations for Tomasito?
- The school principal greets Spanish-speaking parents in Spanish at school. What other things might she do to support Spanish-speaking parents? How might she help staff, the majority of whom are not Latino, better understand the school's Latino families?
- Although this is a small school, Linda was evidently not aware that Tomasito's older brother attended the same school. What staffing communication structures might the principal enact to facilitate a focus on families?
- To enable Ria and Tomas to participate more in their children's education, how would you connect the family with services available at the school? What additional resources might you search for in the community for them? Which additional resources would be especially useful to have in the school building?

RECOMMENDED READING

Eccles, J. (1999). The development of children ages 6 to 14. *Future of Children, 9*(2), 30–44. Available online at: http://www.futureofchildren.org/information2826/information_show.htm?doc_id=71891

Edwards, R., & Alldred, P. (2000). A typology of parental involvement in education centering on children and young people: Negotiating familialisation, institutionalisation, and individualisation. *British Journal of Sociology of Education, 21*(3), 435–455.

Case 2: A Special Education Plan for Anabela

Does Supporting Her Needs Mean Holding Her Back?[2]

by Margaret A. Vaughan

Characters:

Anabela, second grader

Connie, Anabela's resource room teacher

Jean, Anabela's teacher

Magda, Anabela's mother

Gaspar, Anabela's father

Arturo, Anabela's grandfather

Ms. Layton, La Paz Elementary School Principal

TEACHER TO TEACHER: TALKING OVER ANABELA'S PROGRESS

Connie York, the resource room teacher, enters Jean Harfleur's second-grade classroom at La Paz Elementary School. She and Jean have a close working relationship. Connie sighs, "I just can't get Anabela's mother more involved!" Jean sympathetically puts her arm around Connie's shoulder.

Several months have passed since Anabela Vicenti's placement in special services and, though her mother, Magda, was initially eager and involved, she has not attended any parent-teacher conferences since the initial IEP (Individualized Education Plan) team meeting in November.

Connie sighs again. "It's easy to see that Anabela's family gives her a lot emotionally, but I'm still not so sure about academically. I really want them to be more involved with the goals of Anabela's IEP.

"I know we've been back and forth on this, but I feel strongly that Anabela should be retained next year to avoid a more restrictive full-day placement. Retention will give her the same model of services for another year and let her have time in the regular classroom with her peers. It's worked so well for her this year. I don't want to rock the boat now. I'm afraid the demands of the third-grade curriculum and schedule will overwhelm Anabela, even with the resource room services."

Jean nods her head slowly. "Oh, Connie, I hear you, but so few kids are retained here at La Paz. I just don't want Anabela to feel left out and perhaps even more insecure."

As you read this case, consider applying the following theoretical lenses to your analysis:

- Developmental-Contextual: What are Anabela Vicenti's self-regulatory skills like, including her mastery motivation and social-emotional regulation? What are Magda and Gaspar's stress levels like in relation to parenting two children with special needs? What are their coping skills and social support networks like?
- Motivation to Learn: What are Anabela's motivation-related feelings, including her sense of competence, control, and social connectedness?

ANABELA'S CUMULATIVE RECORD

According to Anabela's cumulative record from Sandia, her prior elementary school, she was classified as a nonreader at the end of kindergarten, not knowing all her letters and sounds. She was referred for educational testing then, but never received it.

File notes indicate that the first-grade teacher worried about the effect of this delay in receiving services on Anabela's progress. Without resource room help, the teacher created her own set of goals for Anabela related to reading, writing, adding, and attention span. At the end of first grade, she recommended retention, but only as a backup strategy—provided Anabela did not get into the resource room in second grade. Anabela's parents consented to testing and advocated strongly for an IEP for their daughter. They also complained adamantly to the principal about the recommendation to retain.

Fortunately, when Anabela transferred to La Paz in October of her second-grade year, she received testing, an IEP, and resource room services, as well as additional assistance from the resource room aide in her regular classroom.

ANABELA'S MOTHER MAGDA AND HER AGENDA

"Anabela's grandpa and I went to the principal at Anabela's old school a lot. Her first-grade teacher was always late or absent. Her special education referral was delayed. And Anabela was placed in a modified bilingual class. I later discovered that Anabela was the only one identified as English Only in her class, so the teacher spoke mostly in Spanish. We are Mexican and have a Spanish last name, but we don't speak Spanish at home. That class did not help Anabela, and I let the principal know it.

"My husband, Gaspar, has been ill for the past few years. I have to help take care of him. This past year I injured my knee. My husband Gaspar worries. Gaspar did not ask many questions when we went to school to sign the IEP, but after the meeting, he said to me, 'I want to understand Anabela's disability and to be there when she needs me.' Though he does not help much with her homework, he spends all the time with her that he can.

"My father, Arturo, and my older kids have to help me. My father is the one who walks Anabela to school. He says to me, 'I like that the teachers see me every day. They know that I always keep an eye on our Anabela.' If he tells me something I don't like, I go to the principal to work it out. I also get to school for the important things like the IEP team meeting.

"After Anabela's first special education referral at Sandia, I felt relieved and wanted her tested right away. You see, I know about special ed. My older son, Richard, is in a resource room. They tested him so late, and I always wondered why he was not referred sooner. Now testing was being delayed with Anabela too!

"Then our family moved to a new neighborhood, and I decided to enroll Anabela at La Paz. What a difference—the school is so well run, and the principal knows every child by name! I am so impressed.

"I am also relieved. I can stop fighting for a while. The resource room is giving Anabela what she needs. At the IEP meeting, they explained that her problems are both academic and social. She has a learning disability, and I guess she depends on the teachers too much. I know because she can be like that at home too. She is my baby, my youngest. I spoil her, I know. I don't make her do chores, but she likes to help me if I ask.

"Lately my knee is better and I feel busy again. We're a close family and spend a lot of time together on sports. I think Anabela's soccer team is good for her. I told the coach to go easy on her though. I'm not going to let him pressure her. It's a game and supposed to be for fun. She's a sensitive child.

"At Sandia they would 'bench' Anabela for things like forgetting her homework. We'd go crazy looking for homework in the morning, and she'd be so upset. It's easier now that we have a routine. Besides, Ms. Harfleur and Ms. York seem so understanding. I can tell they're nice because Anabela is happy now. I just don't want her to feel pressured. My dad can see the difference too. Finally, all my work and this new school have made a difference.

SPECIAL EDUCATION AT LA PAZ

Both Sandia and La Paz are predominantly Latino schools, but La Paz is smaller and more economically diverse. La Paz makes concerted efforts to follow special education guidelines and timelines. The principal, Ms. Layton, expects the teachers to value families and views the school as a community.

State and district policies also shape special education placement at La Paz. For example, the state requires that placements in special education verify that a child's second language was not the deciding factor in determining delays, and specialists are expected to distinguish learning disabilities from problems stemming from environmental factors. The district has guidelines on retention of special needs students, and La Paz generally discourages it. Teachers must provide a detailed rationale, and decisions are made on a case-by-case basis.

JEAN HARFLEUR, ANABELA'S TEACHER, ON ANABELA AND HER FAMILY

"I don't know Anabela that well because she's in the resource room or with the classroom aide so much. But I do know she's eager to learn, and somewhat fearful. She tries to prove herself in class, yet all the kids know she is low academically. Anabela visits the resource room for two hours every day, which limits her opportunities for friendship. She's babied by the other girls in the class and maybe by her family too.

"The delay in special education placement at her last school put Anabela in a tough spot. Overall, she has adapted well, and her behavior is not a huge issue. These things bode well for third grade. But she's also immature and distractible, getting out of her seat often and constantly asking for help. She needs more individual time than I can offer.

"Anabela's parents came to the IEP team meeting, but since then verbal communication has been scarce. They sign the papers I send home, but that's it. I recently learned that family health issues prevented Magda from attending the parent-teacher conference a few weeks ago. Anabela's grandfather brings her every morning, but he observes more than asks questions. I should try to talk with him more."

CONNIE YORK, ANABELA'S RESOURCE ROOM TEACHER, ON ANABELA AND HER FAMILY

"Anabela's family is so pleased with La Paz, but Magda views my resource room as the cure to Anabela's needs. According to testing, Anabela needs comprehensive help—particularly in reading and writing. Her strength is in verbal reasoning—she tested two years above grade level.

"I share goals and progress regularly with the family, but I want more involvement from Magda with homework and IEP goals. I don't know Anabela's parents that well, but I do know they've had stressful health issues recently and I think they both work.

"At the IEP meeting, Magda and Gaspar made it clear how unhappy they were with Anabela's prior school. Dad seemed caring and expressed his interest. I haven't wanted to create stress by bringing up the idea of retention, even though I'm convinced it's best for Anabela. It would be easier to raise this issue with Magda if I saw her more. She tends to communicate directly with Ms. Layton, our principal. She talked directly with Ms. Layton about a child who was bothering her daughter, before even talking with Jean.

"Anabela needs intensive work and time to gain confidence. Anabela is talkative, but more tentative. I encourage Anabela to learn to work on her own and believe in herself. We can do a disservice if we don't encourage independent work and thinking among children with learning disabilities."

ANABELA, ON FAMILY, LEARNING, AND SCHOOL

"I never read at home by myself. It's not fun like it is when I read with Mom. I don't read with my dad, but he takes me to work with him sometimes. When my mom hurt her knee, I cried and asked her if I could stay at home with her. She let me if it was real rainy, but otherwise I had to go to school. She's working again now, but I still help her put on her socks and pick up her things. My mom teaches me things like my preschool teacher did. Mom taught me how to tie my shoes and got me to be brave and try soccer too.

"My grandpa takes me to school every day and gives me two dollars too. My grandpa says, 'Seeing you in school makes the family proud. I want you to do your learning and do your work.' He has a desk at his house down the street for me to do homework, and he helps me. I like when we go for walks to the coffee shop for a donut. I like having a bigger family. My mom says you have more people to help you.

"I go to the resource room with two kids from my class. Sometimes we have to sit alone so we won't talk. We have a lot of work there. I know I'm good at thinking even when it's hard for me to read. Ms. York says to use my thinking to help me read. She says, 'You just have to believe in yourself.' I'm not so good at writing, but I'm good at jumping rope. Ms. Harfleur helps me too. She's nice to me and never yells. I can read sentences now and all my number words. Math and writing—ugh! I do like when we sing in math. When I grow up, I want to be one of those singers that dances too."

PUTTING THE PIECES TOGETHER

Jean sits in her classroom at the end of the day and stares out the window. It's her responsibility as classroom teacher to make retention recommendations to the principal shortly before the close of the school year. Her head is beginning to hurt.

"I think of Connie as my savior, and I usually defer to her. Besides, she knows Anabela the best and certainly made a convincing case for retention. But I still feel ambivalent. And given the climate here, I'd have to make a really airtight case for retention to Ms. Layton. And then there are the parents. I hardly know them, but they opposed retention when Anabela was at Sandia. Who knows how they would respond to the idea now?"

Jean rests her head in her hands. "How am I going to put all these pieces together?"

DISCUSSION QUESTIONS[3]

Major Issues

The purpose of this case is for educators to consider how children's development influences parents' and teachers' educational decision making, and how to promote collaborative educational planning and placement among school staff and between school staff and families, particularly for children with special needs. The case is designed to help educators understand the following:

- How the child's development influences parents' and teachers' decisions around special services and school learning

- The role of family involvement in the referral and placement process for special education
- Communication and collaboration processes with school teams and with families of children with disabilities

Describing the Situation

- What is the central problem in this case?
- How do Connie and Jean define their roles with children and families differently?

Exploring Contributing Factors

- How do Anabela's social skills and needs affect her academic progress?
- How do family relationships shape Anabela's social-emotional and cognitive development?
- How do the teachers' and mother's view of Anabela affect their decision making?
- How do beliefs held by Connie and Jean influence the communication and referral process?
- How does the extent and nature of Magda's executive functioning differ across the two school contexts (Sandia and La Paz)?

Articulating Possible Next Steps

- What factors should Connie York and Jean Harfleur consider to determine whether Anabela should be retained?
- How might Magda react to requests for more family involvement and the suggestion of retention by Connie or Jean? How should Connie and Jean communicate recommendations and requests to Magda?
- How can Magda make a difference in the decision-making process about third grade?
- How, if at all, should Anabela be a part of home-school communication, given her verbal skills and self-awareness? How might other family members be engaged in home-school communication?

Replaying the Case

- How would Anabela's school life be different if she had stayed at Sandia? How would Magda's involvement differ if Anabela were still untested and without an IEP?
- How would the dilemma change if the school district and La Paz had a different policy on student retention?
- Jean admits that she doesn't know Anabela or Magda well because she hasn't spent much time with them. How might Jean's opinion on retention change if she knew Anabela and Magda better?

Looking at the Bigger Picture

- How can teachers explain "holding back" to parents when a child is making progress? When retaining a child, how can teachers and parents maintain that child's motivation to learn?
- How can schools support parents of children with disabilities?
- What is the principal's role in bridging communication between family and teachers?
- How can schools create an environment that responds quickly and effectively to children's needs, without causing families to relax their level of engagement with the child or the school?
- Considering your perspective or situation, are there populations in your community about whom people make general assumptions (given that Anabela was not a Spanish speaker)? Who do you know in your community who could help you best communicate with Anabela's family? What programs or agencies would contact that would help Anabela's family?

RECOMMENDED READING

Lake, J., & Billingsley, B. S. (2000). An analysis of factors that contribute to parent-school conflict in special education. *Race: Remedial & Special Education, 21,* 240–251.

Sanders, M. (2000). Creating successful school-based partnership programs with families of special needs students. *School Community Journal, 10,* 37–56.

Case 3: My Favorite Subject Is Lunch

Motivating a Disengaged Student

by Phyllis Blumenfeld

Characters:

Anthony, fourth grader

Jason, Anthony's teacher

Cynthia, Anthony's reading teacher

Sue, Anthony's mother

Thomas, Anthony's father

Caroline, Anthony's grandmother

ANTHONY BARBARIN AT SCHOOL

"And time is up" Jason Mitchell said. "Put your pencils away, hand me your test, and grab anything you need for lunch." The classroom rumbled as 25 fourth-grade students jumped up, pushed in their chairs, made their way to Mr. Mitchell's desk and then scattered out the door for the cafeteria. Anthony was the last to reach Mr. Mitchell and walked at a distinctively slower pace than the rest of his classmates. Anthony handed in his exam.

"You didn't answer all the questions, Anthony," said Mr. Mitchell as he glanced quickly at Anthony's test and then at his student.

Anthony mumbled, "Yeah. It was too hard."

Mr. Mitchell sighed. "I know its only November, but I've seen your work starting to get worse, Anthony. And you're getting lazier. We've talked about having to pass fourth-grade tests to do well. That means working hard."

Anthony nodded his head, "I know." He then shrugged his shoulders and walked with his head down out of the room by himself for lunch.

As you read this case, consider applying the following theoretical lenses in your analysis:

- Parenting Children with Disabilities: How might Anthony's self-regulatory skills relate to his difficulties in school? How do family processes impact his development?
- Motivation to Learn: In which areas does Anthony exhibit feelings of competence, control, and connectedness? What behaviors might point to a lack of motivation in school?
- Ecocultural Understanding: What are the daily routines and activities that shape Anthony's development? How do these cultural activities take on various functions beyond their most explicit purpose?

ANTHONY

In the cafeteria, Anthony got his lunch and then sat at the end of the long fourth-grade table.

"Hey guys, look at this," he yelled down the table to a few of the other boys in the class.

When he got their attention, he flipped his eyelids inside out.

"Gross!" everyone yelled.

Anthony enjoyed getting a reaction from his peers. He thought to himself, "I'm glad it's lunch time. At least now things will get exciting. That math test was too boring! It was just one problem after another, and they took such a long time to do. I used to like math, but now I think it's boring. Sometimes I feel like Mr. Mitchell is trying to confuse us with talking about how to use a protractor, do angles, and add and multiply fractions. Mr. Mitchell says I'm getting lazy. But really, what's the point?"

Anthony is an eleven-year-old African American fourth grader. When asked about school, his notions about what's fun include watching movies, art class, and lunch. Although Anthony doesn't enjoy most school work, he thinks positively of his teacher, Jason Mitchell.

"He treats all of us the same, and I know that he cares. He gives us a lot of work so we'll pass the grade. He usually jokes around a lot and is pretty fair and helps students with their work. Sometimes I get up in a bad mood, but when I come to school, he like jokes around, and I get happier because he makes school more fun. The only thing I don't like is that Mr. Mitchell yells a lot, and sometimes he doesn't listen to what kids have to say. He also gives lots of punishment and homework when our class is bad."

The only subject Anthony doesn't have with Mr. Mitchell is reading.

His stomach dropped as he thought about going to reading class after lunch. "I hate reading. It makes me sleepy. The only good thing about reading is that our teacher Ms. Hague gives us 15 minutes of quiet time for reading, so we don't have to do work the whole time."

At that moment, a boy in Anthony's class yelled out to a girl passing by.

"Yo! Devon says you're ugly." All of the boys at the table began to laugh and hoot.

Anthony laughed out loud too. Although Anthony didn't necessarily like all the teasing and fighting that went on at school, he didn't have a best friend and really wanted to be accepted by the other boys. He went along with it, which sometimes left him in trouble at home and in school.

"Some boys in class act tough, and some boys don't like to do their work. They like to play and don't care if they get in trouble. There are girls too who think they're all that. Like if someone is doing a problem on the board, and that person gets it wrong, the class will start laughing. I guess it's really not that funny, because they were trying. But I'll tease them too.

"Sometimes kids get on my nerves. Like when we're play wrestling. We don't hit each other for real, we just pretend hit each other. Sometimes, though, kids will fight for real. That's when I don't want to fight no more 'cause we get in trouble. I try to tell other kids that, but they don't listen to me. And then when the teacher comes over, they say it's my fault."

The one thing Anthony does like about school is art class.

"I wish there were time to do art all day. Like last year, we got together and made a mural on the wall outside of the school for Black History Month. I even went in one Saturday to help out and liked walking around the school when it was empty."

Anthony mostly looked forward to the end of the school day when he could meet his father at the corner store and help him with the cash register.

"I really don't like school. Everybody says it's like a jail for kids. They keep on saying that one day—when we're in school—they're going to lock up all the doors so we won't ever get out. I know they're joking. But it's still hard. I'm getting lazier, and I know I'm gonna have to get better. I'll have to be reading more, which I hate in the first place."

JASON MITCHELL AND CYNTHIA HAGUE, ANTHONY'S TEACHERS

Meanwhile, in the teachers' lounge, Jason Mitchell sat down to eat. Mr. Mitchell is African American and has been teaching for nine years, all in the fourth- and fifth-grade level at Northside Elementary School. He has a master's degree in education and a certificate to teach mathematics in grades 6–8, although he enjoys the younger grades more. Northside is a typical elementary school that runs from grades K–4. Mr. Mitchell is very structured and usually well prepared for his classes. He has good management skills, although he raises his voice quite often. He usually addresses his students with respect and is known for his ability to joke and be friendly.

Recently his district had been going through a number of structural reform initiatives including reducing student-teacher ratios, increasing supports and opportunities for students and adults, instituting more flexible procedures for allocating resources, and setting clear and fair academic and conduct standards. Mr. Mitchell worried that these reforms were taking away from his ability to do project-based work in his classroom. For the past few years he had focused mainly on the skills the kids needed to pass the fourth-grade math statewide exam.

His friend and fellow fourth-grade teacher, Cynthia Hague, sat down next to him to eat her lunch. This was Cynthia's third year at Northside. She was one of the few white teachers and one of the younger teachers in the school. She had a BA in elementary education and was thinking about returning to school for her master's degree. In the beginning of the year, Cynthia and Jason decided to decentralize their classes to help prepare the students for the transition to middle school next year. Specifically, their classrooms switched for math and reading depending on ability, with Cynthia taking the lower reading class and Jason taking the lower math class. They also hoped to carry out a large combined class project on family histories and immigration and migration patterns in the United States. However they had not had a lot of time to plan it out yet.

"Cynthia" he asked, "How is Anthony doing in your reading class?"

"You know I'm glad you brought it up. He's not doing so well. I get the feeling that sometimes he's just staring off into space. And lately, he hasn't been coming in with any of his homework assignments. He tells me he forgets them at home."

"I've been seeing the same thing. The work is getting more difficult, and he's not approaching his new assignments with sincere effort or persisting when confronted with difficult problems. His work involvement is just declining. He didn't even finish all the answers in the test I gave him this morning. He doesn't participate in a lot of classroom discussions, and he seems withdrawn and uncommunicative. He talks about how he likes art class, but art is not as demanding as other subjects. More and more, he's interfering with other people's work and getting into fights. He listens for directions, but doesn't ask for help when he needs it."

Cynthia joined in, "I know. I really try to talk to the kids in my class about strategies to do well in school and later in life, such as reading things more than once, thinking about and engaging in what they're reading, and organizing their thoughts to make sense of text. I try to get my kids to relate new information to existing knowledge and go back over things they don't understand."

"Right!" Jason said, "I might tell them on math exams to skip problems they don't understand and go back to work on them more in depth later. But I think Anthony just skips them altogether. He's not making sense of the work we do."

The two began to brainstorm reasons why Anthony wasn't doing well. They also discussed the fact that he didn't seem to have many friends. They bounced ideas off each other such as perhaps a learning disability, problems transitioning between the two teachers for math and reading, and little support at home.

"I'm not sure how organized things are for Anthony at home—and I don't know what kinds of routines his family has set up around homework and study habits. I don't know what they do together as a family. Hopefully, I'll meet his mother next week at parent-teacher conferences, but maybe I'll give her a call before that."

THE BARBARIN FAMILY

Anthony lives at home with his mother, father, and his grandmother. He is an only child. His mother, Sue, age 28, works as an aide in a nursing home for the elderly. She is married and lives with her husband, Thomas, who manages a small convenience store that is popular in the community. Sue and Thomas met in high school, graduated in the same class, and got married shortly after she became pregnant with Anthony. Sue's mother, Caroline, recently moved into the house and has taken over a lot of the cooking and cleaning responsibilities, leaving time for Sue to start taking nursing classes at the local community college.

After a hectic morning of getting Anthony out of bed, ready for school, and out the door, Sue and Caroline sat down to have breakfast together before Sue left for work.

"Wasn't that a tough morning!" said Caroline.

"You said it. Maybe Anthony needs to go to bed a little earlier so he doesn't wake up in such a haze," Sue offered.

"Or maybe he should stop going to the store after school and come straight home. Now that I'm here, the minute he walks in the door, he can get right to work on his homework. That way he can be done before dinner and get a good night's sleep," suggested Caroline.

"It's just that I know he loves going to the store. It became such a routine over the past few years, I left work to pick him up at school, brought him straight to the store and then went back to work. Now that he's older, he's allowed to walk there himself. Now I also let him help out his dad when he first arrives at the store, rather than make him finish his homework right away. He can do his homework after dinner. Thomas is always telling me how much Anthony likes working the register. He's gotten real good at doing the calculations in his head and always gives the customers the right amount of change. Just the other day I went by, and he rang me up and flipped my penny change in the air to me with his thumb."

"He really is a smart one," Caroline said. "How's he doing this year in school? I know he had some trouble last year."

"Good. He hasn't gotten in any trouble that I know of. We talk about it a lot. I tell him that he better stay out of trouble, or else he'll be punished here—and that means not getting to go to the store with his father or watching television. He knows better than to mess around. We're always telling him to study hard and do good in school so he can get a good job later on. We tell him to behave so that he doesn't grow up to be a crackhead or seven feet tall in fifth grade."

Caroline began to laugh at the image of Anthony towering over his peers if he were not promoted past the fifth grade. Yet, Caroline also had some serious concerns and questions. Why didn't she see more of Anthony's friends around the house or the neighborhood? Should she start taking him to the park or for walks around the neighborhood? Then she could tell him more about what it was like when she was growing up and his family history. Was experience at the cash register really the kind of math he needed to be able to do well in school? Why didn't she know more about what was going on at Anthony's school? Sometimes Sue helped Anthony with homework, but most nights he went straight to his room after dinner and shut the door. Was he really getting his work done?

When Caroline asked about what Anthony did at school, he usually responded "nothing" or talked about hanging out with his friends at lunch. Surely there was more to school than just lunch. Caroline vowed to ignite some passion for learning in her grandson.

DISCUSSION QUESTIONS

Major Issues

The purpose of this case is for educators to gain an understanding of children's motivation in school and how it relates to the home-school relationship. The case is designed to help educators consider the following:

- The influence of student motivation on the home-school relationship
- The different contexts shaping children's affective, behavioral, and cognitive engagement
- Ways that families and school personnel might work together to engage children

Describing the Situation

- Which school and after-school activities does Anthony enjoy?
- How does Anthony feel about reading and math?
- What does Anthony communicate about his school life to his family?
- Describe the relationship between Ms. Hague and Mr. Mitchell and the Barbarin family. How is this relationship affected by Anthony's level of engagement?
- In what contexts does Anthony feel most successful?
- Describe Anthony's relationship with his peers.

Exploring Contributing Factors

- How does Anthony's work at the store contribute to his sense of self?
- What external motivators do Anthony's parents and teachers employ?
- What are Anthony's expectations about rewards and punishments for his behavior and performance in school?
- What messages does Anthony receive from his teachers about who he is and who he should be? From his family? From his peers?
- What are Ms. Hague's and Mr. Mitchell's perceptions of Anthony? What assumptions do they make about him and his family?

Articulating Possible Next Steps

- Identify opportunities for home-school communication in this case. How might the school better capitalize on them?
- What is Anthony's homework routine like? What other routines does Anthony have in his life outside of school? Which routines are meaningful? How can Anthony's parents and teachers shape and harness his home routines to foster school learning?
- How might Mr. Mitchell talk with the Barbarins about Anthony's abilities?
- How might Anthony's teachers, Mr. Mitchell and Ms. Hague, and his parents learn more about each other? How could better relationship between home and school be utilized to increase Anthony's motivation to learn?
- What would you do to learn more about a student like Anthony in your own school and community?

Looking at the Bigger Picture

- How might larger educational policies influence children's overall motivation and engagement in school?
- Brainstorm ways that families and local community groups can help shape classroom curriculum in ways that are authentic to students and help motivate and engage students.
- How can schools and families collaborate on matters of instruction and curriculum? How can school leaders and teachers apply learning that takes place in children's homes and communities to the school curriculum?
- What can teachers and school leaders do to address the emotional and social needs of parents and their children?

RECOMMENDED READING

Stipek, D., & Seal, K. (2001). *Motivated minds: Raising children who love learning.* New York: Henry Holt.

Notes

1. An earlier version of this case was originally published on the Family Involvement Network of Educators, Harvard Family Research Project, Web site: http://www.gse.harvard.edu/hfrp/projects/fine/resources/teaching-case/tomasito.html

2. An earlier version of this case was originally published on the Family Involvement Network of Educators, Harvard Family Research Project, Web site: http://www.gse.harvard.edu/hfrp/projects/fine/resources/teaching-case/anabela.html

3. We would like to thank Jonathan Alderson for contributing to an earlier version of these discussion questions.

References for Stipek

Bandura, A. (1977). Self-efficacy: Toward a unifying theory of behavioral change. *Psychological Review, 84,* 191–215.

Kazdin, A. (1988). The token economy: A decade later. In G. Davey & C. Cullen (Eds.), *Human operant conditioning and behavior modification* (pp. 199–237). New York: Wiley.

Kazdin, A., & Bootzin, R. (1972). The token economy: An evaluative review. *Journal of Applied Behavior Analysis, 5,* 343–372.

Lepper, M. (1973). Dissonance, self-perception, and honesty in children. *Journal of Personality and Social Psychology, 25,* 65–74.

Mace, F., & Kratochwill, T. (1988). Self-monitoring. In J. Will, S. Elliott, & F. Gresham (Eds.), *Handbook of behavior therapy in education* (pp. 489–522). New York: Plenum.

O'Leary, K., & Drabman, R. (1971). Token reinforcement programs in the classroom: A review. *Psychological Bulletin, 75,* 379–398.

Ryan, R., & Grolnick, W. (1986). Origins and pawns in the classroom: Self-report and projective assessments of individual differences in children's perceptions. *Journal of Personality and Social Psychology, 50,* 350–358.

Shapiro, E., & Cole, C. (1994). *Behavior change in the classroom: Self-management interventions.* New York: Guilford Press.

Stipek, D. (2002). *Motivation to learn: Integrating theory and practice* (4th ed.). Needham Heights, MA: Allyn and Bacon.

Stipek, D., & Seal, K. (2001). *Motivated minds: Raising children who love learning.* New York: Henry Holt.

References for Hauser-Cram et al.

Bandura, A. (1977). Self-efficacy: Toward a unifying theory of behavioral change. *Psychological Review, 84,* 191–215.

Bronson, M. B. (2000). *Self-regulation in early education.* New York: Guilford.

Bullock, M., & Lutkenhaus, P. (1988). The development of volitional behavior in the toddler years. *Child Development, 59,* 664–674.

Hauser-Cram, P., & Howell, A. (2003). The development of young children with disabilities and their families: Implications for policies and programs. In R. M. Lerner, F. Jacobs, & D. Wertlieb (Eds.), *Handbook of applied developmental science* (pp. 259–279). Thousand Oaks, CA: Sage.

Hauser-Cram, P., Warfield, M. E., Shonkoff, J. P., Krauss, M.W., Sayer, A., & Upshur, C. (2001). Children with disabilities: A longitudinal study of child development and parent well-being. *Monographs of the Society for Research in Child Development, 66*(93, Serial No. 266).

Knitzer, J. (2000). Early childhood mental health services: A policy and systems developmental perspective. In J. P. Shonkoff & S. J. Meisels (Eds.), *Handbook of early childhood intervention* (2nd ed., pp. 416–438). New York: Cambridge University Press.

Lerner, R. M. (1991). Changing organism-context relations as the basic process of development: A developmental contextual perspective. *Developmental Psychology, 27,* 27–32.

Minuchin, P. P. (1988). Relationships within the family: A systems perspective on development. In R. A. Hinde & J. Stevenson-Hinde (Eds.), *Relationships within families: Mutual influences.* New York: Oxford University Press.

Shonkoff, J., Hauser-Cram, P., Krauss, M., & Upshur, C. (1992). Development of infants with disabilities and their families: Implications for theory and service delivery. *Monographs of the Society for Research in Child Development, 57*(6, Serial No. 230).

Stipek, D. J., Recchia, S., & McClintic, S. M. (1992). Self-evaluation in young children. *Monographs of the Society for Research in Child Development, 57*(1, Serial No. 226).

Section 2

The Mesosystem

In Section 1 of this volume, we presented theoretical lenses and teaching cases for which microsystemic processes were most salient. In this section, we focus on the **mesosystem**, which in ecological systems theory refers to the relationships and interactions among the immediate contexts in which child development occurs. These interactions can occur at multiple levels, such as between and among settings (e.g., the school and the afterschool program), or between and among the individuals inhabiting those settings (such as the teacher and the afterschool program director). Examples of the types of interactions occurring in the mesosystem include the effects of children's experiences within the family context on their experiences at school (and vice versa) or the effects of neighborhood characteristics on family functioning.

Ecological systems theory defines the mesosystem as comprising "the linkages and settings containing the developing person," or "a system of microsystems" (Bronfenbrenner, 1989, p. 227). Microsystems are those contexts that contain the developing person (in the case of this volume, the focal child), many of which can overlap. For example, a child's friendship and peer networks at home and at school often overlap, because many children attend school in their neighborhoods. This is an example of linkages among several microsystems—peers, neighborhood, and school—all of which contain the developing child on an almost daily basis. A number of different processes can emerge from these linkages and may have significant influences on the child's development. For example, a child may be drawn to a different peer group at school than at home but nonetheless may feel obligated to "hang out" with the neighborhood kids at lunch time. Tensions such as this are likely to influence the child's interactions in each of these settings.

Section 2 contains two theoretical lenses and four teaching cases that effectively illustrate how processes in the mesosystem can relate to children's development. First, Pamela Davis-Kean and Jacquelynne Eccles present a model of Social Executive Functioning that draws heavily upon and extends ecological systems theory. The social executive functioning model represents children's development as being dependent on the effectiveness of parents and other significant adults in coordinating the connections among children's microsystems. That is, parents or primary caregivers are the principal conduits through which children receive information about the world and how it operates, and about what their roles in the world might be. Moreover, parents and caregivers use that information in guiding their children's experiences. In this way, the family acts as an executive functionary, or a body that manages information processing and decision-making on behalf of the developing child. The ultimate goal is for children to develop into well-functioning adults who will themselves become executive functionaries for both their own and others' children's lives.

The social executive functioning model is essentially a mesosystem model, as one of its critical tenets is that executive functionaries must work closely together to ensure children's optimal development. Specifically, the connection and coordination among microsystems can support or inhibit the flow of information about children, the management of their learning opportunities, and the development of their executive functioning skills. The model asserts that the relative influence of one executive functionary—such as the school—is dependent on the executive functioning of another, such as the family. For example, to the extent that the family is an efficient manager of information and experiences for the child, less is required of the school in its capacity as an executive functionary.

The executive functioning model can provide a useful framework for understanding and analyzing the cases in this volume. In this section, we have included four particular cases because of their emphasis on the connections between family, school, and community—or the mesosystem. In "Defining 'Fine': Communicating Academic Progress to Parents," we meet first-grader Nathan, whose teacher has recommended that he attend summer school to maintain his reading progress. In this way, Nathan's teacher has acted as an executive functionary, using and analyzing information about Nathan's abilities and making decisions about how to enhance his progress, based on the information she has obtained. Nathan's mother, however, is surprised by the recommendation, as his teacher has communicated all along that he was performing at grade level in reading. Although both Nathan's mother and his teacher are acting as executive functionaries, managing information and organizing his experiences pertaining to his academic progress, problems occur because of the breakdown in communication between the microsystems of school and family. As a result, both systems continue to work at full capacity as executive functionaries, but not necessarily in concert. Similar issues arise in "Bilingual Voices and Parent Classroom Choices," where a mother, teacher, and school principal have different notions about whether bilingual placement would be best for first-grader Nina Campos.

The second lens in this section, "How Do Communities Support Family Involvement? An Exploratory Framework," by Heather Weiss and M. Elena Lopez addresses the role of community institutions in facilitating greater continuity across children's contexts. The authors' definition of community is broad, encompassing socially interdependent groups of people ranging from neighborhoods to racial and cultural groups. Their bottom line is that communities are self-defined, provide their members with a sense of belonging, and are committed to upholding a set of practices, beliefs, and values shared among them.

Community institutions can provide resources that facilitate the connections between children's families and their schools. For example, many contemporary afterschool programs transport children from their schools and provide homework supervision and assistance. These resources are particularly beneficial to families who don't have flexible work schedules, have multiple obligations at home or are not confident about their own capacity for helping their children with homework.

In the case, "Staying on a Path Toward College," we are introduced to Paulo, a sixth-grade, Mexican-American youth whose working-class parents have aspirations that he will take "the good path" in life, and ultimately graduate from college and get a well-paying job. As his parents worry that he is slipping from the path, they enlist assistance from members of their community. Paulo's godmother's son, who is an alumnus of a community college outreach program for low-income youth, helps him with homework and encourages him to apply for the program. The director of the program, Rachel Marquez, is committed to the program's mission of creating networks of youth who share the goal of going to college. In Paulo's case, resources from both community institutions (the college, the outreach program) and individual members of his and his family's cultural community (his godmother and her son) provide bridges across Paulo's worlds of family and school. Similarly, in "Lunchtime at Sunnydale Elementary School," grandmother Beatriz Hinojisa relies on members of her cultural community to give voice to her growing concerns about her granddaughters' safety at school.

As with the theories in Section 1, we encourage readers to consider the theoretical approaches in this section for other cases, aside from the cases included here. The point of this section is to illustrate the ways in which theory regarding properties of mesosystems can be applied to real-life dilemmas related to family educational involvement. Children's development occurs at home, at school, in neighborhoods, and in community institutions, all of which are interdependent contexts in many ways. What happens at home affects a child's experiences at school; what happens at school can affect a child's peer relationships outside of school; and so on. Readers are encouraged to explore the interrelationships among children's many microsystem contexts when trying to understand the dynamic underpinnings of their individual situations.

3

Theoretical Perspectives
on the Mesosystem

The theoretical perspectives included in this chapter focus most centrally on the linkages across children's developmental contexts, or across their microsystems. Hence, these perspectives are useful illustrations of processes occurring at the level of the mesosystem in children's ecology. Specifically, Pamela Davis-Kean and Jacquelynne Eccles present a model that positions parents and caregivers as executive functionaries in children's lives, managing the flow of information regarding the target children's development and using that information to organize those children's experiences. Importantly, the social executive functioning model works at the levels of both individuals and institutions, and the effectiveness of executive functionaries is largely dependent on the coordination of information flow among and between them.

Heather Weiss and M. Elena Lopez provide an empirically supported theoretical framework for understanding how communities and the institutions within them can support the links between families and schools. Although the community microsystem is emphasized in this perspective, it represents a mesosystem approach in that it focuses on the role of the community in connecting other systems. The authors define community broadly, describing it as being anchored in feelings of belonging and common objectives among its members.

We encourage readers to consider real-life situations to which these theoretical perspectives might be applicable. As examples of such applications, we have clustered the perspectives in this section with four teaching cases in the next chapter. Each of these teaching cases describes families' experiences in multiple contexts—home, school, neighborhood, cultural group—and how they are interconnected. Thus, the theories contained in this chapter can be readily applied to each of the cases.

Social Executive Functioning

*by Pamela Davis-Kean
and Jacquelynne S. Eccles*

Research suggests that home-school relationships that involve high levels of effective coordination and communication promote school success for children (Comer, 1980; Comer & Haynes, 1991; Epstein, 1990). Yet research also indicates that such coordination and communication among parents and teachers is rare and, if it does occur, is based on specific characteristics of parents, teachers, and schools (e.g., parents' backgrounds, teacher beliefs, and principal leadership; Comer & Haynes, 1991; Epstein, 1990; Hoover-Dempsey & Sandler, 1997). In this piece we introduce the *social executive functioning model*, which highlights how some schools and families jointly manage the healthy development of children through the effective coordination and communication of information and resources.

The social executive functioning model draws on both cognitive psychology, which focuses on the individual's ability to perceive, process, and produce information, and systems theory, which stresses the dynamic and complex relationships among individuals, institutions, and their various contexts. Within the individual, executive functioning is a cognitive process that occurs as people manage, evaluate, and respond to information and resources in their environments (Borkowski & Burke, 1996; Fletcher, 1996). We believe executive functioning can also occur at the group (or systems) level, as schools and other institutions manage and organize information coming into and flowing out of their organizations (Davis-Kean & Eccles, 2002).

To function effectively, individuals and systems must learn how to manage and coordinate the flow of information and to organize and carry out necessary tasks. At the individual level, children learn this through interacting with their physical and social environments. They take in and process information, leading to cognitive and social learning (Flavell, 1999). This flow of information occurs in a rich set of social contexts, and there are multiple avenues through which information and resources reach each child. Early in life this information is generally managed by parents or parental figures through both their daily practices and the decisions they make concerning the types of information and resources the child receives (Eccles, 1992; Fursternberg, Cook, Eccles, Elder, & Sameroff, 1999). As the child matures, teachers, religious figures, relatives, peer groups, and other significant people come to influence the informational flow and resources available to the child. Thus, over the years of childhood and adolescence, multiple significant others are engaged in managing the information and resources available to both inform children about their world and shape their growing knowledge and skill repertoire.

Moving beyond the individual, the concept of executive functioning can also help us think about how families (and other institutions such as schools) manage the healthy development of children. Just as individuals must process information and act on it to accomplish tasks, so must families and other institutions. Family management theorists, for example, propose that families' daily practices, particularly their managerial activities, are important influences on children's social and cognitive development (Furstenberg et al., 1999). These theorists argue that families orchestrate their children's daily lives in ways that provide them with opportunities and resources and protect them from risks and dangers.

Institutions and individuals beyond the family sphere (e.g., schools, communities, and teachers) also manage children's daily lives in ways that are intended to promote their healthy development. We describe the managerial and organizational process that occurs in systems (e.g., social institutions such as families, schools, and neighborhoods) as **socially organized executive functioning** and refer to the systems and individuals doing this work as **executive functionaries**. For example, schools act as children's executive functionaries when they institute schedules to organize children's time and activities. Similarly, families act as executive functionaries when they establish procedures for managing the tasks related to childrearing, such as mealtime, getting ready for school, afterschool activities, doing homework, and bedtime. Ideally, with the help of important individuals and institutions, children will eventually learn to perform these managerial and organizational tasks for themselves and ultimately become self-regulated socially connected adults.

Our model, derived in part from Bronfenbrenner and Morris's (1998) nested context model, depicts the role of executive functionaries in children's daily lives (see Figure 3.1). What is not depicted is the critical importance of these executive functionaries working closely together. Individuals and institutions can only be effective executive functionaries for children when they have sufficient and appropriate ways to take in, evaluate, and share information and resources with each other. Our model shows that individuals and institutions interact with and affect each other.

The model shows how some individuals and institutions (e.g., parents, schools) are close to children, while others (e.g., school board, mayor) may be more distant. However, closer elements are not necessarily more influential than more distant ones. Effective functioning is a dynamic property of the entire system. For example, the community context may not have a strong influence on one child if her family and school are effective executive functionaries on her behalf. By contrast, the community contexts may have a stronger influence on another child if his family and school are less effective in the area of executive functioning. Similarly, when a community and school have few resources, the family system will have more demands placed on its executive functioning as it attempts to provide the child with greater opportunities and minimize risks.

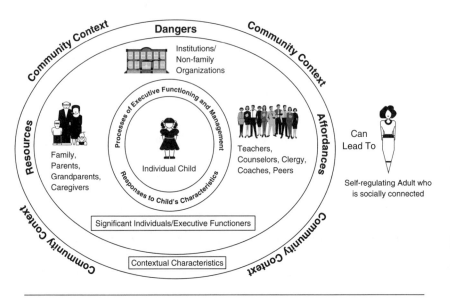

Figure 3.1   Social Executive Functioning Model

Note: The spheres are dynamically interacting such that contexts are affecting and being affected by executive functioners and the individual child.

For example, in poor communities, where there are few organized out-of-school activities and where schools are underfunded, parents must work hard to locate appropriate and safe activities for their children. The difficulty of this task may be even more challenging because the family itself also has limited resources. Thus, there is a dynamic interaction between the elements of this model, which produces a unique configuration of influence and outcomes.

At the heart of this model is *the individual child,* who receives resources and processes information from his or her world. Children bring to the situation their own cognitive abilities, temperament, and other individual characteristics. This is where the connection is made between the socially organized executive functionaries and children's internal executive functioning. As they mature, children must gradually incorporate information, strategies, and resources from their environments. For example, in order for children to have good social skills and learn to be self-regulated, parents or significant adults in their lives must explain what skills are needed for positive interactions and self-control. Children must then process, incorporate, and apply this information in an appropriate manner.

The next sphere in the model refers to *significant individuals and institutions.* These are the groups most likely to interact directly with and influence children. These groups manage information coming in from the other spheres and adjust them in response to children's characteristics. In the early years of life, management and resources generally flow through *parents or primary caregivers*. These caregivers provide important physical (e.g., food, transportation, health care), psychosocial (e.g., social and emotional support and skills, adaptability) and internal (e.g., self-discipline, self-awareness, and values) resources to children.

When children begin attending daycare or school, some executive functioning shifts to these new arenas. Like parents and other primary caregivers, daycare centers and schools, as well as the teachers working in them, provide children with physical and psychosocial resources. For teachers in these settings to be effective executive functionaries for children, they must coordinate their activities with children's primary caregivers. Without this connection, the two parties will not have the information they need to effectively manage children's lives and promote their well-being.

Recent calls for greater collaboration between school and families indicate a growing awareness that children's executive functionaries must have better coordination with each other. For this collaboration to occur, however, the two systems must have access to the same information and must have shared goals against which each system can evaluate progress and identify potential problems.

As children mature, more individuals (e.g., peers, counselors, religious leaders, coaches) may act as executive functionaries on their behalf. Similarly, executive functioning must occur in a greater number of social institutions (e.g., community programs, Head Start, juvenile court). In addition, children and their executive functionaries must manage more opportunities and dangers. In many cases, the dangers become increasingly risky, and the opportunities become more difficult to manage. As these demands increase, stronger coordination among the executive functionaries is needed. Unfortunately, such coordination becomes difficult as children move into middle childhood. This is because children of this age must navigate contextual systems that tend to be independent of and disconnected from each other.

Community contexts, such as neighborhoods, surrounding communities' characteristics, and shared cultural contexts, represent the outermost sphere. These are contexts that influence children indirectly through the executive functionaries. These contexts interact with the primary caregivers' own demographics and put certain constraints on what resources they can draw on to help them manage. Community contexts vary in the extent to which children's primary caregivers must intervene and manage their children's experiences. When primary caregivers agree with the norms and values of the community and trust their neighbors to help them raise their children, their executive functioning for children is more easily distributed among and shared with other community members. By contrast, when primary caregivers feel their neighborhood is not safe for their children, they may have to exert considerable energy as executive functionaries to protect them.

When executive functionaries manage resources and information well for the child, the end result is an adult who has good self-regulation skills and who is well integrated into the community. When there is a failure in the executive functioning system, this goal is more difficult to achieve. Thus, problems with children's executive functioning can be similar to a cognitive disability. For example, when a primary caregiver cannot effectively model self-regulation for the child, the child is less likely to learn this important skill. Sometimes, however, resources may be unavailable in one social context (such as the family), but are provided in another (such as the school). For example, providing free/reduced lunch programs, helping children develop emotional self-regulation, and teaching children important social skills are school resources that can augment the family's economic, information, and social-emotional resources. Individuals at school can also connect families and children with other organizations, such as community outreach programs, that may provide this assistance. Conversely, schools may also receive resources and information from families. For example, if parents feel the schools are not adequately teaching their children, they may become more involved in teaching at home, or may obtain tutoring from other institutions. Hence, a certain amount of compensation can and should occur between the executive functionaries to aid in the development of a self-regulated adult. Such compensation is likely to work best when the various systems are working together on behalf of the child.

Conclusion

The social executive functioning model demonstrates how adults inside and outside the home can work together to promote healthy progress for children. Because children spend many of their hours outside the home in educational settings, teachers, coaches, and other school personnel can make important contributions to children's positive development. The children develop not only their academic skills in these settings, but also their social skills through dealing with peers and adults. Academic and social skills are equally valuable talents to foster, and predict success in adulthood. Thus, it is important that avenues are created whereby communication, management of information, and coordination are the tools to foster both the social and academic talents of children.

Implications for Educators

The social executive functioning model has implications for teachers' and schools' interactions with families. In particular, teachers and other school personnel must begin with the assumption that parents can and want to be effective influences in their children's education. Inherent in the social executive functioning model is the notion that one way to be effective is to improve and maximize the connections between children's homes and classrooms.

Reduce barriers to parents' effective family participation. Parents and families can be dissuaded from participating and communicating with schools for many reasons. Logistical, cultural, and informational barriers should be identified and strategies put in place to reduce them. Teachers and schools can solicit feedback from parents on what barriers they face. Identifying and involving parent leaders who share the same cultural or linguistic background as other families can facilitate this process.

Cultivate schools and classrooms that welcome and integrate families. Schools must cultivate an environment in which parents and families are welcomed and integrated into the school community. Providing a space inside the school for parents to gather with each other, meet with school personnel, and access information and resources sends a strong message that parents are a valued constituency and welcomed visitors at the school.

Establish and utilize effective systems of communication between home and school. On a systems level, school administrators and other personnel should ensure that they have effective communications systems in place to convey and receive important child and family information. Updated telephone systems and other technologies, language translation services, and contact persons who can orient parents to the school system and its practices provide necessary infrastructure for the effective transmission of information between schools and families.

Help children and families improve executive functioning skills. This model suggests that teachers should attend to how well information flows (or is blocked) between families and their school and/or classroom, and how that information is managed. When feasible, teachers can develop classroom strategies that optimize communication and collaboration between themselves and families. For example, teachers can provide parents with suggestions and tips about how to help children plan, organize, and complete homework assignments. These suggestions should be matched to parents' educational and linguistic backgrounds.

Help families navigate school-related tasks and activities. Some parents may need help understanding basic educational practices in contemporary U.S. schools, such as those who attended school in other countries. Teachers and schools should not take it for granted that parents will be able to help their children complete homework assignments and navigate course requirements that will prepare them for college. Instead, teachers and other school personnel may need to provide some parents with resources and information that will allow them to effectively guide their children through the education system.

Community Support for Family Involvement in Children's Learning

by Heather B. Weiss and M. Elena Lopez

Ecological theory views the neighborhood as an important context for children's development (Bronfenbrenner, 1986). As mentioned in the introduction to Section 2, children's development is influenced by children's immediate contexts (microsystems such as home, school, and community) and the relationships among these contexts (the mesosystems).

The relationship of neighborhood circumstances to children's development has long been of interest to developmental researchers. In general, neighborhood influences on child and youth outcomes (ages 11–16) tend to be modest, and the processes by which they occur through family management strategies are still not well understood. For example, one study found little evidence to indicate that neighborhood circumstances improve adolescent outcomes as a result of family management practices, which refer to how parents react to the world outside the home, either by monitoring youth activities or linking youth to resources, such as neighborhood programs (Ran-Kim, Chan, Settersten, & Teitler, 1999). Other studies, however, suggest that neighborhoods affect youth because neighborhood features influence parent perceptions and monitoring activities. Parent perception of neighborhood problems is related to regulation of children's activities, which, in turn, is associated with children's increased social competence (O'Neil, Parke, & McDowell, 2001). Parent perceptions of neighborhood as a community—for example, how closely knit the neighborhood is and how likely neighbors will help in time of trouble—alter parenting practices. Neighborhoods with a greater sense of community encourage more intensive parental monitoring, which in turn is associated with better youth outcomes (Rankin & Quane, 2002).

Children and youth grow up in multiple contexts: home, school, neighborhood, and friendship groups. Only recently has there been an attempt to understand the relative importance of each context as well as the joint influence of all four contexts for child and youth development. The better the quality of each of these contexts, the better the outcomes for them; however, the joint effect of all four contexts matters most for child and youth development (Cook, Herman, Phillips, & Settersten, 2002). Strengthening all of these contexts to promote positive development holds the best promise for child and youth success now and in the future.

This theoretical lens focuses specifically on how neighborhood and community contexts can support families and the home context, especially in relation to children's school success. Although much has been written about school practices to involve parents in their children's learning, we know less about how such involvement is promoted by the community and, in particular, by parents' social networks and organizations other than the school. **Community** refers to "a group of people who are socially interdependent, who participate together in discussion and decision making, and who share certain practices that both define the community and are nurtured by it" (Bellah, Madsen, Sullivan, Swidler, & Tipton, 1985, p. 333). It includes people who typically develop a sense of belonging by virtue of geographic location such as neighborhoods, purposive activity such as the workplace, or cultural affinity such as language, ethnicity, and religion. Community support for family involvement consists of the informal processes and formal organizations that provide the resources and opportunities for families to become involved in children's learning and development. This article highlights in particular "community bridging strategies" available to parents and the expansion of family involvement roles through community organizations.

Community Bridging Strategies

Low-income families often seek to overcome negative neighborhood conditions that threaten their children's lives through community bridging strategies that promote youth development (Jarrett, 1999, 2000). **Community bridging strategies** refer to a complex set of parent actions that link children and youth with "mainstream opportunities and institutions" (Jarrett, 1999, p. 46). They include monitoring children's time, space, and friendships, seeking local and extra-local resources, and using in-home learning strategies.

Communities as networks of people provide a context for parents to create bridging strategies. As parents develop informal networks in the community, they expose their children to people who can enrich a child's developmental experiences. In middle childhood, children develop the ability to understand different perspectives and behaviors and their consequences for interacting with others (Eccles, 1999). A study of Boston neighborhoods showed that when parents had strong neighborhood ties that extended beyond the family, children's social behaviors and school performance were better. One explanation for this finding is that children who were exposed to more heterogeneous social networks had more opportunities to spend time with other adults in socially and cognitively stimulating activities (Marshall, Noonan, McCartney, Marx, & Keefe, 2001).

Community-based employment can provide opportunities for low-income parents to gain access to resources that enhance their child's learning. In a study of low-income mothers' involvement in their elementary school children's education, Weiss and colleagues describe how mothers used the workplace to call teachers by phone and access resources such as computers, educational advice from colleagues or employers, and tutoring or homework help for children (Weiss et al., 2003). Their children also came to the workplace after school to do homework. The study shows that full-time working parents are less involved at the school than part-time working mothers, but that the workplace provides a space other than the home or school in which involvement can occur. Mothers who used these workplace opportunities exemplify the community bridging strategies that direct their children toward new resources or those that are not available in the home.

A growing number of communities provide afterschool programs for children that not only serve working parents by providing safe places for children to engage in activities, but also engage families in the programming. Some parents ensure quality services by participating in surveys and focus groups, although a core group of parents takes on leadership and governance roles. Parents may also participate in children's activities, help raise funds, and find paid positions as coordinators and tutors in these programs (Blank, 2001; Caspe, Traub, & Little, 2002). Through afterschool programs, they monitor their children's activities and use these programs as bridging strategies to expose children to new learning environments.

As children grow into early adolescence, their relationships with parents change. Although children seek to distance themselves from their parents in some aspects of their lives, they also want to develop close relationships with nonfamilial adults (Eccles, 1999). Afterschool programs complement and support parent roles by offering adult guidance for children. In some situations, they function as cultural brokers among immigrant families and mainstream institutions and provide resources beyond what families and schools offer, such as counsel and assistance for college preparation. The Bridging Multiple Worlds model guides university-community partnerships designed to increase access to college among low-income, ethnic minority, and immigrant youth. The model has been used extensively to help Latino youth in California feel confident and safe in their neighborhoods, learn alternatives to violence, and gain bicultural skills needed to succeed in school. Program staff members provide cultural continuity by reinforcing Latino families' beliefs that success in life is measured in both moral and academic terms. Staff also offer youth a view of life opportunities through resources of mainstream institutions, including schools, colleges, and banks (Cooper, Chavira, Mikolyski, & Dominguez, 2004).

Expanded Family Involvement Roles

Community organizations act as change agents by providing the resources, occasions, and supports for parents to take proactive roles in their children's learning, and more broadly, in public education. Community organizations refer to public service agencies, faith-based organizations, and an array of non-profit entities that serve the community. Although schools are the most important institutions for directly engaging families in their children's education, many of them lack the capacity to provide low-income and immigrant parents with the level of support they need to become engaged in their children's learning. In different parts of the country, community organizations are fulfilling this function. They provide a forum or space for parents and community members to deliberate on educational issues; they expand parent roles as learners, teachers, advocates, and leaders; and they organize parents and community members to use their collective power to effect school change.

Ethnic associations, for example, provide a forum in which immigrant parents can communicate in their native languages about their aspirations and frustrations and construct the goals they have for their children. Among various Southeast Asian groups, the associations connect the school and the community by facilitating meetings among parents, teachers, and community leaders (National Coalition of Advocates for Students, 1997). These convening activities familiarize school personnel with the culture of students and families and may help them to better align school practices with parental wishes and needs. They also convey to parents, in whose cultures the separation of school and home is the norm, that their participation in schools is important.

As mentioned in the introduction to this volume, parents may experience social, psychological, informational, and practical challenges that limit their involvement in children's education. In addition, family involvement practices tend to reflect school priorities and terms of parent participation. In recent years, some community organizations have worked directly with families to expand their roles in schools and to create a more equitable role for parents in shaping their involvement. Although these organizations differ on many important characteristics, they tend to adopt a similar philosophy, namely one that seeks to give parents the opportunity not only to engage in their children's learning and development, but also to influence schools and to become resources for other parents, teachers, and students.

The Jane Addams School for Democracy, a community-based initiative of higher education institutions and a neighborhood service center in Saint Paul, Minnesota, offers a good example of expanding the educational roles of a diverse group of Hmong and Latino parents. By joining the school's study circles, parents are *learners* who study to gain citizenship and improve their English skills. Through their interactions with community members of various ethnicities, and with professionals and students, parents also learn to apply the principles of democracy as they plan and carry out the school's activities. Furthermore, their involvement with the school opens new opportunities, such as access to the Community Education Program, sponsored by the St. Paul public school district. Through this program Hmong and Latino parents become *teachers* and offer courses in cooking and reading and writing in their native language. Building on the opportunities for dialogue and newly formed networks of relationships, parents have also become *leaders* in initiating school change. A small group of core parents, with the assistance of the Jane Addams School, organized a series of meetings to train other parents about the school system and work on common concerns. Beyond giving input at meetings, parents seek to influence school actions. One of their concerns is the way schools communicate academic progress, particularly the lack of specific information from teachers about how children are doing in school. Another concern, and one around which the parents have organized, is changing the school lunch menu so that children have more nutritious food and Asian food as an option. As part of this campaign, parents have designed a strategy that includes recruiting more community members to be involved, conducting a parent survey about the school lunch menu, meeting with the food services director, presenting a plan to the school board, and developing a media effort (Harvard Family Research Project, 2002).

Schools have high expectations of parental involvement at home and in school, and yet the conditions of impoverished families often make such involvement difficult. Although there are well-intentioned teachers and principals who are interested in reaching out to low-income parents, there are also those who view them from a deficit perspective. This perspective is evident in negative attitudes about parents' failure to complement school efforts to educate their children and beliefs about the need to change families rather than to understand how parenting roles can be supported. Community-based social service organizations can provide opportunities for low-income parents to become *advocates* of improved relationships with schools. Bloom's ethnography of impoverished single mothers, for example, illustrates how a community-based grassroots organization developed an advocacy plan with mothers and school administrators to address the strained relationships between parents and school staff at meetings to discuss a child's academic difficulties (Bloom, 2001). The mothers felt intimidated by these meetings, where they were alone in confronting as many as seven to ten school staff that wielded their professional status in demeaning ways. To address the mothers' concerns about these meetings, the advocacy plan consisted of a role play that involved a mother and several school staff to resolve a fictitious fourth-grade boy's poor performance, and a debriefing session. Through the role play, the mothers could air their concerns in a safe environment and feel empowered. The school staff also gained a different perspective to the meetings, that of an impoverished parent wanting her child to succeed. In addition, the mothers have insisted on having a community volunteer attend the meetings with them to serve as an ally.

Community organizing groups that advocate for improved housing, economic development opportunities, and neighborhood conditions for low-income residents are also turning their attention to education reform. They have recruited parents to become leaders in improving the quality of schools, and have made impressive gains in addressing parents' concerns about children's safety, afterschool activities, school size and school climate (Gold, Simon, & Brown, 2002a; Shirley, 1997). Unlike other forms of family involvement, education organizing is political and focuses on building parent and community power. This approach can make it suspect among school officials who are not accustomed to demands for public accountability. When schools resist change and discourage parent activism, organizing groups resort to confrontational tactics that deepen conflict. When community organizing groups, however, maintain working relationships with schools, home-school connections have improved (Gold, Simon, & Brown, 2002b). Parents increase their presence and roles in schools. They serve as tutors in class and in afterschool programs, lead parenting workshops, and help maintain school safety.

Conclusion

The conventional portrait of community partnership in education emphasizes the use of community resources for schools and students. Communities, however, have an untapped potential for supporting and promoting family involvement in education. Families turn to community members—such as coworkers, neighbors, and friends—to enhance their children's learning opportunities. Community organizations open up opportunities for parents to learn about and participate in educational issues affecting their children. We are just beginning to understand the ways that communities can be a force in involving families in children's learning and development. Future research needs to deepen and expand the ideas we have explored in this chapter.

Implications for Educators

Teachers and school leaders should expand notions of parent involvement beyond home and school to include community. This suggests the need for educators to develop greater awareness of the community settings and institutions that provide opportunities for family involvement. Some specific actions that schools can take include the following:

Take a tour or revisit the community. Whether an educator lives in the community or outside it, visiting neighborhoods and talking to people in the community about the places families frequent and the activities that their children access when school ends can provide a wealth of information about children's lives outside of school. Educators can develop lists that document the resources, supports, and occasions for family involvement that currently exist, and those that could be created. Home visits also provide educators with an opportunity to listen to parents and to observe how the home supports children's learning. This exploration in the home and community can generate ideas about ways to connect with families and how community activities can intersect with classroom experiences.

Expand parent networks. Educators can help connect parents to each other and expand their social ties. This connection can enrich parents' knowledge about involvement practices to support children's learning. It also can stimulate children's access to other people in the community who can enrich children's social and educational experiences. Family resource centers, for example, provide a space where parents can go to meet each other informally and build a sense of community. With the help of educators, family resource center staff can build parent interest for supporting children's learning in school and afterschool.

Make connections with community organizations. When schools collaborate with community organizations, they can interact with parents that may be difficult to reach individually. Holding parent meetings in community settings can make parents feel more comfortable, especially when they can communicate in their native languages and gain access to community translators. Educators can also learn more about their students and families from those who have contact with them in their broader roles as community members. This exposure also lends itself to exploring new ideas and roles for parents in their children's education. One advantage of creating alliances with community organizations and leaders is their credibility among parents. The message of family involvement becomes more powerful for parents when community leaders express and demonstrate support for it.

4

The Cases

In this section, we have included four teaching cases that highlight the linkages across several microsystems and encourage readers to consider the theoretical lenses in Chapter 3 as analytical tools for further exploring the dilemmas these cases describe. The cases contained herein—"Lunchtime at Sunnydale Elementary School," "Defining 'Fine'," "Bilingual Voices and Parent Classroom Choices," and "Staying on the Path Toward College"—all illustrate the ways in which microsystems are connected, and the ways in which coordination across these systems can facilitate (or be disruptive to) children's positive development. The theoretical lenses in the preceding chapter provide but two ways of uncovering some of the specific processes and mechanisms by which such coordination can help or hurt children's outcomes. Lenses appearing in other sections of this volume might also be applied and may lead to different ideas about how one might resolve the dilemmas presented here.

Case 4: Lunchtime at Sunnydale Elementary School

What Do First Graders Need?

by Barrie Thorne

Characters:

Rosa and Maria, first graders

Beatriz, Rosa and Maria's grandmother

Tish, Maria's 16-month-old sister

Lena, Maria's mother

Linda, Sunnydale Elementary School principal

Matty, cafeteria worker

Mary, P.T.A. parent

As you read this case, consider applying the following theoretical lenses in your analysis:

- Executive Functioning: How is the family acting as an executive functionary in this case? How is the school acting as an executive functionary? How can better coordination be achieved between the families and the school?
- Family Support: What is the nature of parent participation in decision-making to effect schoolwide change? How can it be improved? To what extent is the school demonstrating cultural competence?
- Ecocultural Understanding: What are the different perceptions of development in middle childhood expressed in this case? How can the principal and the parents develop greater awareness of their own culturally-based expectations of children?

BEATRIZ, ROSA AND MARIA'S GRANDMOTHER

Beatriz Hinojosa worried that her granddaughters didn't get enough to eat at school. Rosa, the six-year-old, had asthma and was small for her age. Rosa's cousin, Maria, was five-and-a-half; they were in the same bilingual first-grade class at Sunnydale School. On weekdays, the grandmother was responsible for Rosa, Maria, and Tish, Maria's 16-month-old sister, from early in the morning when the girls' mothers set off for work until they returned at dinner time. Beatriz's daughters were both single mothers in their mid-twenties. They and their children shared an apartment a block away from the apartment where Beatriz lived with her son and his wife. Early each morning, Beatriz picked up her three granddaughters and drove to the school, aiming to get there by 7:30 a.m. so that the girls could participate in the free breakfast program.

Maria and Rosa were so little that the grandmother wasn't comfortable just dropping them off. On the first day of the school year, she began a routine of parking the car and, with the toddler in tow, guiding the girls through the school, across the upper playground, and into the small portable building that housed the school cafeteria. A parent volunteer organized the orange juice, cereal, and milk and stood to the side as Beatriz helped Maria and Rosa prepare their bowls and choose where to sit. The atmosphere felt rushed, and one time a group of older kids threw food. Maria and Rosa often dawdled, eating only a few bites before the bell rang. After the bell, Beatriz said goodbye to her granddaughters as the parent volunteer guided them and the other younger kids toward their classrooms in the main building. Then Beatriz drove home and took care of Tish until 2:45 p.m., when it was time to return to the school to pick up Rosa and Maria.

Two weeks into the school year, when Beatriz pulled into the pick-up area, Rosa and Maria bustled into the car, full of news. "When we got our lunches today, some big kids shoved us around," Rosa said. "Yeah, they shoved us, and I was so scared, I nearly dropped my tray," Maria added.

The girls had even more to tell: Their classroom had been moved from the main school building and into a portable across the playground. The only bathrooms were in the main building, and if one of them had to go during the class period, they had to choose a partner, get a pass, and walk across the playground to the bathroom and back again by themselves. This bit of news startled Lena, Maria's mother, and she observed, "Little kids shouldn't be allowed out on their own like that; it would be easy for one of them to wander off." The three adults talked it over and agreed that the grandmother, who was the family's main connection to the school, should find out what was going on.

The next day Beatriz and Tish went to the school at noontime. They walked alongside Rosa and Maria in the first-graders' queue as it slowly moved from the portable, across the playground, up the stairs, and into the cafeteria. When they finally got inside, Beatriz watched as the girls pointed to their names on the free lunch roster, got trays, and reached for prepackaged food items and cartons of milk. The grandmother leaned over and pointed out that they were supposed to choose between pizza or a cheese sandwich. Then she looked around the crowded room and squeezed her granddaughters and herself (with Tish on her lap) onto the bench at one of the tables.

It all felt noisy, chaotic, and hurried. Young kids take a long time to eat, but the bell was already ringing, and other kids were standing up to leave with their lunches only half finished. Beatriz didn't think her granddaughters were eating enough. And when they walked across the busy playground toward the portable classroom, they had to skirt around bigger kids who were playing jump rope and kickball and just hanging out. Rosa said that the day before when she got a pass and was walking to the bathroom with Gloria, some big kids were out at recess and almost ran into them. Beatriz grew more and more perturbed. Didn't the teachers care about the safety of the little ones? What would happen if one of her granddaughters got hurt, or somehow wandered out of the school yard?

LINDA CHANG, PRINCIPAL

The principal, Linda Chang, always had a lot to juggle when the school year began, but this year was especially pressed. For the first time the school had a breakfast program for lower-income students, but there was no one to oversee it, and she had had to ask quite a few parents until she found one willing and able to volunteer to run it every day. The school was not only short of staff, but also short of space. The spring before the state had mandated smaller class sizes for the first three grades, and there weren't enough classrooms. After the first set of enrollment figures came in, Linda had to hire two additional teachers and arrange for the delivery of three portable buildings in order to create enough classrooms. Then a long-awaited donation of computers arrived, which she had promised to the fourth grades. But one of the fourth-grade classrooms was in a portable, and the portables didn't have enough wiring for computers. There weren't many choices, and Linda ended up moving the first-grade Spanish bilingual class into the portable, which opened a well-wired room in the main building for the fourth graders and the new computers.

There were other changes that fall. Linda had to persuade the teachers, whose contracts specified that they did not have to be on duty during lunchtime, that they needed to take the time to walk their students, single file, down to the playground by the cafeteria. At the end of lunchtime, they also were supposed to come down and meet their students and lead them, single file, back to their classrooms. This routine was part of a new system of playground discipline that was developed in response to a crisis the previous school year, when a fifth-grade boy threw rocks and injured a younger child. Rumors circulated about playground violence, and parents phoned the school and e-mailed the principal to express concern. Several teachers met with the P.T.A. Board, and then with Linda, the principal, and worked out a new set of policies.

Getting 420 students fed and back to class within roughly an hour was a real challenge. When she had time, Linda did her best to be an ordering presence in the cafeteria, helping Matty Harris, who oversaw the distribution of food and kept an eye on students eating at the tables. The cafeteria didn't have enough space for all, or even half, of the school's students to eat at the same time. Students ate in two age-ordered shifts. The older grades went first, because older kids eat more quickly. Thirty-five minutes later, a second bell rang, and queues of students from the first and second grades moved from classrooms to the upper playground, with "bag lunch kids" settling in at the picnic tables and "school lunch kids" lining up to go into the cafeteria. The school lunch line was longer than ever that fall because the number of students qualifying for free or reduced-price lunch had gone up. Lower-income immigrants were moving into the school intake area, and there had been an increase in transfers to the school from low-income, predominantly African-American areas of the city.

THE GRANDMOTHER ENCOUNTERS SCHOOL STAFF

One day, early in the school year, the principal saw an older Latina woman, holding a toddler, move along the lunchline in tandem with two girls from Mr. Turner's first-grade Spanish bilingual class. She guessed that it was the girls' grandmother and went over and introduced herself; then she was paged and had to hurry back to the office. The next day the grandmother and the toddler again showed up walking next to Rosa and Maria at the end of the line. The principal was away at a meeting, and Matty Harris, the sole cafeteria worker, was especially hassled because they were once again way behind, and the bell would ring in ten minutes. Matty asked the students to choose an entrée more quickly.

Carefully holding their loaded trays, Maria and Rosa followed their grandmother to the tables, but there was no space left, so Beatriz, the grandmother, went over to Mrs. Harris and asked, "Where can I set my girls to eat?"

"You'll have to go outside," Mrs. Harris said.

Beatriz took the toddler's hand, and with the other hand she gently guided the girls, still carrying their trays, down the stairs and to an empty space at one of the picnic tables. They settled in and began to eat. Then one of the playground aides came over and said, "You can't take school lunches outside; you have to eat them inside."

Beatriz was exasperated. "There was no room inside. What are we supposed to do?" The aide shrugged and walked away.

When Beatriz returned at the end of the school day, she parked the car and went to an area near the portables where she had sometimes seen parents of the Spanish-speaking first graders gather to talk while they waited for their children. She joined the group and discovered that they were also upset that the first-grade bilingual class, which began the year secure in the main building, had been bumped out to a portable. Some of the mothers had also heard about big kids shoving little kids in the cafeteria and about scary walks to the bathroom. They agreed that first graders were too little to put up with these problems.

Discussion of "the cafeteria and the bathroom problems" continued in phone and other conversations, until one of the first-grade parents, Mary Ramos, an Anglo woman married to a man from Mexico, suggested that they go as a group to the monthly P.T.A. meeting that was scheduled for the following Thursday evening. Mary, who was college-educated and studying to be a bilingual teacher, was the only one in Latino circles who was active in the P.T.A. She said that she would present the group's complaints to the principal.

THE P.T.A. MEETING

The small core of parents active in the Sunnydale P.T.A. were nearly all middle-class and college-educated. Most of them were White, with a handful of African Americans. The "P.T.A. parents," as they were known around the school, were aware of and troubled by the mismatch between the educational, income, and racial/ethnic makeup of the P.T.A. and the overall composition of the school (See Table 4.1).

Table 4.1   Sunnydale Elementary School

Location	Large Western city, population over 1,000,000
Grades served	K–5
Enrollment	420
• Latino	18%
• Asian and Southeast Asian	25%
• African American	45%
• White	10%
• Other	2%
Students eligible for free and reduced-priced lunch	48%
Certified teachers	90%

The P.T.A. parents worked hard to bring more resources to the school. They organized fundraisers and ran a scrip program at the grocery store. They served on the school site committee and attended and spoke out at school board meetings. They had also tried various forms of outreach to other Sunnydale parents, such as free spaghetti dinners, and, when they could get expert help, having key announcements translated into Spanish and Cantonese. They knew that there were big gaps of language and cultural understanding among families at the school and that many of the other parents worked long hours in inflexible jobs and had extremely difficult lives.

Several of the Latino parents had tried coming to P.T.A. meetings in the past, but even if they understood some of the English, half the time they couldn't figure out what was being talked about. Back home in places like Mexico and Guatemala, teachers were the experts, and schools didn't talk about parent involvement. The immigrant parents felt inadequate and excluded when they were with the Americans who seemed to run things. But this time Mary Ramos, the Spanish-speaking Anglo mother who was friendly with them and active in the P.T.A., would be there speaking out on their behalf, and they were attending as a group with a purpose.

When Beatriz and her daughter Lena entered the auditorium, they went over to sit with the other six Spanish-speaking parents. Mary Ramos sat near the front of the group and softly paraphrased the content of the discussion in Spanish. Beatriz (who migrated to the United States from Mexico when she was 15) and Lena (who was born and raised in the United States) were the only other fluent English speakers in the Latino group.

After an hour of discussion about issues such as the format of report cards, fundraising, and planning for a school Halloween party, the P.T.A. president, an African-American man, asked if there were any new items for the agenda. Mary Ramos stood up and turned toward the principal.

"Ms. Chang, these parents and I have children in the same first-grade class. We are coming to the meeting to figure out if there is some way that our smaller children can be safer. They were moved to a portable outside and have to walk across the playground to the bathroom and older kids bump them."

Lena chimed in, "The younger ones are out by themselves without supervision." Beatriz added, "One of my girls has asthma. She's little, and she doesn't remember to put on a coat and take an umbrella."

The principal responded by describing the various pressures that led to the decision to switch classrooms and put the first-grade bilingual class in a portable. She reminded them that the bilingual class was lucky because they not only had a teacher, but also a Spanish-speaking aide who came three mornings a week. Then she addressed the bathroom policy:

"Other first graders also have to have hall passes and walk by themselves to the bathroom. Children are dismissed to go to the bathroom during the two recess times, and otherwise only in an emergency, when they go with a partner, take a pass, and go straight to the restroom." In short, she tried to reassure the parents that school policies were being evenly applied, and that there were reasons for the switch of classrooms.

But Mary, who was intent on being a spokesperson for a group of parents she felt the school was neglecting, wasn't satisfied. She responded, "They feel that their children are being tossed around. They would like to be involved and help make it smoother for their children."

Beatriz wanted the principal to know about the troubling things she had seen during her visits to the school. "I started going to school breakfast and lunch, to make sure my girls are eating," she said. "I saw kids throw food, and there isn't enough time for younger kids to eat. And the big kids are on the playground at the same time as the little kids go to the bathroom, and they run into the little kids."

The problems spilled out, one on top of the other. Linda Chang, feeling she had already addressed the bathroom issue, picked up on Beatriz's complaints about school meals. "Last year children were handed individual servings. The District is doing things a new way this year, with a choice of two entrées, and the food is better because it's hotter, but it takes more time. I agree that supervision is limited. If you can," (she looked pointedly at Beatriz) "volunteer to help with breakfast."

Beatriz replied, "I teach my granddaughters to take this and this. The problem is the big kids; you should have the older ones come after the little kids."

Linda responded, "We tried, but we feed over 250 every day. Lunch periods are only 35 minutes long, and the older children go first. It's too slow if the little ones eat first. I don't like to see big boys and girls pushing little ones. It was a mistake that the older ones came in late that day."

Beatriz wasn't satisfied: "Where can I sit my girls to eat? There was no room in the cafeteria, so we went outside, and then the woman, she came and told us, 'You can't take your food outside.' Where are my girls supposed to sit?"

Linda once again suggested a course of action: "We welcome volunteers."

Then a kindergarten parent spoke up with a different issue, and attention turned away from the first-grade parents and their concerns. At the end of the meeting, the principal, Linda Chang, went over to the Spanish-speaking group and gave them flyers prepared by the P.T.A. that read: "We need volunteers— room parents, library, breakfast, lunchtime, fundraisers, in the classroom. Your involvement benefits your child. Please get involved. They will be proud of you and knowing you care raises their self-esteem."

Beatriz, Lena, and the other Latino parents once again felt shoved aside. As they left the meeting, Lena turned to her mother and asked, "What about some kind of caring?"

DISCUSSION QUESTIONS

Major Issues

The purpose of this case is for educators to consider divergent perspectives on children's development and family-school relations and how school and family cultures shape these views and practices. The case is designed to help educators understand the following:

- The relationships between schools and immigrant families
- The ways cultural beliefs and practices shape families' perceptions of child development and their subsequent school involvement
- The concerns of parents and other caregivers and their efforts to change school practice

Describing the Situation

- What are Maria and Rosa Hinojosa like?
- How does Beatriz Hinojosa view Maria and Rosa?
- How much personalized adult help and supervision does Beatriz believe a first grader needs? What is the principal, Linda Chang's, perspective?
- What concerns do Beatriz, Lena, and the other first-grade bilingual parents have about the school? What strengths and assets do they bring to the situation?
- How does the spokesperson, Mary Ramos, frame the situation?
- Describe parent-based changes that have already emerged at Sunnydale Elementary.
- What is the dilemma in this case?

Exploring Contributing Factors

- How and why might a family perspective of the lunchtime situation at Sunnydale differ from the perspective of a principal responsible for an organization of over 400 students?
- How do different cultural beliefs and practices, for example, about food and safety, relate to the situation?
- How does Beatriz's view of volunteering and family involvement in the school compare with the principal's view?
- What are Beatriz's underlying beliefs about professionalism versus caring? The principal's? How do these differences contribute to miscommunication in the case?

Articulating Possible Next Steps

- How might Beatriz and her two daughters become more involved in the school P.T.A.? How might this involvement lead to the school becoming more responsive to diverse groups of students and caregivers? What impact might this have on Beatriz's lunchtime concerns?
- If a similar situation happened in your community, what kinds of organizations might help the Latino parents develop a strategy for changing school practices?
- How might the school support informal parent interactions and facilitate parent networking that has organically emerged?

Replaying the Case

- What strategies has the P.T.A. tried to involve parents who are immigrants, non-English-speaking, and lower income that have not succeeded? What else might they do differently given practical constraints?

- Identify situations in the case where teachers and school staff were insensitive to family needs. How might the school better help teachers and school staff develop the attitudes, beliefs, and practices to build stronger relationships with families?
- How might the principal have responded more appropriately to Beatriz and other first-grade bilingual parents' concerns? Why was her suggestion of volunteering more insensitive?

Looking at the Bigger Picture

- How much supervision does a first grader need?
- How might an administrator manage the organizational needs of a school while remaining responsive to individual family concerns?

RECOMMENDED READING

Delgado-Gaitan, C. (2001). *The power of community: Mobilizing for family and community*. Boulder, CO: Rowman & Littlefield.

Fine, M. (1993). [Ap]parent involvement: Reflections on parents' power and urban public schools. *Teachers College Record, 94*(4), 682–710.

Lawrence-Lightfoot, S. (1978). *Worlds apart: Relationships between families and schools* (pp. 20–42). New York: Basic Books.

Thorne, B. (in press). Unpacking school lunch time: Contexts, interaction and the negotiation of differences. In C. R. Cooper, C. García Coll, T. Bartko, H. Davis, and C. Chapman (Eds.), *Developmental pathways through middle childhood: Rethinking contexts and diversity as resources*.

Case 5: Defining "Fine"

Communicating Academic Progress to Parents[1]

by Margaret Caspe and Holly Kreider

Characters:

Dick, Peterson Elementary School Principal

Nathan, first grader

Molly, Nathan's mother

Margot, Molly's friend

Tammy, Nathan's teacher

In a small rural state, an act is signed into law. The act ensures overall educational quality in the state's schools through equitable school funding via changes to the property tax system and adoption of rigorous statewide and local academic standards. Under the new act, every school in the state is required to create an action plan for improvement. The action plan must be developed with input from parents, teachers, and community members. The statute further requires each school to assess student performance under the plan, so that there is some measure of how well the plan is working. Student performance results must then be delivered to community members. Therefore, committee members will need to know how to interpret and act on school performance data, as well as how to communicate the information to the community at large.

THE PRINCIPAL, DICK LEONARD

Dick Leonard, a principal of 24 years, was returning to his office at Peterson Elementary School after a long day of meetings at the District Office. Peterson Elementary is a relatively modern school facility with a small-town feel. The school has 13 full-time teachers along with a number of part-time aides and specialists. The only language spoken in the school is English, and the population is about 99 percent White. The school enjoys minimal safety concerns and few discipline problems. Nearly everyone in the school knows one another and many of the teachers taught the parents of current students or know their parents through community connections (see Table 4.2).

As you read this case, consider applying the following theoretical lenses to your analysis:

- Executive Functioning: What are the opportunities and challenges in coordinating children's various social executive functionaries relating to academic progress? What are the similarities and differences in how each actor in the case evaluates Nathan's progress?
- Community Support: What is the role of the larger community in communicating academic progress? How does the new legislation impact the community's role in the school?
- Family Support: What parent-to-parent informal networks exist in this case and can be harnessed for school decision making and parent empowerment?

Dick rolled down the window and started to recap the important points of the day's events. Although controversial, he didn't think the law, which was the topic of the meeting, was all that bad. He was told that state test results would be coming back soon, and with that data, staff, parents, and community would all need to come together to form an action plan for approval by the school board.

Table 4.2   Peterson Elementary School

Location	Rural New England town, population 2,500
Grades served	K–6
Enrollment	$N = 310$, 96% Caucasian
Students eligible for free and reduced-priced lunch	20%
Average class size	20
School staff	13 full-time regular teachers (100% Caucasian & female)
Percent of students meeting or exceeding state math standards	86%
Percent of students meeting or exceeding state reading standards	85%
School-based services	Regular evaluation of all children and provision of educational enrichment to any child deemed eligible (either because they are above or below the "accepted criterion"), reading enrichment program, summer school
Parent involvement opportunities	Parent/teacher council and classroom-specific opportunities including portfolio nights, parent-teacher conferences, field trips, classroom volunteering, and Grandparents Day
Community events	Fundraisers, church-based events, sporting events, Girl Scouts, Boy Scouts

He knew that on the systemic level, this meant making tough decisions about which programs to keep and which to let go in order to increase student success. He had already done away with some of the less academically oriented parent events. Parents would need to be involved in the decision-making process. They would need to understand the standards and what it looked like for a child to successfully meet those standards. He believed these changes would start at the classroom level with the parent-teacher relationship.

"When parents come to school, we have to get them on the same page as us. This starts with the relationships between teachers and parents. Parents don't come to conferences to talk about social stuff. They want to know what their kids can and can't do. I am very clear with my teachers on how they should run their parent-teacher conferences. I don't say the specifics, but I remind them that we're dealing with the state standards and frameworks, and that we need to articulate this to our parents. We need to educate parents because our academic system is different than when they came to school. We need to talk about new assessments. We need to talk about math, reading, and writing performance. They need to understand why we're choosing certain books for reading."

Dick believed from experience and research that what parents and families want most from schools is a good experience for their kids. Parents want schools first and foremost that are safe and treat kids with care, understanding, and fairness. There was no question in his mind that different parents wanted different things, but he knew they all wanted to see their kids succeed.

"Parents need to understand what success is. They need to talk to their kids about the importance of school and listening to their teachers. On the flip side, teachers need to be able to articulate to parents what their kids should be able to do. You can't have high standards and low expectations for kids and families at the same time."

Dick had initiated a number of new school-wide policies based on these beliefs. He had eliminated the practice of giving letter grades. At the beginning of the school year, he distributed a summary of first- and second-grade standards for language arts and math to all parents of first- and second-grade students. He required teachers to use these standards to develop curriculum and evaluate student performance. At the meeting that morning, he was quite vocal in explaining his rationale to his colleagues.

"A kid might get an *A*, and the parents think they know what their kid learned. Well, they don't know. They only know he got an *A*. We need to show what that *A* means, what the content and performance standards are, and where a kid is in relation to the standards. We have to explain if a kid is meeting the standards, exceeding them or below them. That's why standards were developed in the first place. You can tie your *A* to standards. Standards are a tool that let teachers and parents monitor the rigor of the work children are expected to do. Unfortunately, standards might be public documents, but they're not accessible and understandable. I think that we in education need to take more responsibility in explaining to parents what standards mean. This will get directly at the issue of parents not having trust in the system."

Dick had talked about building trust back into the system. Over the years, he believed that deteriorating confidence was one of the main problems that existed between the public and public institutions. If teachers and schools could communicate progress and standards with families better, then that would be the first step in building more confidence in the system.

Dick thought of his own situation as a father. He had stopped going to parent-teacher conferences for his daughter when she was a sophomore in high school. During one back-to-school night, he asked his daughter's math teacher to talk about the standards in her classroom. Dick was shocked that the teacher could not clearly express what she expected from his daughter and the others. Nor could she show him some of his daughter's work when he requested it. He felt his time had been wasted.

As Dick drove into the parking lot, he saw the usual crowd of parents waiting to pick up their children. He noticed Molly Burnham among them. She was one of his involved mothers, and he was always pleased to see her in her son Nathan's classroom. He believed that this was one of the best ways for parents to learn how to be their child's first teacher. Understanding assessment, from his perspective, was just another level of this. As he pulled into his parking spot he renewed his vows to make things different at his school from how they had been in the past.

THE PARENTS, MOLLY AND MARGOT

Molly and her friend Margot, both parents at Peterson Elementary, stood in the parking lot waiting to pick up their children. Molly was upset because her son, Nathan, who was in first grade, had been recommended for summer school. She knew that he was reading on grade level, so was surprised to hear the recommendation two weeks ago at parent-teacher conferences. She and her husband decided not to send their son to the summer classes. As a 30-year-old White mother of two, Molly worked only part time so that she could spend more time at home with her children. Much of this time was spent on making Nathan a strong reader. She confided her concerns to her friend Margot.

"Reading is one of the areas where it took him a long time to pick it up, because he resists when he has trouble learning. But we're really working on helping him understand that just because things are a little difficult doesn't mean it can't be done. I keep telling him it's like playing Nintendo—not that I like him to sit there hour after hour—but there are things that are hard, and then he'll get help, and he'll do it. So eventually this year, he really did pick up his reading. He can read fluently and understand what he's reading. He's now on grade level exactly. And that was important to me."

Molly had advocated for her son to be in the special enrichment school-day reading program but other kids were ahead of him so he couldn't enroll. Because of this, she worked on reading with him a lot at home.

"We read all the time, even if it's the back of a cereal box. We read signs, we look at the board at the bus station, and if he recognizes that something looks colorful and interesting, he'll read that. We read a story every night. It's mostly the same books all the time, but he likes the repetitions and knowing words immediately.

"His teacher told me he was doing well, that he was on grade level. But now she's recommending him for summer school. I really don't think it was fair. Why is she concerned about summer slippage when we spend so much time reading with Nathan at home? We have nearly twenty library books taken out! Besides, I kept trying to get him help during the year, but there were other special needs kids ahead of him. And he's not even special needs. And now they want him to miss his summer, and he's only in the first grade. Why would she suggest summer school out of nowhere?"

Margot, the other mother, responded. "This school just has a lot of trouble letting us know how our kids are doing. My oldest son is in fourth grade, and his report cards have been getting stupider and stupider over the years. By fourth grade, you really need to have some kind of letter grade. Let me know where he stands! I just can't figure it out. Last quarter I got this report that says 'he's meeting the standard,' or 'he's not meeting the standard,' or 'he's exceeding the standard.' These report cards don't even tell you if your kid is really doing okay. I mean they moved my son up a level, which is great. But we're also a little worried about that because I don't know if he's doing A work, B work, or C work. You don't have any control over how they do the report cards anymore.

"And at the parent-teacher conferences, teachers just present a portfolio and tell a parent that the child is doing fine. Teachers need to *show* what fine means. It needs to be concrete. You know, we come into school and they go over the kids' progress, their report card, and their strengths and weaknesses. Yes, you meet the teacher. You get the report card. Then she has folders with some work in them, but what does it all mean? What do I have to compare it to?"

Molly thought more about it. She didn't mind having standards or benchmarks to show progress. Because of her loose work schedule, she was in the school a lot and felt she had a good handle on what was going on. She understood the different strategies the teachers used in reading and how she could help Nathan beyond asking him to sound things out. But she also felt the curriculum was a bit overwhelming, and that the new standards made it hard to read letters and notes sent home by the school. She was worried sometimes that even though she was actively involved, she was not getting the total picture and not getting a lot out of the communications with the school.

Molly looked at Margot and said, "I think the school also needs to send home information in between quarters to let you know how your kids are doing. I know that when the kids leave school, teachers are allowed to have their time. But if they could have progress reports or open houses or a potluck dinner—they don't do those things anymore."

Margot and Molly agreed that they missed the monthly school potluck dinners where families from the community would come together for relaxing evenings. It gave parents time to catch up with one another and children a chance to play together.

At this point, Nathan came bounding out of school and gave his mom a big hug. "Let's go play in the park," he yelled.

THE TEACHER, TAMMY GRAY

Tammy Gray, Nathan's teacher, began to clean up her room after dismissal. Teaching at Peterson Elementary for over 10 years, Tammy was a respected educator and friend to many in the building. As she straightened out the reading record folders, she smiled as she ran across Nathan's. He was the success of her year. He came into her class in the fall with a lot of difficulty reading and was very behind with his sounds and his retention of words. She worked one-on-one with him for most of the year.

"Without the one-on-one, I'm not sure what would have happened. He might have picked it up, but because he was so much lower than the others, it's hard to say. But now I expect him to continue reading at the average level next year. He's doing well with his research on zebras, and he's just so excited about anything he reads and writes. His mom's in school a lot, and if she's walking by, he'll bring her something that he's written and show it to her."

But Tammy was also concerned.

"I just don't want him to lose what he's learned—we've worked so hard this year and he's come along so well. I don't want him to hit the 'summer slide' so to say. Molly acted surprised when I suggested he attend summer school to prevent this. Hasn't she been tracking his progress through the year? I don't even think she realizes how low he was coming in."

Tammy looked out her window and saw Nathan and his mother walking to the park. She had an unsettled feeling in her stomach. She finished tidying up her room and walked down the hall to the main office. She thought about all the times parents were surprised at the end of the year when their children's promotion to the next grade was questioned. But Tammy felt she did her best.

"I send home numerous report cards and progress reports throughout the year. I even have my own progress reports that I try to send out during the report periods so that the door is open if parents want to discuss any problems. We hold report cards until the parent-teacher conferences to make sure that they arrive home and so that we can talk to the parents about them. In my class, I explain what the different standards are, the way the report cards are marked with a four-point rubric and what it means. I tell them how their child's doing in the different areas and let them know the concerns I might have. And then I ask the parent if they have questions for me, and quite often they don't. I don't know if that's because I've explained it so clearly or they just have no idea what to ask!"

Tammy always felt her discussions with parents were positive experiences. She believed educators need to go into conferences with an attitude of "What can we do to make this situation better for your child?" or "These are all the wonderful things your child can do." She walked into the office to check her mailbox. Inside, a flyer invited her and other teachers to take part in the school-design team created as a result of the new law. She wondered under her breath, "What a waste of time! I recognize many of the parents in this school have a lot of strengths and a lot to contribute. But, if parents don't even understand about their own kids' progress, how are they ever going to be able to participate in these school-wide teams to assess the progress of the entire school?"

DISCUSSION QUESTIONS

Major Issues

The purpose of this case is for educators to learn how to effectively communicate with families about children's academic progress. Special attention is given to parents' and teachers' divergent attitudes toward various types of assessment, including traditional letter grades and alternative tools such as portfolios. The case is designed to help educators understand the following:

- Parents' concerns about children's academic progress
- Ways to communicate children's progress to parents
- The influence of state policy on engaging families in school reform

Describing the Situation

- Describe the challenges the school faces in conveying student progress to families. Why has the principal stopped relying on letter grades as a way to describe students' academic performance?
- How do Molly Burnham and other parents feel about the school's assessment practices?
- How do parents' attitudes affect their relationships with teachers and their reactions to teachers' educational recommendations?
- What do Molly and Nathan do together at home and in the community to learn? Is the teacher aware of these activities?

Exploring Contributing Factors

- What factors outside of the school have contributed to the shift away from letter grades?
- Why are some parents responding negatively to new forms of student assessment?
- What is Tammy Gray's attitude toward parents in this case? How does this attitude influence her reaction to parent involvement on the school-design team?

Articulating Possible Next Steps

- As principal, what should Dick Leonard do to facilitate parents' understanding of children's academic progress in relation to the standards?
- As a teacher, what should Tammy do to respond to parents like Molly who are surprised by their children's end-of-the-year performance, despite having been informed of their progress throughout the year?
- How should Molly approach the school and/or teacher to convey her dissatisfaction with the school's ability to convey this information to parents?

Replaying the Case

- What could Dick, Molly, or Tammy have done differently in any part of the story? For example, what if parents had been involved in Dick's decision to eliminate letter grades? What if Tammy had told Molly about her concerns for Nathan earlier in the year? How would these actions have changed the evolution of the case?
- What legislation in your hometown, community, or state has been passed lately that sounds like the dilemma faced by this school and its families? What can you do in your area to influence legislation?

Looking at the Bigger Picture

- Is it more important to understand where children perform in relation to others in the class or to understand what they know and are able to do?

Why might educators and parents differ in their perspectives on this issue? What can be done to resolve these differences?

- What are some of the key elements that define parent-teacher relationships?
- What role can Dick Leonard play in building trust and confidence in his school?
- Do you agree that letter grades tell parents nothing about their children's academic performance? Why or why not? What meaning do letter grades have for parents?
- What strategies can the principal adopt in developing a school-improvement action plan? Who should be the main stakeholders in developing this plan?
- How does the culture of power in the school serve to discourage parent participation?
- Identify a school where genuine parent participation in decision making occurs. What structures are in place to facilitate parent involvement? How have school leaders developed a culture of participation?

RECOMMENDED READING

Barksdale-Ladd, M. A., & Thomas, K. F. (2000). What's at stake in high-stakes testing: Teachers and parents speak out. *Journal of Teacher Education, 51*(5), 384–397.

Christenson, S. L., & Sheridan, S. M. (2001). *Schools and families: Creating essential connections for learning.* New York: The Guilford Press.

Epstein, J. (1995). Family/school/community partnerships: Caring for the children we share. *Phi Delta Kappan, 76,* 701–712.

Case 6: Bilingual Voices and Parent Classroom Choices

Family Involvement in Language and Literacy²

by Margaret Caspe

Characters:

Nina, first grader

Inés, Nina's mother

Sonya, Nina's teacher

Andy, school principal

In 1968, Congress, for the first time, endorsed funding for bilingual education through the Bilingual Education Act. This was significant because up until this time, students were discouraged from speaking non-English languages. In 1974, the Supreme Court followed Congress's lead and ruled in *Lau v. Nichols* that schools are not free to ignore the need of limited-English-speaking children.

Today, bilingual education continues to be controversial. Many critics argue that the approach keeps students in a cycle of native language dependency that ultimately inhibits significant progress in English language acquisition. Proponents reason that if students first learn to read in the language in which they are fluent, they can then transfer the skills to English and develop stronger literacy in the long term. Complicating the debate is the range of programs that fall under the definition of bilingual education.

A growing movement within the debate argues to give families more control over deciding the placement of their children. Under most policies, parents are permitted to pull their children out of bilingual education only after the students are in such classes; schools are not required to seek the parents' approval before making placements. Schools are increasingly required to provide descriptions of program options and seek parental approval of students' placements in advance. However, proposals concerning parents' rights to choose often draw criticism. Opponents fear that the school system will not make information easily available to immigrant parents, especially those who speak little or no English, negating any informed parental choice.

The No Child Left Behind Act (NCLB) requires that English Language Learner (ELL) students participate in statewide assessments, regardless of language ability—a huge challenge for many states and districts. Each state must specify how it will assess English Language Learners and develop a standard for measuring proficiency and progress.

MOTHER AND DAUGHTER BATTLE OVER HOMEWORK

Inés Campos didn't know what to do. Her daughter Nina sat under the kitchen table crying, refusing to continue with her homework. "I don't like it! Don't like it! *¡No me gusta!*" Nina screamed. Inés was exasperated. She had been helping Nina with her homework assignment for the past three hours and was beside herself. Inés wondered where her creative and artistic daughter was—the girl who loved to paint portraits of the neighbors. Nina's homework difficulties were beginning to make her hate school. Nina was not doing well academically and did not have many friends. Inés wondered if in choosing a monolingual classroom for her daughter she had made a poor decision.

As you read this case, consider applying the following theoretical lenses to your analysis:

• Executive Functioning: How is Inés' role as a primary caregiver and executive functionary influenced by school policies and practices regarding bilingualism and homework?

- Community Support: What resources in the community support and inhibit Inés' involvement with her daughter's learning?
- Ethnic and Racial Minority Parenting: In what ways do the cultures of Nina's home and school match and not match? Look for examples of community acculturation in this case.

CHOOSING AN ENGLISH-ONLY CLASSROOM FOR NINA: INÉS, NINA'S MOTHER (TRANSLATED FROM SPANISH)

"I know I am the defect for my child. She's not doing well in school because she doesn't speak English well. She doesn't like to read English books. She loves to hear stories—but she always asks that I read Spanish language books. She asks for Spanish because I put some flavor into it. You know when I read in Spanish I get animated. But in English, no. So, she doesn't even want to bring out a book in English."

Inés came to the United States from Mexico for a short vacation. She had not intended to remain in the United States and had never imagined coming to the country to work. In Mexico, she was a schoolteacher in good economic standing and surrounded by a loving family. When she became pregnant with Nina, however, she changed her mind.

"I feel that here Nina can do something. I don't say that in Mexico she can't do it, it's just that I think she has better chances to do it here. But the key in America is English. Nina has to learn to speak English quickly. I know from my own experience. Everything is hard for me. I work at a childcare center, sell products door-to-door, and clean houses, and I still depend on the government welfare. I sometimes feel trapped. I need to learn English so that I can undertake my own business and my own dreams. Right now I can't work with Americans because I don't understand English. So that is my goal—to learn English."

Inés reflected on her own struggles in not understanding the English language and was determined that her daughter should learn English first and foremost. Inés enrolled in adult English classes at the nearby high school and knew how difficult acquiring a second language was. She was adamant about placing Nina in an all-English classroom to bypass her own hardships. As well, she had been instructed by close friends at her church group not to speak with her daughter in Spanish so that she could develop a better grasp of the language.

In the beginning of the year, Nina was placed in a bilingual first-grade classroom. Inés went to the school and talked with the principal to request the all-English setting. She was grateful that the principal permitted the switch, but then faced the problem of not being able to help her daughter with homework.

At the parent-teacher conference in the beginning of the year, Inés was afraid to tell the teacher, Sonya Chesin, about her difficulties in helping Nina with homework and understanding what was being sent home. Nina translated throughout most of the meeting. When Inés asked the teacher for more direction on how to help, Sonya encouraged Inés to read with her daughter in Spanish at home.

"The teacher says it doesn't hurt for children to learn both. So that's what I've been trying to do. I try to teach her Spanish because I promised the teacher that I would. I was a teacher in Mexico myself, and I notice that the different sounds get her a little confused—you know, the vowels all make different sounds. But we work on it. I've also been getting help from my friend Cora at church. She speaks both English and Spanish, and I send Nina over to her house to practice her English. But I don't like being so far from her. I feel a little like I'm losing her, and I don't want her to know how little English I know."

Inés did not tell Sonya that they were working on homework assignments for up to three hours each night.

"I don't want to tell the teacher too much because I don't want Nina in a bilingual class. I think where she is now is better as far as I understand. She has to learn English. If she learns Spanish, she will go down. But it worries me because I know she's very far behind. Too far behind. I ask her questions when she reads to me in Spanish, and I give her reading comprehension to see if she knows what she's reading—but she doesn't know. I wonder if she'll even go to second grade."

A BILINGUAL CLASSROOM MAY SUIT
NINA BETTER: SONYA CHESIN, NINA'S TEACHER

"I'm going to send Nina to second grade. I think it's normal that she is having so many problems in school because English is her second language. It's very hard for children who speak Spanish to learn English. Because English is her second language, I expect her not to do as well as some of the other children. I'd be more concerned if she were a native English speaker. I guess Nina wouldn't be in my room if she really needed more Spanish support because I'm not the bilingual classroom. But I definitely think she needs remediation. She'll never be at the top of the group. You know, she just doesn't have the support at home. These are working people, you know, they're working people, and they don't have access. They probably don't go to the library a lot or go to museums or go to plays. They don't come from that kind of background, so it's pretty hard for them to give their children that kind of knowledge. Getting a job, staying alive, and putting food on the table is just a big chore."

As a veteran teacher at Morrison Elementary, Sonya believed that a bilingual placement might be a more enriching experience for Nina (see Table 2.1 in Chapter 2 for demographics about Morrison Elementary). She worried about Nina's reading and writing skills as well as her social emotional progress. Nina was very sensitive and cried a lot, especially when things were too difficult for her. Sonya attributed these difficulties to Nina's second-language acquisition. Sonya's homework policy followed the school guideline of 20-minute assignments every night except Fridays and holidays. She attempted to individualize the work and send notes in two languages, but due to the time constraints and a busy teaching schedule, this often did not happen. She wished she had more regular communication with parents.

"I mentioned to Nina's mother at the first parent-teacher conference that she should really consider a bilingual placement for her daughter. She seemed very negative toward this suggestion. I think Spanish is a beautiful language and a real asset if she can speak both. So, I made some suggestions about how she might work with her daughter at home and work on beginning sounds. We have to abide by the parents' wishes."

IDENTIFYING BILINGUAL ISSUES AT MORRISON ELEMENTARY: ANDY BEBER, PRINCIPAL

"A number of parents in our school advocate for their children, and bilingual education has been a hot topic around here. Parents will often come to me and request one program or the other. What's interesting is you never know where someone will come out on the issue. The controversy is not just one side against another. I speak Spanish, so I think it's easier for parents to come to me. Some native speakers will come requesting a bilingual placement for their children although others come demanding a monolingual one. In our school, I think the most common problem that parents and teachers in our bilingual programs face is when children's English becomes stronger than their Spanish. The bilingual program becomes hard for them. So the system is often hard for language-delayed and English-improved students."

Morrison Elementary has transitional bilingual, two-way bilingual, and monolingual classrooms. Transitional bilingual education students spend the majority of their time learning in their native language, but spend a certain amount of the day developing English skills. At Morrison Elementary, the transitional bilingual class includes basic instruction in Spanish and 20 to 30 minutes a day of English instruction for English language development. Two-way bilingual or dual immersion bilingual education is instruction divided equally in two languages. This approach is intended for equal numbers of language minority and language majority students in the same classroom, with the ultimate goal of students becoming proficient in both languages. In monolingual classrooms, instruction is entirely in English. Andy Beber is responsible for determining children's placement in the monolingual rooms, then a random-number system assigns whoever is left to the dual classrooms, creating a mixture of language-ability children.

Third grade is typically the year when full bilingual students start making the transition to English instruction, but this is dependent on passing a Spanish test. The test is difficult for some students. For many who can never pass the test, the school eventually places them into English out of desperation. They often do poorly.

"I grapple with what the best system is. We have a wide range of families in our school coming from diverse communities, so it is hard to target our resources and audiences. I have parents who live in palaces, and I have families who live in one-bedroom apartments. The majority of parents are very unresponsive and hard to reach. We don't have a lot of parent involvement in this school, so it's just hard to know what kinds of supports parents need."

INÉS WONDERS WHAT TO DO NEXT

Exasperated, Inés did not know what to do. Her daughter Nina continued to sit under the kitchen table crying, refusing to complete her homework. With the spring parent-teacher conference coming up in the next few weeks, Inés was prepared to ask again for help with the homework, but she also anticipated Sonya recommending a bilingual placement. She wondered if she had made the wrong decision by choosing a monolingual classroom for her daughter. Would Nina be better served in a bilingual classroom? How could she know? "I am the defect for my child," she thought.

DISCUSSION QUESTIONS

Major Issues

The purpose of this case is for educators to consider choices parents make around bilingual education and the responsibility of the school to help parents make informed decisions. The case is designed to help educators better understand the following:

- The meanings and contexts of bilingual education for immigrant families
- Different ecological contexts shaping the child's development
- How schools can help families in their placement choices and their support of children's homework

Describing the Situation

- When are Nina and Inés most vitalized in their mother-daughter relationship? When do difficulties arise?
- What does Inés hope for Nina's future? What does she believe is the key in helping her obtain this? In what ways is Nina struggling?
- What do Inés and Sonya believe about bilingual education? How do their two perspectives come into conflict?

Exploring Contributing Factors

- How does the bilingual structure of the school affect Inés' choice of classroom placement for Nina?
- What assumptions does Sonya make about Inés? How do Inés and Sonya communicate? What effect might this have on Nina?
- How does Nina's placement in Sonya's classroom contribute to her academic performance and social-emotional development?

- What strengths does Inés bring as a parent to this placement dilemma? How might Sonya or Andy capitalize more on these strengths?
- In what ways does Sonya support Nina and Inés?
- How well does the school communicate with parents about issues of bilingual education? What impact does this have on Inés and Nina?

Articulating Possible Next Steps

- How might Inés initiate a conversation with Sonya about her homework difficulties at the next parent-teacher conference?
- If Sonya were aware of the homework situation, what might she suggest to help Inés?
- Who in the community might Inés turn to for support?

Replaying the Case

- How could Sonya have supported Inés and Nina more?
- What can Morrison Elementary do differently in terms of providing parents with the key information they need to make a good placement decision for their children?
- Suppose Inés had talked with other parents from the school to see how their children are learning English, furthering their Spanish, and gaining skills in the subject areas. How might this have changed Inés' placement decision or confidence in talking with Sonya?

Looking at the Bigger Picture

- What school structures impede or facilitate Inés in helping Nina with homework?
- What does Inés perceive as some of the structural barriers to resources?
- What kind of school culture (school norms, attitudes, behaviors, beliefs, and expectations) is needed to affirm the identities of the students in the school? What role should the principal play in nurturing this kind of culture?
- What is the role and responsibility of local institutions like public schools in helping immigrant families make decisions around bilingual education?
- What might be the role of parent or community groups who advocate for Latino children in helping Inés in this case?
- What should the key elements of an ESL policy for this school be?
- Is bilingual education a hot topic in your home area? What policies exist in your state related to English Language Learners? What resources in your community could you draw from to help Nina and Inés?

RECOMMENDED READING

Delpit, L. (1995). *Other people's children: Cultural conflict in the classroom.* New York: The New Press.

Luz Reyes, M. de la, & Halcón, J. J. (Eds.). (2001). *The best for our children: Critical perspectives on literacy for Latino students*. New York: Teachers College Press.

Case 7: Staying on the Path Toward College

One Boy at the Crossroads

by Catherine R. Cooper, Elizabeth Dominguez,
Margarita Azmitia, Erica Holt,
Dolores Mena, and Gabriela Chavira

Characters:

Paulo, sixth grader

Rachel, community college outreach program director

Alberto, Paulo's father

Sarita, Paulo's mother

Alicia, family friend

Miguel, Alicia's son

Nancy, Paulo's math teacher

INTRODUCING PAULO

Paulo Dominguez sat around a table with a number of his fellow sixth graders eating potato chips and cookies. He and his classmates listened as a woman named Rachel Marquez talked about a program that would help prepare them for college. All sixth graders in the community were being recruited to submit applications to the program, which was designed to support them through middle and high school in learning the study habits and decision-making skills needed for college preparation and careers. The program, named Más Allá (connoting the meaning "beyond" in English), represented a long-term partnership between the town's community college and the larger nearby university. Its mission is to engage girls and boys into a program that builds long-term networks for academic success and support for pathways to college.

"Your lives consist of many worlds," she began, "and each world contains all the different people or groups in your life, like a family member or a friend, or sports teams, classmates, and church groups." Rachel began passing out colored pencils and paper to the students and invited each sixth grader to think about the different worlds in their lives. As Paulo began to draw pictures of his family, school, and church he thought about his present life in California and his future dreams of working with computers and maybe even designing video games.

Rachel then urged the youths to think about the positive and negative influences in each of these worlds. Paulo looked over at his two best friends making faces and amusing gestures behind Rachel's back. Paulo began to feel self-conscious about following Rachel's instructions, turned his paper over, and started drawing video game characters instead.

As you read this case, consider applying the following theoretical lenses to your analysis:

• Executive Functioning: Who are the significant individuals scaffolding Paulo's thought processes? What factors make this a critical period in the development of his ability to self-regulate?
• Community Support: How can community programs engage parents to support the learning and development of youth? What community bridging strategies are available to the parents in this case?
• Ethnic and Racial Minority Parenting: How are Paulo's parents' parenting practices affected by their past experiences? How do their beliefs influence their goals for Paulo?

When school let out, Paulo walked home. He lives in a small trailer in an RV lot with his parents, older brother, and two younger siblings. His parents came to California as Mexican immigrants.

"If I tell my friends I want to join the college outreach program, they'll think I'm a schoolboy. But Mama always says that if I don't go to college I won't have a good future. My mom loved to go to school, but had to quit school to start working when she was 12. Her mom didn't let her do her homework, even though she really liked to do homework. Instead, she had to do chores. Mama tells me that I need to go to college if I want to get a good job and buy a house. Going to college helps you get a job instead of being a drug dealer or other things that cause you to get in trouble with the cops."

However, Paulo, who was always a good student, had been slipping. His math teacher had recently recommended him for the remedial track, and more and more frequently, he was not turning in homework assignments. When Paulo reached home, his mother was in the kitchen cooking dinner while his father was reading the newspaper at the kitchen table. He had been in the fields picking strawberries since five in the morning. "*Hola mi'jito* (hello my son)," his father said as Paulo poured himself a glass of water, "*Como te fue en la escuela?* (how was school?)"

PAULO'S FAMILY

Alberto Dominguez, Paulo's father, spent his childhood in Mexico and completed an elementary education at a *primaria* (elementary school) in a rural village where there was no middle or high school. When he moved to a nearby town in an adjacent state to find better work, he met his future wife, Sarita.

After Sarita and Alberto were married, they decided to make the trip to California to find work and give their children a better start in life. Sarita started working in a factory on an assembly line while Alberto worked in the fields picking strawberries. Sarita took English classes at night until she became pregnant with their first child, Raul. She attended other classes in Spanish, including birthing and child care. Since then she has had three other children and continues to work part time in the factory.

SARITA, PAULO'S MOTHER

"I'm quite concerned about Paulo. His father and I want him to be safe, both physically and emotionally, and we want him to have an equal chance to learn and succeed. But lately, I see him being less with the family and more with his friends. I know this is a time for him that's difficult. He's getting older, and relationships and friendships get harder, but I want to help him make the right decisions so we can guide him to college and to stay on the good path. I don't want him to get into drugs or a gang, or get a girl pregnant.

"But I do worry. At the same time that we want Paulo to succeed in school, I'm afraid we're not able to help him. I don't like to go to the school much. Raul, my oldest son, dropped out of school a few months ago, but when he first started having trouble, I got a call from one of his teachers. They called me to go there. I was very scared because I was unfamiliar with the system and the language. No one spoke my language except for the principal and one other teacher who translated for Raul's teacher. I asked them both about the problem involving my son, and the principal and the teacher weren't very helpful. I just felt like they wanted me to leave. Raul dropped out a few months later.

"We aren't here in the United States because we like working here or love living here. We live better in Mexico. But I make this sacrifice because I want my children to study, to learn English, and have a better life than me and their father. It's not that I don't think we have a good life; it's just I want Paulo to have a better life. We provide encouragement and use our own lives as examples of how limited your options are with a poor education.

"And now I see Paulo, just like Raul was a few years ago, at this crossing in the road. He's on *el buen camino de la vida* (the good path of life) now, but some of his friends, I think, are making it hard for him to stay on it. I know that his father and I can't always help with his school learning. I still don't feel comfortable going to the school like I probably should. Already, he has more education than me and his father. I'm worried about him."

ALBERTO, PAULO'S FATHER

"Any type of job is acceptable for my son, as long as it isn't in the fields. When I was very young, I started to pick vegetables on the rancho, and I wouldn't want him to do that. Right now, Paulo is a very serious and good boy. I would like for

Paulo to get to college, but the way things are now, who knows? We don't have much money to send him to school. I know that college is not the only definition of success in life, but I look at our lives in the factories, fields, hotel kitchens—and we want our son to be a doctor, teacher, lawyer. I'd like him to live well. Really, that is the dream that one always has, that one's children succeed, that they are better off. That they do the things one was not able to do.

"His mother and I, we are very poor, but we don't give our children bad examples about anything. We behave well, hoping that they will learn to behave. If they see that we behave and are good parents, hopefully they will do the same. This will keep him away from *malas amistades* (negative friendships)."

COMADRE[3] ALICIA (MADRINA) AND HER SON MIGUEL

There was a knock on the door, and Paulo put down his pencil and homework assignment and went to answer it. His madrina Alicia Robles and her oldest son Miguel had arrived for dinner. Alicia greeted Sarita with a kiss on the cheek and began to help her fix dinner. Meanwhile, Miguel went over to Paulo and asked if he needed any help with his homework. Alicia and Sarita met at a Sunday church soccer game in which their husbands were playing and quickly became close friends. Alicia's oldest son Miguel was only a few years older than Raul. Because her family had been in the United States longer than Sarita's, Alicia felt like it was her job to take Sarita under her wing.

Lately, Alicia had been sending Miguel over to help Paulo with homework. Miguel was one of the first students involved in the community college outreach program and currently attends the local community college, with the scholarship from the outreach program.

As the two boys worked together, Paulo put down his pencil and rested his chin against his fist.

"This work is getting really hard—especially these word problems! I never get them right. If you're not here, I don't even have a chance. I know my mom wants to help, but she just doesn't know this kind of math. I should just quit. What did you do when you were my age?"

"I know where you're coming from, Paulo. This math work is hard, but it's important that you stick with it, stay in school, and go to college."

"I know. You're always telling me that. That lady Rachel came to school today to tell us about that program you're in."

"Hey, that's great, Paulo! Do you have the application? We can get to work on it right now. You know, it was the program that really opened up a lot of doors for me. They helped me get a job tutoring other kids when I was in high school and have kept me employed since then. And that scholarship sure helped me pay for college. Now I work at the program's partnership with the university as a researcher to help make the program better and as a college mentor. So take that application out. Let's look at it!"

When Paulo explained that he was too embarrassed to get the application form, Miguel talked to him about all the reasons he really should get involved. Miguel added that besides all the benefits for the future, there were also cute girls who often attended.

BACK AT SCHOOL

The next morning Paulo got up and went to school. He was still thinking about the community outreach program. The night before, Miguel had reawakened his desire to approach Rachel and ask for an application. As he entered the school, Paulo glanced at the quilt hanging in the lobby. His math teacher, Nancy, and another teacher had asked their students to create a picture of their hopes and dreams, then asked families in the community to sew on the different parts. Paulo's patch showed a computer video game.

"Hey Paulo!" Robert yelled as Paulo approached his math class. "Come over here!"

Paulo walked over.

"Yo. A few of us after school today—we're gonna meet up with some guys up the street. You in?" asked Robert.

Paulo hesitated, "Um . . . well, I might need to stay after school and work on some math homework. I'm failing."

"Paulo, man. Don't worry so much about your homework and school. It's not worth studying so hard. There are easier ways to get a job and money," answered Robert.

"Maybe man, yeah, I'll see," answered Paulo just as the bell rang.

Paulo breathed a sigh of relief and continued to walk to math class. Robert was starting to remind Paulo more and more of his brother Raul who had dropped out of school to hang out all day with his friends and was now on probation for stealing bikes to sell. He knew his parents suspected Raul was in a gang and saw how much they worried about his future.

NANCY BROWN, PAULO'S MATH TEACHER

Nancy Brown had been teaching math for nine years. During her first years teaching at the high school level, she had witnessed several students, especially low-income, ethnic minority, and immigrant boys leave school and its career opportunities too early. So she switched to a sixth-grade math classroom at Bay Vista Middle School a few years ago, hoping to help get youth in the community on the right track to math earlier in their school careers while they were still on "the good path." Bay Vista is a primarily Latino, low-income school with high numbers of English Language Learners who speak Spanish (see Table 4.3). Families mostly come from Mexico to work in the fields picking strawberries and lettuce, and in the packing plants.

"I see it as my job not only to teach mathematics but to also try to encourage the dreams and goals of Latino children and their families. Lately, I am concerned about Paulo. I see him spending time with some really questionable kids, and I'm worried about his math and his goals. I had to recommend him for the low-level sixth-grade math class. This upsets me because I see all the assets he brings with him. I told him that he's got a lot of potential, but that he's not working hard enough. Then he surprised me and started talking about his frustration with word problems.

Table 4.3   Bay Vista Middle School

Location	Mid-sized West Coast city, population 45,000
Grades served	6–8
Enrollment	871, 95% Hispanic
Students eligible for free and reduced-priced lunch	80%
Percent of children who do not graduate from high school	56%
Mobility rate	13%
English Language Learners	59%
Percent of sixth graders scoring at the proficient level or above on math standards-based tests	6%
Percent of sixth graders scoring at the proficient level or above on English language arts standards-based tests	9%

"It seems he has an older friend at home who helps him, but when he's on his own, he just can't figure it out. So now I know he's trying, but there's only so much I can do. There are standardized benchmarks of achievement that determine eligibility for college-prep classes in high school like Algebra 1, Geometry, and Algebra 2, and if you're in low-level math in sixth grade, it's really hard to place into a higher level afterwards and pass Algebra by ninth grade. I just can't put him in these classes without him being prepared.

"I see so many times a disproportionate number of our Latino students placed in low-level math ability groups early on that sends these students towards these remedial tracks. I want to work to untrack these youths, but they need support—as well as the skills—to know they can succeed. In Paulo's case, he hasn't been doing his work and has made some new friends who seem to value school less than he does. It's really affected his grades."

RACHEL MARQUEZ, COMMUNITY COLLEGE OUTREACH PROGRAM DIRECTOR

Rachel Marquez walked into the cafeteria at lunch with her friend Nancy Brown. Rachel wanted to invite more thoughts and questions from students about applying to the program. She had directed the outreach program, Más Allá, since its start six years earlier. The program currently enrolls 500 low-income youth and offers tutoring by college students, Saturday academics and summer institutes, family involvement activities, and academic guidance from sixth grade through high school to help students stay on track to college. Upon graduation from high school, students are awarded $1,000 scholarships to attend the community college.

Más Allá also uses a research-based partnership with a local university to better understand student and family perspectives about resources and challenges to getting into and succeeding in college. In an ongoing cycle of action research, the program hosts regular meetings between program and research staff, as well as youth leaders, to identify ongoing questions and integrate data collection and analysis into program activities. Findings from the research suggested that both males and females see their peers as the greatest source of difficulty in attaining their academic and career goals. At the same time, mothers were the greatest resources. And students who continued in the program drew increasing positive support from both peers and mothers over time, a pattern that makes Rachel think that one key way her program works is by building networks of college-bound peers.

Rachel explained to Nancy the latest problematic trends developing from their research. "Younger students are more interested in program activities than older students. It's the older students who are under more pressure from peers to join gangs, ditch school, spend their time going to parties, and not attend program activities. At the same time, many of them need to work and make money. We also see more girls than boys attending activities. A lot of boys are not applying to the program in sixth grade because even then they think it looks 'uncool.' Some older boys have just stopped coming altogether. These gender patterns worry me, and I struggle with how I can enroll more boys. But one thing that is working is Daniel, who is a student teacher from the university who teaches math at the high school. He's great teaching the math enrichment class at our Saturday Academies. The attendance of the older boys has gone way up. A few bring their 'homeboys' and sit in the back of the class, and Danny just pulls them right on into the math."

Just then, Rachel caught the fleeting and embarrassed eye of a boy sitting amidst his other friends in the cafeteria.

DISCUSSION QUESTIONS

Major Issues

The purpose of this case is to consider how schools and communities can work with Latino families to increase youth opportunities to go to college. The case is designed to help educators understand the home, school, peer group, and community factors that influence Latino youth to take *el buen camino de la vida* (the good path of life) or *el mal camino* (the bad path) and how to get back on the good path. Specifically, the case focuses on the following:

- The influence of family relationships and personal networks on youth identity
- Academic socialization, including building pathways to college

- The different ecological contexts shaping the development of youth or children in the upper range of middle childhood
- Ways that schools might link with low-income immigrant families and communities

Describing the Situation

- What crucial decision(s) must Paulo make?
- How would the different characters who have a relationship with Paulo identify the problem he faces? How are they similar and different in their assessment?
- Identify references to "pathways" and "paths" in this case. What might be some of Paulo's different possible pathways or life trajectories to high school, college, and a career?

Exploring Contributing Factors

- What do Sarita and Alberto want for Paulo's future? How do these expectations influence his social-emotional and academic identity?
- How does Raul (Paulo's brother) influence Paulo?
- Describe Paulo's relationship with his peers. What resources and challenges do they provide?
- What are some of the natural parent networks that exist for families in this community? How have they served as a resource to Paulo?
- How would you describe Paulo's relationship with his teacher, Nancy?
- What are some of the barriers Rachel faces in her work as the program director?

Articulating Possible Next Steps

- What should Nancy do next to support the potential she sees in Paulo?
- What can the school do to develop relationships with Latino parents whose children are at risk of dropping out?
- How might Rachel and Más Allá take a bigger responsibility in helping to engage families in their children's education?
- How might Rachel redesign the efforts to sell the program to Latino boys like Paulo?

Looking at the Bigger Picture

- What are children like during the upper range of middle childhood? How does developmental level influence home-school-community relationships and vice versa?
- How does the social and cultural position of first-generation immigrant Latino families put them at risk for unfavorable youth educational

outcomes? What school and community supports should be available to Latino families? To what extent are the supports offered in this case sufficient to keep Latino youth on the right track?

- In what ways can teachers come to better understand the cultural contexts of the students they teach and how these contexts influence the students' school experiences?
- What other institutions/community organizations can support the school in helping Paulo, and in what ways can they do this?
- Who are the "Paulos" in your school and community? What is being done to reach the needs of these families and children? Identify programs like Más Allá that are available in your community.

RECOMMENDED READING

Cooper, C. R., Chavira, G., Mena, D., Mikolyski, D., & Domínguez, E. (2004, January). *Bridging multiple worlds: Building pathways from childhood to college*. Retrieved April 15, 2004, from http://www.gse.harvard.edu/hfrp/projects/fine/resources/research/minority.html (see www.bridgingworlds.org for related materials and tools for partnerships).

Hoover-Dempsey, K., & Sandler, H. (1997). Why do parents become involved in their children's education? *Review of Educational Research, 67*(1), 3–42.

Moll, L., Amanti, C., Neff, D., & Gonzalez, N. (1991). Funds of knowledge for teaching: Using a qualitative approach to connect homes and classrooms. *Theory Into Practice, 31*(1), 132–141.

Notes

1. An earlier version of this case was originally published on the Family Involvement Network of Educators, Harvard Family Research Project, Web site: http://www.gse.harvard.edu/hfrp/projects/fine/resources/teaching-case/progress.html

2. An earlier version of this case was originally published on the Family Involvement Network of Educators, Harvard Family Research Project, Web site: http://www.gse.harvard.edu/hfrp/projects/fine/resources/teaching-case/bilingual.html

3. A *comadre* or *compadre* is a godparent (godmother or godfather) who helps parents guide their child through life and school. This person is called a *madrina* or *padrina*, for women or men, respectively, in their relation to the child.

References for Introduction

Bronfenbrenner, U. (1989). Ecological systems theory. In R. Vasta (Ed.), *Six theories of child development: Revised formulations and current issues* (pp. 185–246). Greenwich, CT: JAI Press.

References for Davis-Kean and Eccles

Borkowski, J. G., & Burke, J. E. (1996). Theories, models, and measurements of executive functioning: An information processing perspective. In G. R. Lyon & N. A. Krasnegor (Eds.), *Attention, memory, and executive function* (pp. 235–261). Baltimore: Paul H. Brooks.

Bronfenbrenner, U., & Morris, P. A. (1998). The ecology of environmental processes. In W. Damon (Series Ed.) & R. M. Lerner (Vol. Ed.), *Handbook of child psychology* (5th ed., Vol. 1, pp. 993–1028). New York: Wiley.

Comer, J. P. (1980). *School power: Implications of an intervention project.* New York: The Free Press.

Comer, J. P., & Haynes, N. M. (1991). Parent involvement in schools: An ecological approach. *The Elementary School Journal, 91*(3), 271–277.

Davis-Kean, P. E., & Eccles, J. S. (2002, December). *Influences and barriers to better parent-school collaborations.* Paper presented at the National Invitational Conference on School-Family Partnerships and Social and Emotional Learning, Washington, DC.

Eccles, J. S. (1992). School and family effects on the ontogeny of children's interests, self-perceptions, and activity choice. In J. Jacobs (Ed.), *Nebraska Symposium on Motivation, 1992: Developmental perspectives on motivation* (pp. 145–208). Lincoln: University of Nebraska Press.

Epstein, J. L. (1990). Single parents and the schools: The effects of marital status on parent and teacher interactions. In M. T. Hallinan, D. M. Klein, & J. Glass (Eds.), *Change in societal institutions* (pp. 91–122). New York: Plenum Press.

Flavell, J. H. (1999). Cognitive development: Children's knowledge about the mind. *Annual Review of Psychology, 50,* 21–45.

Fletcher, J. M. (1996). Executive functions in children: Introduction to the special series. *Developmental Neuropsychology, 12*(1), 1–3.

Furstenberg, F. F., Jr., Cook, T. D., Eccles, J., Elder, G. H., Jr., & Sameroff, A. (1999). *Managing to make it: Urban families and adolescent success.* Chicago: The University of Chicago Press.

Hoover-Dempsey, K. V., & Sandler, H. M. (1997). Why do parents become involved in their children's education? *Review of Educational Research, 67*(1), 3–42.

References for Weiss and Lopez

Bellah, R., Madsen, R., Sullivan, W. M., Swidler, A., & Tipton, S. M. (1985). *Habits of the heart: Individualism and commitment in American life.* Berkeley: The University of California Press.

Blank, S. (2001). *Good works: Highlights of a study on the Center for Family Life.* Baltimore: The Annie E. Casey Foundation.

Bloom, L. R. (2001). "I'm poor, I'm single, I'm a mom, and I deserve respect": Advocating in schools as/with mothers in poverty. *Educational Studies 32*(3), 300–316.

Bronfenbrenner, U. (1986). Ecology of the family as a context for human development: Research perspectives. *Developmental Psychology, 22*(6), 723–742.

Caspe, M., Traub, F., & Little, P. (2002, August). *Beyond the headcount: Evaluating family involvement in out-of-school time.* (Issues and Opportunities in Out-of-School Time Evaluation Brief No. 4.) Cambridge, MA: Harvard Family Research Project.

Cook, T. D., Herman, M. R., Philipps, M., Settersten, R. A., Jr., (2002). Some ways in which neighborhoods, nuclear families, friendship groups, and schools jointly affect changes in early adolescent development. *Child Development 73*(4), 1283–1309.

Cooper, C. R., Chavira, G., Mikolyski, D., & Domínguez, E. (2004). Bridging multiple worlds: Building pathways from childhood to college. Retrieved July 28, 2004, from Harvard University, Harvard Family Research Project, Family Involvement Network of Educators Web site: http://www.gse.harvard.edu/hfrp/projects/fine/resources/research/minority.html

Eccles, J. (1999). The development of children ages 6 to 14. *Future of Children, 9*(2), 16–30.

Gold, E., Simon, E., & Brown, C. (2002a). *Strong neighborhoods, strong schools: Successful community organizing for school reform.* Chicago: Cross City Campaign for Urban School Reform.

Gold, E., Simon, E., & Brown, C. (2002b). *Strong neighborhoods, strong schools: The indicators project on education organizing.* Chicago: Cross City Campaign for Urban School Reform.

Harvard Family Research Project. (2002). University-community partnership: The Jane Addams School for Democracy. *FINE Forum, 5.* Retrieved June 28, 2004, from http://www.gse.harvard.edu/hfrp/projects/fine/fineforum/forum5/spotlight.html

Jarrett, R. L. (1999). Successful parenting in high-risk neighborhoods. *Future of Children, 9*(2), 45–50.

Jarrett, R. L. (2000). Neighborhood effects models: A view from the neighborhood. *Research in Community Sociology, 10,* 305–323.

Marshall, N. L., Noonan, A. E., McCartney, K., Marx, F., & Keefe, N. (2001). It takes an urban village: Parenting networks of urban families. *Journal of Family Issues, 22*(2), 163–182.

National Coalition of Advocates for Students. (1997). *Unfamiliar partners: Asian parents and U.S. public schools.* Boston: Author.

O'Neil, R., Parke, R. D., & McDowell, D. J. (2001). Objective and subjective features of children's neighborhoods: Relations to parental regulatory strategies and children's social competence. *Applied Developmental Psychology, 22,* 135–155.

Ran-Kim, J., Chan, W., Settersten, R. A., & Teitler, J. O. (1999). How do neighborhoods matter? In F. F. Furstenberg, T. D. Cook, J. Eccles, G. H. Elder, & A. Sameroff (Eds.) *Managing to make it: Urban families and adolescent success* (pp. 145–170). Chicago: The University of Chicago Press.

Rankin, B. H., & Quante, J. M. (2002). Social contexts and urban adolescent outcomes: The interrelated effects of neighborhoods, families, and peers on African American youth. *Social Problems 49*(1), 79–100.

Shirley, D. (1997). *Community organizing for urban school reform.* Austin: University of Texas Press.

Weiss, H., Mayer, E., Kreider, H., Vaughan, P., Dearing, E., Hencke, R. et al. (2003). Making it work: Low-income working mothers' involvement in their children's education. *American Educational Research Journal, 40*(4), 879–901.

Section 3

The Exosystem

The **exosystem** is defined by Bronfenbrenner (1979, 1989) as the level of a developing person's ecology encompassing linkages and processes between at least one setting that contains that person (i.e., a microsystem context) and at least one other setting that does not. Importantly, events taking place in the latter setting must influence processes occurring in the former. Perhaps the clearest example of the exosystem is the relationship between a parent's workplace and the family. In this case, if the child is the focus, the parent's workplace is a setting that does not contain the developing person, and the family is a setting that does. One way in which the workplace can affect the family setting is through its influence on how much time parents have to spend with their children.

Here we have clustered two cases with one theoretical lens to illustrate some of the processes that can occur at the level of the exosystem. The theoretical lens, "School-Based Family Support," is offered by Heather Weiss and Holly Kreider, and provides an empirically supported perspective on the ways that schools can support families in their involvement in their children's education. This lens reviews a body of literature documenting how some schools have connected families with resources ranging from childcare to mental health services. From this perspective, the school and the family (parents or caregivers) represent developing children's microsystems, whereas parents' adult contexts—such as social networks, mental health services, professional development training—represent settings that do not contain the developing child yet can directly influence interactions in the settings that do. Importantly, the perspective offered by this lens conceptualizes parenting as a skill that progresses developmentally. Thus, as parents mature and acquire more knowledge, they can incorporate these developing skills toward more effective parenting.

The two cases in this section, "Afterschool for Cindy" and "Piecing It Together," illustrate processes occurring at multiple levels—the micro, meso, and exosystems. We include them here, in Section 3, to facilitate applications of theoretical perspectives focusing on the exosystem. In "Afterschool for Cindy," single-mother Marla faces multiple challenges in caring for her daughter. Marla has struggled with a series of unhealthy romantic relationships, low-wage jobs, and a lack of social support networks. These are all settings that comprise Marla's, but not Cindy's, microsystems. But all of the issues with which Marla is contending have effects on processes occurring in Cindy's microsystem of family, which ultimately affects her schooling. Applying an exosystem-based approach to Marla's and Cindy's case may reveal different solutions than would a single-sided approach focusing only on Cindy's family setting, for example. Whereas the latter might lead one to view Marla as an uncaring parent because she does not arrange for supervised afterschool care for Cindy, focusing on the exosystem might shed light on how Marla's own immediate circumstances have impacted on this decision.

In "Piecing It Together," Karen Carson struggles to properly care for two sons, one of whom is diagnosed with a behavioral disorder and the other with a learning disability. Karen herself must deal with issues of drug use and poverty; and, like Cindy's mother, Marla, Karen lacks sufficient social support. In this case, we witness sixth-grader Dionte's trajectory through eighth grade, when his attitude toward and behavior at school worsen dramatically. Although Karen values schooling and wants both of her sons to succeed, she lacks many of the skills and resources necessary for ensuring positive outcomes for them.

In Dionte's and his brother Tamaal's case, however, we meet two other adults who want to see them succeed and do not write Karen off as a bad mother. Social worker Kofi Hunter, who handles Tamaal's case with Child Protective Services, focuses on helping Karen acquire the skills she needs to effectively care for both of her sons. Dee Johnson, Dionte's teacher, watches as he becomes more and more disengaged from school and commits herself to getting him back on track. The problem, however, is in the breakdown of communication across the various systems. Because Karen, Kofi Hunter, and Dee Johnson are each working independently of one another, they each are also working with only limited information. While Karen focuses primarily on improving Tamaal's situation by placing him in foster care, Kofi focuses primarily on improving Karen's circumstances, and Dee focuses on engaging Dionte in school. Little effort is made, however, to make connections across these settings. In this section, readers are encouraged to consider the connections among parents' settings and circumstances and those directly affecting their children.

Processes occurring at the level of the exosystem are apparent in other cases throughout this volume, as well as in situations not addressed here at all. Parents are developing persons just as children are, and their development occurs in a set of microsystems that often do not overlap with their children's.

Aside from the workplace, for example, parents have their own social networks, friendships, and, for single parents, dating and romantic relationships, most of which do not include their children. But parents' experiences in these settings affect their own development, which in turn affects their interactions with their children in the family system. Thus, focusing on the exosystem can often shed a different light on children's experiences at school than does focusing only on contexts that directly influence children.

5

Theoretical Perspectives on the Exosystem

As we described in the introduction to this section, the exosystem is that level of a developing person's ecology that connects that person's microsystems to other systems not containing that person. Importantly, these latter systems must directly influence the developing person's experiences in microsystem settings. Simply said, the significant others in individuals' microsystems have their own microsystems, not all of which overlap. For example, siblings have the family context in common, but not necessarily school, peer, or work (for older individuals) settings. But each has experiences outside of the family setting that can directly influence interactions with other family members. Processes such as these constitute the exosystem and are outlined in the theoretical lens offered by Heather Weiss and Holly Kreider.

Weiss and Kreider, in "School-Based Family Support," describe many of the ways in which schools can work with families to support their children's educational experiences. Their approach, derived from a broad empirical base, highlights especially how schools can link families to other services and institutions that can enhance their own personal development so that they might become better equipped for effective involvement in their children's education. This approach focuses on the connections between family members' (particularly parents or primary caregivers) and children's microsystems, illustrating how even those contexts that do not contain the children can directly affect their development. Because all people conduct their lives both within and outside of family settings, this exosystem approach may provide an overlooked perspective in a variety of school-related situations.

School-Based Family Support

by Heather Weiss and Holly Kreider

Healthy child development requires strong, nurturing families that in turn are nurtured and supported by individuals and institutions within the community (Weiss, Woodrum, Lopez, & Kraemer, 1993). The field of **family support**, which aims to promote the development of children and families, is rooted in this belief and has enjoyed a long history of program initiatives, research experiences, and policies (e.g., Zigler & Weiss, 1985). Historically, family support programs have come in varied forms such as prenatal and infant programs, child abuse and neglect programs, early childhood education and family-oriented day care, parent education and support, and neighborhood-based programs (Weiss, 1983).

Until recently, however, schools have been a less common partner in family support efforts, despite their strategic position in communities as a potential provider of support to families. Specifically, schools have extensive access to children, provide contexts for their growth from early childhood through adolescence, and are located mostly in neighborhoods where students' families live and work (Lopez & Hochberg, 1993; Nissani, 2004). Yet only recently have schools become major players in the family support field. This may be due in part to the fact that scant research literature exists to inform schools about what they can do to be ready for all families and children as they enter into schools (Nissani, 2004). Fortunately, as Christenson and Sheridan (2001) observe, the family involvement focus of schools has begun to shift from how to get parents involved to how to promote positive child and family development. Nissani (2004, p. 3) concurs that "schools are currently the fastest-growing sector for the development of family support programming."

In this chapter, we offer theoretical premises of family support based on several decades of research and program experiences and show how these premises have begun to take hold in school settings, drawing examples from elementary schools that serve students in middle childhood and their families.

Family Support Premises

Dunst (1995) outlines the central premises of family support that are grounded in developmental, social, community-based, ecological, and cultural perspectives. Taken together, these premises place the growth, empowerment, and strengths of families at the center of education and human service models (Dunst, 1995; Halpern, 1999). These premises offer guidance for how professionals, including educators, should interact with families.

A developmental process. Family support experts believe that parenting is a **developmental process**, meaning that parents have the capacity to grow and develop over time just as their children do. The family support movement aims to promote parent development by empowering parents "to act on their own behalf, especially enhancing parental child-rearing capabilities" (Dunst, 1995, p. 4). Thus, this developmental stance is based on family strengths, and enriches families' potential to create healthy home environments for their children (Weiss et al., 1993).

Family resource centers are one example of how schools have begun to institutionalize the developmental and strength-based premises of family support. For example, the Kentucky Education Reform Act of 1990 called for the creation of Family Support Centers in Kentucky to help families and students find local solutions to nonacademic problems. These centers now serve 83 percent of schools in Kentucky and enjoy continued broad support by communities and policymakers. The centers serve children from birth through age 12 and provide services such as child care, afterschool programs, support for parents through home visiting and peer support groups, parenting education, and health services or referral (Denton, 2001). Likewise, community schools bring many partners together into the schools to offer a range of supports and opportunities to children, youth, families, and communities before, during, and after school, every day of the week (Coalition of Community Schools, 2004).

Strengths-based approaches promote parents' abilities to contribute not only to healthy home environments for their children, but to healthy school environments as well. Schools can support and empower families by creating new roles for them in the schools. For example, schools can provide recruitment and training for parents to become family liaisons, classroom aides, afterschool tutors, and even teachers-in-training (Harvard Family Research Project, 2001). It is also important that school opportunities for parents respond to their own interests and priorities. Parent Services Project, a family support organization in San Rafael, California, worked to engage parents in local elementary schools. Their process first involved having parents identify their concerns and develop their vision, before ideas and programs, such as a homework club, were actually implemented in the schools (Harvard Family Research Project, 2004).

Social support. **Social support**, or the resources provided by individuals and groups, contributes importantly to healthy development of children and their families. Strong social support networks are associated with lower stress levels among mothers of children with disabilities. Furthermore, social support can improve parents' emotional resources, involvement in the schools, and adaptability to their children's temperament and behaviors (see Section 1, Chapter 1, this volume).

Schools can enhance parent-to-parent supports by creating opportunities for families to network and socialize with each other. Activities that bring families together to interact with one another promote child and family development, as well as a sense of community. For example, the Families and Schools Together program is an intervention and parent involvement program that has whole families gather weekly at the school to participate in specific activities that are fun and research-based. These meetings aim to foster children's sense of belonging, promote parents' sense of empowerment, create positive family and parent-child interactions, and build social support networks among families (Hernandez, 2000).

Families can also benefit from social support either to help them in time of need or to enhance their personal and career growth. For example, by creating partnerships with local community agencies, schools can connect families to needed social services. To be effective, such support must be responsive to emerging family issues, even when these issues fall outside of the primary scope of the organization (Family Support America, 2001; Schultz, Lopez, & Hochberg, 1996; Shartrand, 1996). In their study of high-performing schools serving migrant populations, Lopez, Scribner, and Mahitivanichcha (2001) found that the main criterion for successful parental involvement programs was "an unwavering commitment to meet the multiple needs of migrant families above all other involvement considerations" (p. 261). For example, school personnel addressed the pressing social, economic, and physical needs through supports like the provision of basic necessities (e.g., food, clothes, and school supplies), vocational training, and frequent home visits. Note, however, that outreach to meet the needs of families is important but not sufficient to engage them as partners in children's learning. Christenson and Sheridan (2001) provide a useful framework for the development of home-school partnerships. They propose a collaborative approach, constructive attitudes, an atmosphere that facilitates collaboration, and school actions that are inclusive of parents and responsive to their desires with respect to children's learning.

Beyond social services, schools can create a learning community that goes beyond the classroom to include families. Activities such as adult computer training, arts and dance courses, and book clubs offer parents and other adults opportunities to gain valuable skills and explore new interests. Providing after-school programs and extracurricular activities can promote both child development and parent well-being, because parents who are concerned about their children's afterschool arrangements may experience more psychological distress and job disruptions (Massachusetts Afterschool Partnership, 2003).

A Community Basis

Child and parent functioning are optimized when families can access resources and supports in their neighborhoods and when families feel a strong sense of community (Halpern, 1999). Historically, the community basis of family support has focused on community-based information and resources to support *individual* family goals. However, in recent years family support efforts have expanded to also improve families' *collective* use of information and to offer community-wide, family-strengthening activities (Halpern, 1999; Lopez, 2002).

Opportunities for civic engagement and social networking, for example, can create **social capital**, meaning the resources that arise from strong social relations among and between parents, children, and school staff. Specifically, relational resources such as shared norms for child behavior and trust allow parents to exchange valuable information and better support their children's education and development (Coleman, 1991). Community-based organizations can serve an important role in facilitating such processes across families (see Section 2, Chapter 3, this volume). For example, the Parent Services Project, mentioned earlier, is a community-based organization that works with groups of parents in several public elementary schools in California to help build a collective sense of community among parents through formal training and informal networking opportunities. Parents then collectively identify and take action around school-wide issues of concern to them (Lopez & Kreider, 2003).

A social ecology. Child and family development also are nested within a broader **social ecology**, meaning that they influence and are influenced by the individuals and systems that interact with families (see Introduction, this volume). Family support professionals strive to create systems that are fair, responsive, and accountable to families (Family Support America, 2001). Family support programs can prepare parents to advocate for themselves and their children, ensuring they are fairly served by schools. For example, The Right Question Project (RQP) promotes parent and community involvement in schools by building parents' individual skills so they can effectively support, monitor, and advocate for their children's education. RQP helps parents learn to think critically, ask the "right" questions, and create plans for action. In this way, RQP helps parents create their own solutions rather than giving historically disengaged and low-income families prescribed solutions to their problems (Coffman, 2000).

Parents can also participate in decision making to effect school- or system-wide change, through school planning, problem solving, and governance. For example, parent representation on local school councils in Chicago has impacted the schools in many ways, including the hiring of new educational leadership that better reflects the diversity of the community. It can also engender a sense of ownership among parents and others who become involved in schools, which establishes a foundation for their ongoing advocacy of children and schools (Lopez & Kreider, 2003).

Cultural competence. Because notions of parenting, community, and child development vary culturally, it is essential that staff working with families develop cultural competence. **Cultural competence** can be defined as the capacity to acknowledge "the knowledge, skills, customs, values, beliefs, and practices that culturally diverse people consider their strengths" (Dunst, 1995, p. 43). Louise Derman-Sparks (1998) describes a three-step process by which educators can become more culturally responsive to the children and families they serve. The first step involves *acknowledging* that cultural differences between oneself and a child's parent may exist and respectfully letting the parent know about an issue needing discussion. The second step entails *asking* questions of oneself and a child's family to better understand varying cultural beliefs and viewpoints about a situation. Using the information gathered, the final step calls for *adapting* one's practice—as part of a resolution that both the educator and a child's parents jointly negotiate to address a conflict caused by cultural differences.

The Funds of Knowledge model developed by Luis Moll at the University of Arizona bridges the cultural divide that sometimes occurs between school personnel and families (see Chapter 7, this volume) by having teachers learn about their students' families and incorporate this knowledge into the curriculum. With the help of experienced researchers, teachers conducted ethnographic research in the homes of their students, who lived primarily in low-income Latino families. Teachers interviewed members of students' families about their personal and labor history to uncover the "hidden" home and community resources of their students. In study groups, teachers integrated these funds of knowledge into their curriculum, creating socially meaningful tasks and active learning for students. One teacher created an instructional unit on building and construction that involved twenty parents and community members. These individuals shared their expertise with students by explaining their tools and how they used measurements and numbers in their work (Harvard Family Research Project, 2003; Moll, Amanti, Neff, & González, 1992).

Conclusion

Schools are institutions with educational and developmental aims, are nested within local communities, and serve an increasingly culturally diverse population of children and families. These features make them ideal locations for acting on the theoretical premises of family support. In the following section, we present some practical implications of these premises for educators.

Implications for Educators

Focus on family strengths. Educators must begin with the assumption that all parents strive to be good parents, but need opportunities and support to do the best they can for their children (Weiss et al., 1993). Educators therefore must build on family and community strengths, empower parents to enhance their parenting and parent involvement skills, and create school environments that help parents overcome self-doubt and effectively advocate for their children.

Acknowledge social supports and services important to all families. All families can benefit from social supports and services. By responding to families' self-identified needs, educators can in turn facilitate families' involvement in their children's learning and schools. Schools can use or build on existing resources and mechanisms, such as family resource centers. But schools cannot do everything alone and must also look to other resources in the community to which they can refer families for support.

Educators can also be supportive by building trusting relationships with families over time (Bryk & Schneider, 2002). For example, when teachers listen attentively and share very specific information about children with parents, this can help to reduce defensiveness and reticence among parents who sometimes bring their own negative childhood experiences with schools into their interactions with teachers. These practices can keep the exchanges between parents and teachers focused on their common interest in the child (Lawrence-Lightfoot, 2003).

Promote community through social networks and civic engagement. Educators can also support families by creating opportunities for them to connect with each other and to the community. Organizing social events, providing needed services, and establishing a space in which families can meet together helps to provide the structures necessary for community building and social action to take place.

Respect the culture of families. Educators should examine and understand their own cultural perspective and how this relates to their views of families' child-rearing practices and developmental goals. Educators must take it upon themselves to understand the contexts in which their students are raised, and make efforts to address conflicting attitudes and beliefs when they interfere with children's educational experiences and/or relationships between families and schools.

6

The Cases

The cases in this chapter illustrate with great detail how what goes on in parents' personal lives can have effects on their children's outcomes. The theoretical perspectives that precede this chapter, in Chapter 5, can be useful tools for understanding precisely how these relations emerge. In "Afterschool for Cindy," readers might consider how Cindy's school might have intervened further in her mother's struggles to provide stable afterschool care for Cindy. How might Cindy's mother's personal situation have influenced her reactions to school personnel's recommendations? Or in "Piecing It Together," does the school's obligation to students' success end with the student, or should it extend to parents to ensure they are equipped to support their children's education? These and other questions are raised in the context of the theoretical perspectives offered by Weiss and Kreider in the preceding chapter, who argue that schools can provide important links between parents' and children's worlds. Readers might consider similar questions in an attempt to view the cases that follow from multiple angles.

Case 8: Afterschool for Cindy

Family, School, and Community
Roles in Out-of-School Time[1]

by Ellen Mayer

Characters:

Cindy, second grader

Nikki, Cindy's teacher

Ed, Willow School principal

Marla, Cindy's mother

Shellie, school counselor

> I Went to camp
> I Went on a Horse.
> I like Horses.
> My mom Love
> Horses.

—*Cindy Potter*
Willow School
Second-grade portfolio

PERSPECTIVES ON CINDY AND HER MOTHER: NIKKI, CINDY'S TEACHER

Nikki, a second-grade teacher in a large town, was grocery shopping after school when she noticed her student Cindy playing unsupervised in the parking lot near the photo-processing store where her mother worked. Although Nikki felt this to be a safe and peaceful community, she nevertheless felt some concern. Cindy was skipping around, peering into car mirrors, waving frantically to anyone who exited the store.

Nikki was accustomed to thinking a lot about all the needs of her students. She worked at Willow School, a small K–6 school offering a safe, caring, and nurturing environment for students and families. The school looked holistically at the needs of its students and helped them with a range of needs, sometimes even with clothing or food. The principal, Ed, expected his teachers to be advocates for the kids in their classrooms.

Nikki had been working hard with Cindy over the course of the school year to improve her social skills and help her to be more compliant in the school setting. If Cindy could learn to be less impulsive, she could focus better on her academics; if she could learn to make appropriate social overtures to her peers, she would feel better about herself, and even feel more confident in her learning. To Nikki's way of thinking, helping Cindy develop socially was a critical key to unlocking improved reading and math performance.

Enriching afterschool experiences were a fundamental ingredient in this formula. If Cindy's out-of-school time could reinforce the work Nikki was doing in the classroom with her around social skill building, Nikki was convinced that Cindy would see academic gains at school. Nikki saw her community as rich in afterschool opportunities for elementary school children, many providing a context for social skills development. There were programs in the arts, a vast number of athletic programs offered through the Recreation Department, and programs through Youth Services such as Big Brothers/Big Sisters. Nikki wished more than anything that Cindy could be involved in soccer. A big strong girl with lots of energy and enthusiasm, it would do Cindy a world of good to be part of a team, learn the rules of the game, and have to listen to her coach. It would also be wonderful if Cindy could have a Big Sister. Nikki could just imagine Cindy, such a loving child, throwing her arms around a Big Sister and smothering her with kisses.

Although filled with love, Nikki felt that Cindy's home life was not an easy one. She viewed Cindy's mother Marla as a low-income single mom with a good heart, wanting the best for her daughter educationally, but perhaps lacking the parenting skills and motivation to follow through on good intentions. To Nikki, Marla seemed overwhelmed with life: trying to discipline and control an admittedly difficult child; recovering from a series of unhealthy partner relationships; and coordinating Cindy's afterschool life when she changed job hours or jobs, or managed two jobs at once. Nikki questioned the quality of the out-of-school life that Cindy had with her mother: Mostly, she heard reports that they spent time watching videos that to Nikki seemed appropriate only for grown-ups.

Despite all the times during the year that Nikki had suggested afterschool opportunities for Cindy, Marla never once followed up on any of these suggestions. Before Cindy took home her copy of the school newsletter every month, Nikki always circled all the listings of community enrichment activities. She also had made a point of discussing afterschool activities with Marla in the parent-teacher conference. Still, Marla didn't seem to take advantage of all the wonderful opportunities for Cindy in the community. Nikki just wasn't sure how to get Cindy, or those kids like her with parents like Marla, involved in afterschool activities. All this was very frustrating to Nikki. Meanwhile, Cindy was on her own in the parking lot. In the recent past, Nikki had also seen Cindy playing around inside the photo-processing store and felt it was an unhealthy environment for the child, what with all those chemicals. Plus, it just couldn't be much fun for her.

As you read this case, consider applying the following theoretical lenses to your analysis:

- School-Based Family Support: What strengths does Marla bring to supporting her daughter's growth and development? In what ways do Nikki and the school counselor view Marla in deficit terms? How might they empower Marla, building on her strengths and needs, in supporting her afterschool planning?
- Community Roles: To what extent does the community support and promote families' involvement in their children's education and development? What are the ways that the community offers protective factors that promote children's resiliency?
- Social Executive Functioning: How can the school serve as an executive functionary for children needing afterschool care, managing and organizing information coming into and going out of the school, and coordinating with families?

MARLA, CINDY'S MOTHER

As Marla worked her shift at the photo-processing store, she edged to the window from time to time to check on Cindy outside. Again, an afterschool family daycare arrangement had collapsed, and Marla had had no choice but to bring Cindy along to work for the past few weeks. This one had closed because the provider moved out of town. In the prior arrangement, Marla had withdrawn Cindy from the provider's home for a few weeks, concerned that conditions in the home exacerbated Cindy's allergies. When Cindy improved, she sent her back, but Marla always felt anxious about it and didn't know where to turn for reassurance. Other childcare arrangements were fraught with their own challenges. At one point a boyfriend's mother offered afterschool babysitting help, but Marla felt she and the boyfriend were headed for breakup and didn't want to be obligated to the boyfriend's mother. All her kin lived in another part of the country, and Marla often felt depressed and bereft without a family safety net. She would've loved to have her kinfolk babysit. She was divorced from Cindy's dad, and he was not a part of his daughter's life.

Marla valued working and harbored some small pride at her ability to stay off welfare, but it was a round-the-clock challenge to raise a child and hold down a job. She worried constantly about how to arrange afterschool care for her daughter and all the associated logistics. She wondered when Cindy would be old enough to walk with a schoolmate from school to Marla's job site or directly home. Right now, Marla saw the community as unsafe and lurking with dangers for her daughter—dangerous traffic patterns not far from school, crazy people hanging out on the streets.

More than anything, Marla hoped for a job with hours that would allow her to be home with Cindy in the afternoons. Not that being with Cindy was easy. They lived in a small two-room apartment without much room for Cindy to play. Marla was often frustrated when her daughter came home from school and made a mess, and she frequently lost her temper. In her mind, one big problem was transportation. Marla did not have the money needed to repair or insure her old car. And, unless they had been able to hitch a ride with another family, Marla had had to coax a tired eight-year-old to walk a mile and a half home from her daycare provider when she picked Cindy up at the end of the day. She dreamed about taking Cindy to a big amusement park in a distant state, but as it was, she had to push the laundry in a stroller many blocks to the laundromat.

Marla did enjoy being out of the house with Cindy. Sometimes she walked her to the park. But Marla missed the excursions that she and Cindy used to take as part of their participation in a program for families with preschoolers at The Family Support Place, like the time the group drove to visit a real working farm. Marla had even offered a few times to chaperone one of Cindy's second-grade class trips and ride on the school bus with everyone somewhere. She had hoped to go with the class to a zoo in a nearby city, but although she volunteered, she wasn't one of the ones selected to chaperone. Cindy's teacher, Nikki, had asked her on several occasions to come over and visit Cindy at school in the classroom, but somehow Marla just hadn't gotten around to it.

Marla remembered Nikki mentioning afterschool programs to her at one point, but it was more than Marla could manage to even think about arranging this. The programs probably cost much more than family daycare. And how could she ever pick up Cindy from some program way over on the other side of town without a car? The bus system in the community was slow, practically nonexistent. Marla had tried to save up money to get her old car going again. She had disconnected her phone to avoid those big long distance phone bills from calling her kinfolk, but then it always seemed like Cindy was growing so fast that the money was needed for new clothes and sneakers.

Marla had not graduated from high school, and her school experiences had never been happy ones. But she did trust Nikki, and thought that Willow School was good. She was content to allow the school responsibility for many areas of Cindy's life. For example, the school had arranged for Cindy to attend Friendship Day Camp over the past two summers, and Cindy had loved the camp.

CINDY

Cindy went from a trot to a gallop around the parking lot, hugging the neck of her horse. Of course, it wasn't a *real* horse. But she imagined she was on the horse she learned to ride on at camp last summer. That was so much fun then.

Today it just felt like everyone was telling her "No." This morning when she went to get another breakfast donut, her mom had screamed at her, "No more going inside the cupboards by yourself and making a big mess! You are getting too fat!" Then when she got restless being in her classroom at school and went by herself to the playground, the principal found her and said, "No outside wandering!"

Now she had to be at her mom's work. Cindy hated it that her mom had to work and couldn't spend time with her in the afternoons. Cindy really loved being with her mom. Being here was pretty boring, as boring as hanging out at home inside. No other kids and no other horses here. Cindy made her horse stop and slid off. She sighed and climbed onto the hood of a car to rest.

SHELLIE, CINDY'S SCHOOL COUNSELOR

Back at school, Shellie the school counselor had hung a "Do Not Disturb" sign on her door. The school administered a scholarship fund that allowed some students to attend summer camp, and paperwork deadlines were fast approaching for the camp season. Shellie knew she had a long afternoon of deskwork ahead of her.

Shellie had a Master's degree in Social Work and thought of herself primarily as a coordinator at the school. She helped students and their families get connected to social service help in the community as one part of her job. Shellie had extensive contacts with community service providers. As the other part of her job, Shellie helped teachers and administrators at Willow School identify and work with struggling students. She had had many discussions with Nikki and Ed about Cindy. Shellie also ran a couple of groups for students at school. Cindy was a member of her Social Skills Group and seemed to be enjoying it.

Cindy had attended Friendship Day Camp twice on scholarship. The camp for young boys and girls had a strong one-on-one mentoring component with a focus on social skills development. Shellie and Cindy's classroom teachers knew that the camp counselors worked on appropriate social overtures with Cindy and were pleased for the reinforcement this provided Cindy over the summers. Her teachers noticed that there had been no backsliding come the fall, as they might have otherwise expected with Cindy. And Shellie knew that Cindy had enjoyed herself tremendously, learning to ride a horse and taking outings to recreational sites in the surrounding countryside. It was certainly a quality out-of-school experience for Cindy.

Nevertheless, it was like pulling teeth to get Marla to complete the application process. Although Cindy qualified for a scholarship, there was a small sum for Marla to pay, and it took ages before Cindy came in with the money. Now Marla still hadn't sent any of the required information to the camp, nor returned Shellie's three phone messages left for her at the photo-processing store. Shellie started to draft a letter to Marla to remind her to complete her part of the paperwork, or Cindy would not be permitted to attend camp. To Shellie, Marla was a good candidate for a parenting support group. As things stood, Marla didn't seem to know how to advocate for her child, or indeed what daily practices would support the education of her second grader. Shellie hoped that Marla would come through on the paperwork.

Shellie paused in her typing. She wondered what Cindy was doing right now. Shellie wished she had more resources at her disposal to help kids like Cindy to link them up to appropriate afterschool activities. This summer camp scholarship was a unique thing; many of the regular community afterschool activities were simply not affordable for families like Cindy's. What's more, there weren't even any afterschool activities right here in the school building. Cindy would continue to need the right kind of attention and support throughout the school year to do her best in school.

ED, THE PRINCIPAL

Ed believed that if a student has a problem, you deal with it. Just this morning, for example, he had to cut short a fairly important telephone call to address an immediate concern in the building. Cindy had wandered out of her classroom again, and her teacher couldn't locate her. Ed had found her outside on the swings and spent time with her going over some of the Willow School Social Curriculum rules for appropriate behavior.

Sometimes, too, dealing with a student's problem meant working on the community level. Then the school reached out into the community to find the right kind of help for the child. Ed served on the Board of a local youth organization and enjoyed the connection this provided to the larger community. However, he was concerned about the lack of collaboration across the many community social service agencies, the fighting over turf, and the way the school had to pick up the pieces and coordinate services for a student or their family. Willow School's biggest challenge now was being expected to do more and more with less and less. Not just academics—but support to children and families—were expected despite diminished resources at the school's disposal. Thinking about all these responsibilities heaped on the school, Ed wished for more help from the parents and the community. The school could not do it alone.

Ed knew that Shellie, with her "Do Not Disturb" sign on her door this afternoon, was stressed out trying to do it alone. She worked hard on making out-of-school time connections for some of their students. Ed often despaired at the level of parents' involvement in out-of-school activities with their kids. Although some families would take trips or do educational things with their kids, others simply didn't have a clue as to what enrichment activities would help their kids excel academically. The school tried to help by providing information about community enrichment activities in its newsletter, but he was sure that a fair number of these backpack-carried newsletters never made it home.

Ed also believed out-of-school activities didn't necessarily have to be trips to museums or things like that. He recognized that not all families had access to such resources, and that there were many things to do in town that did not cost anything. He believed that a walk in the woods bordering town, looking at

Table 6.1   Willow Elementary School

Location	Rural New England town, population 12,000
Grades served	K–6
Enrollment	282, 94% Caucasian
Students eligible for free and reduced-priced lunch	38%
Students performing at least one year below grade level in reading	26–50%
Students performing at least one year below grade level in mathematics	26–50%
School-based services	Parenting programs; family counseling and support; student counseling; employment assistance; links to public assistance and social agencies; scholarship money for summer camp
Community out-of-school time programs (sample)	Arts programs; Recreation department athletic programs; Youth services programs such as Big Brothers/Big Sisters; family daycare; Friendship Day Camp

the vegetation, or time just spent by parents talking with the child about life experiences, were valuable and necessary lessons. Parents needed to provide the opportunities for children to learn, whether in formal programs or informal family time together. In fact, Ed actually worried that some of the kids were over-scheduled in afterschool activities—in effect, neglected by their parents. To him, nothing out-of-school was as important as the time parents spent engaged with their children.

AN ENCOUNTER BETWEEN PARENT
AND TEACHER IN THE COMMUNITY

Marla was very excited. She had just this moment received a wonderful phone call at the photo-processing store. She had gotten the new job she had applied for: working at the cafeteria at the local hospital. She wanted this job because the hours were perfect, allowing Cindy to spend all her afterschool time with Marla now. Marla looked across the parking lot and saw Nikki approaching the store. She knew Nikki had a roll of film ready to be picked up. Whenever Nikki came into the store, Marla liked to ask her how Cindy was doing in school. Now she couldn't wait to tell her about this new job.

For herself, Nikki entered the store with some trepidation. All throughout her errands she had worried about Cindy's lack of supervision. Nikki wondered whether she should try to say anything briefly to Marla about Cindy's afterschool time. Although she felt uncomfortable talking about Cindy's issues right there in the store, Nikki thought about more forcefully suggesting a formal afterschool program for Cindy. She could explain that parents could sign up their kids at the Recreation Department at any point during the year. Marla could even sign up tomorrow.

DISCUSSION QUESTIONS

Major Issues

The purpose of this case is to consider the roles of the family, school, and community in promoting children's learning and development in out-of-school time (OST). The case is designed to help educators reflect upon individual decisions about OST care within the context of community service systems. Specifically, the case focuses on the following:

• How families negotiate OST arrangements
• The role of schools in OST arrangements
• The role of the community in supporting children and families

Describing the Situation

• How is Marla involved in Cindy's school and learning?
• What challenges does Marla face in afterschool care for Cindy?
• How does Willow School help the family in OST care provision?

Exploring Contributing Factors

- What do Willow School personnel see as a key problem in afterschool care for Cindy, and OST care in general?
- What are the trade-offs in Marla's decision about afterschool care for Cindy?
- How do Marla and Nikki's perspectives on afterschool care differ?

Articulating Possible Next Steps

- Assume that, upon entering the photo shop, Nikki suggests a formal afterschool program for Cindy. How should Marla respond to the suggestion?
- Assume that Marla tells Nikki about her new job and her desire to have Cindy spend her afterschool time with her. How should Nikki respond?
- How might the school support Marla in her afterschool challenges?
- How can the community (e.g., businesses, transportation services, afterschool programs) support low-income parents like Marla?
- What might an ideal afterschool arrangement for Cindy look like over the course of a week? How would it respond to the visions and needs of the various actors?

Replaying the Case

- What could Shellie and Nikki have done differently to help Marla take the steps to secure afterschool and summer-camp spots for Cindy?
- Describe Ed, the principal's, views on afterschool programs. As a leader of the school and in the community, how might he begin to forge more connections between the two contexts? What might be stopping Ed and others from connecting to community services to get some help in reaching out to Marla?

Looking at the Bigger Picture

- Who holds responsibility for children's afterschool care? Identify the opportunities—resources, occasions, and supports—this community provides to children and families.
- Poverty poses tremendous challenges to Marla's options in providing OST care for Cindy. What do you imagine Marla's budget to be—her income for the month and her expenses? What kinds of OST care might she be able to afford under such circumstances?
- Marla enjoyed her joint participation with Cindy in a community program at The Family Support Place when her daughter was preschool age. What kind of formal afterschool program in the community can you imagine might appeal to both mother and daughter? In what ways might Cindy's participation in a formal community afterschool program bolster Marla's social support network?

NOTE

1. This case was originally presented at the 2002 North American Case Research Association annual meeting, Banff, Canada. We would like to thank Education Track participants for their review of the case.

RECOMMENDED READING

Heath, S. B., & McLaughlin, M. W. (1987). A child resource policy: Moving beyond dependence on school and family. *Phi Delta Kappan, 68,* 575–580.

Vandell, D. L., & Shumow, L. (1999). After-school child care programs. *The Future of Children, 9*(2) 64–78.

Case 9: Piecing It Together

Linking Systems to Support a Student and Family

by Jennifer Romich and
Jennifer Simmelink

Characters:

Dionte, eighth grader

Dee, Dionte's teacher

Karen, Dionte's mother

Tamaal, Dionte's brother

Kofi, social worker

FALL 1999: DEE JOHNSON, DIONTE'S TEACHER

Dee, an eighth-grade teacher at Marcus Garvey Middle School, sits at her kitchen table with a cup of tea as she finishes writing an evaluation referral for Dionte, a child in her class. It is 7:30 in the evening, and Dee is at the end of her rope with Dionte. Since school started, he has been causing problems. She feels that he is disrespectful and aggressive, as well as chronically tardy, and he rarely turns in homework. Dee has called his mother several times, but the phone is often disconnected. She's managed to reach her twice but can't get her to come in to talk about Dionte. Even more importantly, she can see significant problems in his academic work. "How can I begin to get Dionte the help he needs?" she asks herself. She believes an evaluation is a good start, although she maintains some surprise that others haven't previously intervened. "He won't fall through the cracks anymore," she thinks as she signs her name to the form.

As you read this case, consider applying the following theoretical lenses to your analysis:

- Family Support: How can educators provide support and access to social services for students? How can educators approach creating an IEP (Individual Education Plan) with parents whose involvement is limited by health issues or other barriers?
- Executive Functioning: How can the various executive functioning roles in this case achieve better coordination? What problems may arise as different systems try to gain access to the same information?
- Ecocultural Understanding: To what extent is Dionte participating in daily routines that promote his well-being? In what ways is Dionte a successful child and student? In what ways is he struggling?

EARLY WINTER 1998 (ONE AND ONE-HALF YEARS EARLIER): KAREN CARSON, DIONTE'S MOTHER

BAM! BAM! BAM! The rocks hit the side of the bus shelter, barely missing Karen. The young boy across the street screams, "I hate you, I hate you!" as he looks for more rocks to throw at his mother. Karen chases her young son Tamaal down the street and finally regains control of the nine-year-old, as a neighbor calls the police. It is the second time this month that the police have been called because of Tamaal.

A single mother, Karen tries to balance work as a home health aide with raising two young sons. This is made even harder by Tamaal's diagnosed emotional disturbance. Her $7-an-hour job leaves her worn out at the end of the day. Most days her eleven- and nine-year-old sons come home to an empty house. When Karen herself gets home, the first thing she does is put her feet up for a few minutes. Sometimes she smokes some weed, too. It's what gets her through the day.

After the police have left, and Tamaal and Dionte are in bed, Karen lights up a joint. On the table in front of her is a phone number for a social worker that the police have given her. Not for the first time, Karen thinks about sending Tamaal to live with a foster family. It would mean giving up legal custody, but it would also mean that he could get his treatment paid for.

Karen loves both of her sons, but can feel them slipping away from her. Karen also knows that she often ignores Dionte because she is so busy with Tamaal and his problems. Perhaps if it were just the two of them, it would be easier to care for Dionte.

Last fall, the school sent her a note saying that Dionte had been diagnosed with a learning disability. Karen doesn't even know the name of the disability. She has been so busy dealing with Tamaal that she hasn't answered any of the school's calls for a meeting. She is worried about Dionte, but she can barely meet the needs of one child, let alone two. "That's it," thinks Karen. "In the morning, I'll call the social worker."

SPRING 1998: DIONTE CARSON

Hearing the bus pull away across the street, Dionte looks for his mom. Sure enough, she's waiting at the light. "Yes!" he thinks to himself as he spies the knotted plastic bag she's carrying. Her client, Mrs. Stoner, has a daughter who works at a catering company. Sometimes Mrs. Stoner's daughter brings home leftovers for Dionte's mom to take home. Normally Dionte tries to get dinner started before his mom comes home, but they've been out of meat for a week, and he didn't want to cook ramen noodles again.

Nowadays it's only Dionte and his mom at home. Tamaal is in foster care, but he visits most weekends. Sure, it's lonely coming home, but whenever he wants, he can go downstairs to see his uncle's girlfriend, Neesha, and their baby, Nia. Besides, Tamaal messes stuff up so much—Dionte had to spend all Sunday afternoon fixing the VCR that his younger brother broke.

"Hi, Mom, you bring ham?"

"No, it's meatloaf today. Dionte, turn off the TV."

"Mom, it's the science fair presentations—I told you that tonight was my turn to borrow the tape."

As the tape runs, Dionte points out details as the sixth graders present their projects one by one. One boy, Marcus, rides the same bus and has invited him over to play. Karen says that she will need some more information—he can't just go someplace unless she knows where he is and how he'll get home. Dionte also points out a girl he used to like. Finally it's Dionte's turn. His project—"Super Duper Flyer"—compares two different types of toy gliders. He laughs when he sees himself on screen bouncing from foot to foot and says that he was nervous in front of the camera.

"So that's what you have behind the couch," Karen remarks. Dionte pulls out the trifold cardboard display from his project. Dionte points out that they had to have a list of materials, a procedure, and a conclusion. These sections are printed laboriously in pencil bubble-letters: MATTERALS, PROƆEDURE, CONƆLUSON. Karen studies the display for a minute, "Your Cs are backwards," she points out, "here and here."

The camera now scans the entire class—Dionte points himself out again and pauses the tape to show where he sits.

FALL 1998: RIVERSIDE MEDICAL CENTER

Date: *September 19, 1998* **Time:** *11:49 p.m.*
Admitted through ER.
Attending physician: *Dr. Harmon*
Notes: *Patient (Pt.) is African American woman, age 31, height 5'6," weight 168 lb.*

Presenting loss of muscle control in right hand, Pt. reports escalating weakness over past three days, dizziness, and periods of blackout lasting several seconds to several minutes. Pt. was found unconscious by

11-year-old son and brought to Riverside via ambulance. Initial diagnosis: series of strokes caused in part by frequent drug use. Pt. admits drug use (marijuana, cocaine) in past 24 hours.

WINTER 1998: KOFI HUNTER, SOCIAL WORKER

Kofi pulls up to the house a few minutes early. A social worker with Child Protective Services for about two years now, Kofi is still getting used to the ups and downs of the job. He looks over the notes he'd written after his initial session with Tamaal's family.

Assessment Notes for Tamaal and Family

The family includes Karen, Dionte, and Tamaal. Tamaal, the referring case, is currently in a foster placement. Karen is primarily concerned with Tamaal's behavior and emotional disorders, Dionte's academic performance, and her unemployment. She is currently receiving TANF [Temporary Assistance for Needy Families] and trying to qualify for SSI. [Supplemental Security Income] Karen is candid about her use of drugs, including marijuana and cocaine. She has attempted treatment in the past and is currently receiving outpatient treatment through a state-sponsored program. Dionte has been fighting when Tamaal comes to visit, and last week Dionte beat up Tamaal for swearing at Karen.

As Kofi reads through the assessment, he makes a few mental notes for his upcoming session. Last week, Karen said something about Dionte having a learning disability. If it's true, he needs to encourage Karen to contact the school to talk about setting up an IEP. Kofi prioritizes the family's goals: Develop a plan for coping with Tamaal and establish a plan for economic self-sufficiency. Kofi views the Carson family as a unit that must work together to help support Tamaal. He would also like to work with Karen to cut down on her drug use.

SPRING 1999: KAREN CARSON

Karen sits in her living room at midnight, waiting up for her 12-year-old son. Dionte has been coming home later and later every night, and Karen is both worried and angry. "I swear, that kid is so LAZY!" Karen fumes to herself. "It seems that all he wants to do lately is hang out with his friends, sleep until noon, and piss me off."

Dionte has become a new person right before Karen's eyes. She remembers just a year ago how he was so sweet and helpful around the house. He always supported her when Tamaal was acting up, and she could rely on him. But now, Dionte is getting a 1.0 GPA. He barely goes to school, and Karen can't remember the last time she has seen him doing homework. As angry as Karen is about Dionte's laziness, she is also worried about him. He has been hanging out with some neighborhood kids who she knows use and sell drugs.

OCTOBER 19, 1999: DIONTE

BEEEP! BEEEP! The horn of Dionte's bus wakes him up at exactly 8:02 a.m. Karen had awakened him before she left at 6:45 a.m. to catch the bus to Workfare, the job she was required to work to continue to receive her public assistance money, but he'd fallen back asleep. Now he'd have to catch the city bus and would be late for school. Dionte pulls on his jeans and digs through the pile of clothes on the floor to find a shirt with a collar, although the school rarely enforces the dress code.

Because it is Friday, his art teacher will let them play CDs so Dionte makes sure he has the T.H.U.G.S. album and the Will Smith soundtrack that his cousin gave him for his birthday last week, along with his blue bandana. He wouldn't wear it on the bus, but he'd wear it when he got to school.

Dionte gets off the bus a stop early to give himself a little break before going in. "You can't trust no one in this neighborhood," he thinks as he passes a junkie buying drugs. "It's safest to walk around carrying a hammer or something." As he trudges along, he thinks to himself about what a terrible school Garvey is. The other kids are bad in class, the teachers yell, and there are always kids getting beat up.

Reaching the school, Dionte rings the bell to be buzzed in. He peers through the wire mesh covering the heavily tinted windows and sighs, waiting for the guard to put down his paper. It is 10:06, the end of third period. He slides in and heads to the main office to get a tardy slip. He hates school.

OCTOBER 19, 1999: DEE JOHNSON

BRRRIINNGG! The bell rings, signaling the end of third period. Dee gathers her belongings and heads downstairs to the main office to meet with the school psychologist about setting up an evaluation for Dionte. As she reaches the ground floor, she sees a husky boy wearing a baggy blue polo shirt and jeans hanging off his back end walking toward her. It's Dionte.

"Dionte," Dee calls sternly. "Where were you? You missed third period."

"I slept late," Dionte mutters.

Not wanting to be late for her meeting with the psychologist, Dee says, "We'll need to talk about this later." With a frown, she also recognizes the blue bandana wrapped around Dionte's hand. Dee tries hard to enforce the rules against any clothes or accessories associated with gangs. She gestures toward it and says, "Dionte, put that away. You don't want to be looking as if you're in a gang, and you sure don't need to act like it."

Dee has been working at Marcus Garvey for five years now. She teaches the bottom-tracked classes. By the time kids reach Dee's room, they are in danger of being retained, have been expelled, or cause so much trouble that no one else will take them. Dee really feels that she can make a difference in kids' lives—especially older ones that others have given up on.

Lately, though, Dee is feeling burned out. So many students come from households where there is little parental support or involvement. Dee understands that single parents are often stretched thin, but given decreased funding and little support from the school board, Dee often feels like she is the only person who cares about these kids.

Dee knocks on the school psychologist's door, sits down, and begins expressing her concerns about Dionte.

"Dionte Carson," the school psychologist says. "Why have I heard that name before?"

The psychologist goes to her filing cabinet and pulls out a manila folder with Dionte's name on it.

"Dionte's already been evaluated," she says. "It seems he was diagnosed with a learning disability back in 1997."

"What?" Dee asks in disbelief. She feels her face turning red. "If he was diagnosed with a learning disability, why isn't there an IEP?"

"Looks like the mother never signed off on it," the psychologist answers. "There are some other papers here. Looks like the family is working with some-one from Child Protective Services.

Dee doesn't know what to say or do. A flood of questions rushes to her head: How can a child have been diagnosed with a learning disability two years ago and never have been followed up? Is it possible that Dionte is receiving external services that she and the school don't know about? Up until this very point in time, she had viewed the evaluation as the first step in the right direction.

What should she do now?

DISCUSSION QUESTIONS

Major Issues

The purpose of this case is for educators to consider the importance of communication among the various systems in which a child participates. The case is designed to help educators consider the following:

- The impact of fragmentation and lack of communication among systems on teachers, family involvement, and the provision of school services
- The barriers to family involvement among poor families
- The factors that influence developmental pathways in middle childhood

Describing the Situation

- Who are the people and systems involved both formally and informally in Dionte's life? Who is managing Dionte's life?
- What role does Dionte play in managing his life and his family's life?

Exploring Contributing Factors

- What are Dionte's perceptions of his ability, control, and connectedness? How does this relate to his engagement in learning?
- How do the people and systems involved in Dionte's life communicate with each other? Whose responsibility is it to initiate these conversations?

- What resources and benefits does Karen bring to her involvement in Dionte's education? What are some of the challenges and barriers that stand in the way of her realizing this involvement?
- What assumptions does Dee have about Dionte, his family, and the factors that led to the unfulfilled IEP?
- What expectations does Karen have for Dionte? How do family challenges influence these expectations?

Articulating Possible Next Steps

- What would you do next if you were Dee? If you faced a similar situation, who would you approach in your community and why? How might you obtain more information about Dionte's family?
- What are some immediate approaches and modifications that can be applied both at home and in the classroom to support Dionte?
- How can the school create avenues of communication, information management, and coordination to bolster Dionte's social and academic talents?
- What role could Kofi play in facilitating an IEP for Dionte? In communicating with the school more globally?
- How can educators differentiate between formal neglect issues and lack of attention due to other family crises?

Replaying the Case

- What, if anything, might Dee have done differently in the situation? For example, could she have taken any other steps before making the evaluation referral? Consider alternative outcomes that might have resulted from taking different courses of action.

Looking at the Big Picture

- What is the role of the principal in schools that Dionte describes as "kids are bad in class, the teachers yell, and there are always kids getting beat up"?
- What are some perceived developmental trajectories for Dionte? What may be some issues in a year, two years, three years, which Dionte will be facing?

RECOMMENDED READING

Coleman, J. (1991). *Policy perspectives: Parental involvement in education*. Washington, DC: U.S. Government Printing Office.

Halpern, R. (1998). *Fragile families, fragile solutions: A history of supportive services for families in poverty*. New York: Columbia University Press.

Schorr, L. B. (1997). *Common purpose: Strengthening families and neighborhoods to rebuild America* (pp. 282–292). New York: Anchor Books, Doubleday.

References for Introduction

Bronfenbrenner, U. (1979). Contexts of child rearing: Problems and prospects. *American Psychologist, 34*(10), 844–850.

Bronfenbrenner, U. (1989). Ecological systems theory. In R. Vasta (Ed.), *Six theories of child development: Revised formulations and current issues* (pp. 185–246). Greenwich, CT: JAI Press.

References for Weiss and Kreider

Bryk, A. S., & Schneider, B. L. (2002). *Trust in schools: A core resource for improvement* (The Rose Series in Sociology). New York: Russell Sage Foundation.

Christenson, S., & Sheridan, S. (2001). *Schools and families: Creating essential connections for learning.* New York: The Guilford Press.

Coalition of Community Schools. (2004). *What is a community school?* Retrieved August 16, 2004, from http://www.communityschools.org/whatis2.html

Coffman, J. (2000). *The Right Question Project: Capacity building to achieve large-scale sustainable impact.* Retrieved September 16, 2003, from http://www.gse.harvard.edu/hfrp/projects/fine/resources/case_study/abstract.html#cs3

Coleman, J. (1991). *Policy perspectives: Parental involvement in education.* Washington, DC: U.S. Government Printing Office.

Denton, D. (2001). *Helping families to help students: Kentucky's Family Resource and Youth Services Centers.* Atlanta, GA: Southern Regional Education Board. Retrieved August 30, 2004, from http://www.sreb.org/programs/srr/pubs/Helping_Families.pdf

Derman-Sparks, L. (1998). Developing culturally responsive caregiving practices: Acknowledge, ask, and adapt. In *Infant/toddler caregiving: A guide to culturally sensitive care* (pp. 40–48). California Department of Education, Child Development Division.

Dunst, C. (1995). *Key characteristics and features of community-based family support programs.* Chicago: Family Support America.

Family Support America. (2001). *Guidelines for family support practice* (2nd ed.). Chicago: Author.

Halpern, R. (1999). *Fragile families, fragile solutions.* New York: Columbia University Press.

Harvard Family Research Project. (2001). Questions and answers. *FINE Forum, Issue 2.* Retrieved September 10, 2003, from Harvard University, Harvard Family Research Project, Family Involvement Network of Educators Web site: http://www.gse.harvard.edu/hfrp/pubs/onlinepubs/reform/index.html

Harvard Family Research Project. (2003). Program spotlight. *FINE Forum, Issue 6.* Retrieved September 10, 2003, from http://www.gse.harvard.edu/hfrp/projects/fine/fineforum/forum6/spotlight.html

Harvard Family Research Project. (2004). Parent perspective, *FINE Forum, 8.* Retrieved August 19, 2004, from http://www.gse.harvard.edu/hfrp/projects/fine/fineforum/forum8/parent.html

Hernandez, L. (2000). *Families and schools together: Building organizational capacity for family-school partnerships.* Retrieved September 16, 2003, from http://www.gse.harvard.edu/hfrp/projects/fine/resources/case_study/abstract.html#cs1

Lawrence-Lightfoot, S. (2003). *The essential conversation: What parents and teachers need to know.* New York: Random House.

Lopez, G. R., Scribner, J. D., & Mahitivanichcha, K. (2001). Redefining parental involvement: Lessons from high-performing migrant-impacted schools. *American Educational Research Journal, 38*(2), 253–288.

Lopez, M. E. (2002). Learning from families. *The Evaluation Exchange, 8*(1), 2–3. Retrieved October 10, 2003, from http://www.gse.harvard.edu/hfrp/eval/issue18/theory.html

Lopez, M. E., & Hochberg, M. (1993). *Paths to school readiness: An in-depth look at three early childhood programs.* Cambridge, MA: Harvard Family Research Project.

Lopez, M. E., & Kreider, H. (2003). Beyond input: Achieving authentic participation in school reform. *The Evaluation Exchange, 9*(2). Retrieved September 9, 2003, from http://www.gse.harvard.edu/hfrp/eval/issue22/theory.html

Massachusetts Afterschool Partnership (MAP). (2003). Parental After-School Stress (PASS) research at Brandeis: Initial findings from pilot study. *MAP News, 1*(1).

Moll, L. C., Amanti, C., Neff, D., & González, N. (1992). Funds of knowledge for teaching: Using a qualitative approach to connect home and classrooms. *Theory Into Practice, 31,* 131–141.

Nissani, H. (2004). *Are schools ready for families: Case studies in school-family relationships.* Chicago: Family Support America. Retrieved August 23, 2004, from http://www.communityschools.org/AreSchoolsReady.pdf

Schultz, T., Lopez, M. E., & Hochberg, M. (1996). *Early childhood reform in seven communities: Front-line practice, agency management, and public policy.* Cambridge, MA: Harvard Family Research Project. Retrieved October 2, 2003, from http://www.gse.harvard.edu/hfrp/pubs/onlinepubs/reform/index.html

Shartrand, A. (1996). *Supporting Latino families: Lessons from exemplary programs* (vol. II). Cambridge, MA: Harvard Family Research Project.

Weiss, H. (1983). Introduction. In E. Zigler, H. Weiss, & S. Kagan (Eds.), *Programs to strengthen families.* New Haven, CT: Bush Center in Child Development and Social Policy.

Weiss, H. B., Woodrum, A., Lopez, M. E., & Kraemer, J. (1993). *Building villages to raise our children: From programs to service systems.* Cambridge, MA: Harvard Family Research Project.

Zigler, E., & Weiss, H. (1985). Family support systems: An ecological approach to child development. In R. Rappaport (Ed.), *Children, youth, and families: The action-research relationship* (pp. 166–205). Cambridge: Cambridge University Press.

Section 4

The Macrosystem

The macrosystem is the most inclusive, and hence the most complex, of ecological systems, encompassing linkages and interactions among micro, meso, and exosystems. Bronfenbrenner, in a revision of his original theory, described the **macrosystem** as "a societal blueprint for a particular culture, subculture, or other broader social context" (1989, p. 228). The macrosystem refers especially to belief systems, ways of life, and opportunity structures that are available to a developing person within a particular societal context. It is therefore very close in meaning to **culture**, which is typically defined within the social sciences as the set of values, norms, beliefs, and symbols that define what is acceptable to a given society, are shared by and transmitted across members of that society, and dictate behavioral transactions within that society (e.g., Goodenough, 2003; Keesing, 1974; Peterson, 1979; Phinney, 1996). Although cultures and subcultures represent higher-order macrosystems, they are distinguished from other macrosystems in that they both encompass all other macrosystems and are passed down from generation to generation.

Processes occurring at the level of the macrosystem are perhaps best described as the patterns of micro, meso, and exosystems that can be found at a particular **social address** or demographic marker. Examples of such addresses include race and ethnicity, social class, sex or gender, profession, social role. Each of these social addresses comes with a particular script that may vary across cultures and subcultures. For example, race and ethnicity has particular social significance in the United States, but much less so (if at all) in many of the countries on the Asian continent. But the meanings associated with race and ethnicity in the United States, and the history and evolution of those meanings, can have substantial implications for children's development through their influence on families, schools, and other immediate contexts in which children live their everyday lives (microsystems); the interactions among those contexts (mesosystems); and the interactions between those contexts and the contexts containing the significant others in their lives but not themselves (exosystems).

In this section of the volume, two theoretical lenses and three cases are included as illustrations of processes taking place at the level of the macrosystem. Thomas Weisner describes his ecocultural approach, which positions children's development in multiple, interacting contexts bound by cultural proscriptions and constraints. That is, what is beneficial to children's development depends on the particular cultural context within which that development occurs and the extent to which the children's everyday activities in their immediate contexts adhere to those cultural expectations. Cynthia García Coll and Celina Chatman describe processes that are particularly relevant for racial and ethnic minority families, who must often contend with issues that other families do not face (such as cultural or structural obstacles). Both of these theoretical approaches provide deeper analyses of how macrosystem processes can influence interactions at other levels of the ecological system.

Weisner's ecocultural approach stresses the importance to overall well-being of children's having everyday routines that are sustainable, meaningful, and congruent. That is, children's everyday routines must be supported by the resources available to them, must be acceptable by the child's family's and culture's moral standards, and must balance resources across family members so as not to incite conflict. Weisner argues that this approach is sensitive to differences across cultures as to what constitutes "healthy development" for children, and applies universally to many different types of families and children.

This ecocultural approach is readily applicable to the three cases contained within this section of the volume. For example, in "Raising Children Alone: Poverty, Welfare Reform, and Family Involvement," third-grader Aiesha Cobbins is having a hard time both at home and at school. Her young, single mother to four children has been unable to obtain gainful, steady employment, is clinically depressed, and continues to be dependent on public assistance. Both historically and contemporarily, mainstream U.S. culture has been predicated on the Protestant work ethic: Hard work results in deserved rewards. The implication, of course, is that those who do not work hard should and will not be rewarded, and those who lack rewards simply did not work hard enough. Thus, within this particular macrosystem, many may initially conclude that Aiesha's mother does not work hard enough to ensure her children's success.

But Aiesha's mother, Samantha, who is African American, expresses her concern about her children's well-being and makes consistent efforts to keep them clothed and fed. She also espouses a sense of distrust toward Whites, especially those who are economically advantaged. This attitude, regardless of its origins or its validity, can impact on Samantha's interactions with her children in the family context and with school personnel, ultimately affecting her children's success and well-being. These processes, together with those stemming from her socioeconomic circumstances, overlay all that can occur at the micro, meso, and exosystem levels. That is, Samantha's views about social disadvantage based on race and the circumstances of her economic status can gravely influence her and her children's experiences in the family, at school, and in the community. This is particularly clear in Aiesha's inability to develop sustainable, meaningful, or congruent routines either at home or at school.

Similarly, in "Learning in the Shadow of Violence," fourth-grader Thandi, one of several children born to a Cambodian immigrant couple, is struggling in school despite her and her parents' aspirations that she attend college in the future. Thandi and her family live in a community plagued by gang violence, and already one of her brothers is serving jail time for his own involvement in gangs. In this case, the macrosystem becomes even more complex, with Thandi's family having to deal with reconciling the expectations from two different cultures—that which they learned in Cambodia and that which they continue to learn in the United States.

Thandi's daily routines at home are sustainable with her parents and older siblings providing economic and skill-based resources to support her education. For example, her parents own a home with space for the children to complete homework, and both her parents and siblings check and help her with homework. But the meaningfulness and congruence of Thandi's routines are questionable, depending on the cultural context within which they are being evaluated. Thandi's parents hold a tight reign on her social life, rarely allowing her to play with friends around the neighborhood or participate in extracurricular events and activities. Within mainstream U.S. culture, this pattern of protective parenting might be seen as debilitating to children's healthy development, as it limits their exposure to experiences outside of the home. But Thandi's family's negative history of violent experiences overlays their family management decisions and even their relationship with Thandi's school and its personnel.

Theoretical perspectives on cultural mismatch and acculturation are also applicable to Thandi's case, as conflicts are apparent in Thandi's and her family's beliefs and values about education and appropriate ways for children to behave. These issues are also apparent in Aiesha's case (Case 11), as are issues of structural inequalities and obstacles. For example, Aiesha's mother's distrust of Whites may have resulted from her own socialization, wherein she likely learned of the history of social and economic oppression to which Blacks in the United States historically have been subjected.

Issues of social disadvantage are also apparent in "What Words Don't Say: Talking About Racism." Loreen and her first-grade son, Martin, have moved from a public housing development to a house in a mixed-income neighborhood. But Martin has problems with friendships at school and in his new neighborhood, where race and class overlap considerably. Specifically, Martin's mixed-income neighborhood is home to mostly White families, and most of the Black students at his school live in poorer neighborhoods. This dynamic begins to affect Martin's school work, and he begins to spend much of his time in school with a friend who is perceived as troublesome by their teacher. The situation is exacerbated because Martin's mother is hesitant to broach the topic with Martin's teacher, and his teacher seems to be largely unaware of the race and social class issues affecting his experiences at school.

When considering macrosystem processes, it is critical to keep in mind that they encompass linkages and interactions at all other levels of developing children's ecology. The macrosystem binds, constrains, and often dictates processes occurring at the micro, meso, and exosystem levels. Children's roles in the family are prescribed by their society's cultural definition of family structure; connections between family and school depend on a society's notions about the forms and extent to which those connections should take place; and the extent to which places of employment should accommodate family educational involvement is decided according to the norms and values that characterize a given society. All of these issues pertain to all children and families, and thus a macrosystems approach can be applied to any situation pertaining to family educational involvement.

7

Theoretical Perspectives
on the Macrosystem

Macrosystems represent broad, structurally related considerations, such as politics, social stratification, and economic distribution, as well as other important considerations such as culture and history. Macrosystem approaches are based much more in abstractions than are those approaches based on the lower-level systems (micro, meso, and exosystems), and require understandings of processes occurring on multiple levels at once.

In Chapter 7, we have included two theoretical perspectives that lay out, more specifically, how processes at the level of the macrosystem can influence interactions at all other levels of a developing person's ecology. In Thomas Weisner's description of ecocultural theory, we learn how family routines are often constructed within the bounds of cultural dispositions and the availability of resources such as time, money, and social support. These routines can be facilitative of or sometimes debilitating to children's well-being, depending on the extent to which they are supported within a given society or cultural context.

Cynthia García Coll and Celina Chatman describe cultural and structural processes that can directly influence parents' and children's perceptions of and interactions with institutions outside of the family context. Particularly in the case of ethnic minority families, issues such as stereotypes, prejudice, and discrimination, as well as a lack of cultural validation, can seriously interfere with such families' strivings for their children's academic success. Because issues such as these can dictate parents' and children's interactions with the individuals and institutions they encounter in their everyday lives, they are best understood from the level of the macrosystem in ecological systems theory.

Because no family or institution exists in the absence of a larger society or culture, macrosystem processes always overlay interactions at all other levels of individuals' ecologies. When considering individual students' and their families' situations as they relate to education, macrosystem approaches may reveal patterns that cannot be detected from more narrow perspectives. In other words, families and institutions such as schools and workplaces can only operate on the basis of what resources are available to them. These resources can range from sources of knowledge, in the abstract, to more concrete affordances such as buildings and transportation. Thus, the macrosystem provides the boundaries within which other systems can develop and must always provide the context within which these other systems are best understood.

Ecocultural Understanding

by Thomas S. Weisner

Every cultural community provides developmental pathways for children within some ecological-cultural (ecocultural) context. Developmental pathways refer to the different kinds of activities, organized by families and local communities, in which that child could or will engage during development. We have an intuitive sense of this in our own life experiences. There are life paths we have engaged with that took us somewhere, and paths we did not take that others have taken. Those paths had emotional meanings for us, practical consequences with costs and benefits, and important people and experiences. Furthermore, the paths were specific—they were in a particular local community, place, and time. Now imagine a child in your mind's eye. When given this mental exercise, most think of that child as an individual, typically floating alone. But, instead, we should think of that child somewhere on earth—in some particular, local sociocultural community. The child has a family context, a neighborhood, social relationships, resources, and so forth. Now put that child and that place in motion over developmental time through the lifespan. Imagine the pathways the child would engage. Those paths consist of everyday activities and practices with their associated participants, goals, tasks, material resources, and feelings. The ecocultural approach emphasizes the importance of the child and family's surrounding social and cultural environment as it is experienced in their everyday routines (Weisner, 2002).

Certain features of the ecocultural context seem to be particularly important for children's development around the world. Some features influence children and families through economics and demography, such as subsistence and work cycles of the family and community, health and demographic characteristics, and threats to safety. Others shape children's pathways through the social organization of daily routines: the nature of the division of labor by age and sex; children's tasks and work, including domestic, child care, and school work. Still other features influence the social roles and groups and how they are organized: roles of fathers and older siblings, children's play and play groups, roles of women and girls in the community and supports for them. Still other features capture the influences of the wider world: the varied sources of cultural influence and information available and the extent of community heterogeneity in models of care and child activities (Weisner, 1984). The point of view in **ecocultural theory** is that children's daily routines and activities along life pathways are the most important influences on their development. Children's development can be understood as a project of families, parents, communities, and children themselves to achieve goals and find meaning. Families and communities try to provide opportunities for children to achieve valorized cultural and community goals. To do so, they organize daily routines and activities with the resources at their disposal, often under very challenging conditions (Weisher, 2005).

Children's developmental pathways are determined by **cultural activities** that are organized into their daily routines. Because this is where children, parents, and teachers experience and live out ecocultural influences, the daily routine of activities is at the center of our attention. In the United States, for example, children's daily routines and cultural activities might include dinnertime, watching television, cruising the mall, doing homework, and domestic chores. In addition to their explicit purposes, these cultural activities also have purposes and meanings that may be less apparent. For example, cooking dinner with one's best friend gets dinner on the table, but it may well include the goals of sociability, planning the future, and entertainment as well. Cultural activities have five important components: (1) tasks, (2) cultural goals, (3) motives and emotional experiences of those present in the activity, (4) people who participate in it, and (5) the typical scripts or rules for how to do the activity (Weisner, 1998). The activities of everyday life are repetitive, and they are filled with explicit and implicit messages about what families and communities believe are important and what they want children to learn and become. This is one source of their power to influence development.

The Cultural Project of Development

Healthy development is signified by the child's growing capacity for competent, innovative participation in cultural life. Children acquire specific domains of cultural competence and cultural knowledge. For example, children learn rules for greeting, playing with peers, enacting gender roles, or doing domestic tasks. Developmentally, children build on their early learning experiences in the family and with primary caretakers. Development toward cultural competence and well-being occurs when children actively participate and practice within the domains of the culture that are valued by the family or community and in which the child previously could not participate or could do so only with special assistance and scaffolding (Tharp & Gallimore, 1988).

Along with the development of cultural competence, increasingly complex and elaborate schemas for organizing cultural knowledge develop in the mind. Many psychological processes organize how such cultural knowledge is acquired: how it is perceived, experienced, felt, memorized, forgotten, and repressed, as part of human activities (D'Andrade, 1992; Shore, 1996; Weisner, 1996). The mind and its mental processes do not develop in isolation; they are embedded within daily routines in a specific local cultural community.

Hence, socialization is far from a straightforward process of "faxing" information from parents or schools into the child's mind! There is always discontinuity between cultural patterns found in everyday activities and individual development. Children acquire cultural knowledge through relationships with parents and close kin in the midst of emotional attachments and conflicts with them. Furthermore, the cultural knowledge represented to children is ambiguous, inconsistent, and filled with conflicting desires and ambivalences (Nuckolls, 1993). For example, parents may give children leeway in making decisions about peers but discourage friendships with peers whom they perceive as bad influences on their child. As children go to school they acquire new knowledge and behaviors that may conflict with the cultural knowledge embedded in the habits of the home. Children simultaneously desire, resist, and transform cultural knowledge along the way to becoming unique individuals (Weisner, 1998).

Developmental Outcomes

One of the most important outcomes of child development is **well-being**, which can be described as the ability to successfully, resiliently, and innovatively participate in the routines and activities deemed significant by a cultural community. Well-being also refers to the state of mind and feelings produced by participation in routines and activities, such as positive emotions, the internal psychological state of feeling effective, and a sense of satisfaction with oneself in the world as a valued person.

A child's well-being depends heavily on his or her active participation in a daily routine of activities that are sustainable, meaningful, and congruent. A *sustainable* daily routine is fitted to a local ecology, meaning that it is appropriate to the family resource base and the resources and constraints available in the cultural community. Sustainable routines also are stable and predictable for children. A *meaningful* routine has moral and cultural significance and value for family members and fits with cultural expectations for a morally appropriate pathway for children and families. A *congruent* routine balances the competing needs and goals of different family members and is not overly focused on any one member to the substantial detriment of another. Congruence recognizes that children and parents are in relationships of competition for scarce resources, as well as in relationships of cooperation, continuity, and intimate affection. Excessive conflict in a child's life does not generally promote well-being.

These features of daily routines—sustainability, meaning, and congruence—matter to children's well-being. But typically they are not captured in traditional research studies of children's development and well-being. Instead, research studies on children and families tend to measure characteristics that are drawn from Western cultural norms and expectations. For example, characteristics related to children's development that are frequently examined include independence and autonomy, verbal and literacy skills, IQ, social adjustment, or secure attachment. It can be problematic when research relies solely on these types of measures to indicate children's positive development and well-being, because these characteristics may not be relevant to other cultural communities that emphasize different developmental goals for children. They certainly are useful for many purposes, but none captures the overall context of a child's pathway and how that context matters for well-being. Thus, ecocultural theory suggests that outcome measures should go beyond traditional developmental measures and incorporate a more holistic view of successful child development. Ideally, such outcome assessments would attend to children's daily routines and the well-being they experience through participating in them (see Bornstein, Davidson, Keyes, & Moore, 2003).

Middle Childhood as an Ecocultural Project

Middle childhood is a period of important developmental advances that establishes growing competency for the tasks of adulthood. These tasks of adulthood vary according to the ecocultural context. For example, a central issue in U.S. families with school-aged children is the gradual shift away from direct parental control of the child's behavior as children spend more time in activity settings at school and with their peers. Children gradually move from coregulated activities with parents and siblings to those that are self-regulated and peer-regulated. Parents retain overall managerial influence, but children are increasingly capable of directing their own activities for long periods of the day (see Social Executive Functioning Model, Section 2). Children enter new and strange settings (e.g., schools, places of worship, sports teams) and select their friends with some degree of parental or teacher monitoring. Such friendships in the United States usually involve the creation of new, personal, and independent alliances.

In many non-Western cultures, the context of that developmental task is different. Children gradually move from being under the caretaking responsibility of older children and other nonparental members of the household (e.g., grandparents) to becoming responsible caretakers who are in charge of younger siblings and cousins. Children ages 6–12 take on increasingly important family roles, including those relating to child care, as well as attending school and participating in peer groups. Parents have managerial and disciplinary roles, but child care is more diffused and shared. Because children live in kin-based groupings, there are few activity settings in which other children who are strangers are present. The sibling caretaking pattern has as its goal to produce an interdependent, responsible child, rather than an independent, self-directed, highly individuated child. Of course these distinctions are relative, because children everywhere experience both kinds of situations to some degree, but the contrasting cultural patterns are significant.

Conclusion

Ecocultural theory and its long tradition of emphasizing cultural influences on development highlights the diversity of cultural responses in the service of a common goal of families and schools everywhere: to provide a daily routine of life that is sustainable, meaningful, and congruent for children and families. Well-being is a useful and holistic perspective from which to evaluate and understand children's development across diverse communities, because it requires understanding community goals and perspectives and does not pre-determine the content or contexts that will have meaning in that community. A cultural approach to development can offer schools an expanded and more inclusive definition of what constitutes successful development. It provides a framework to use in understanding cultural continuities and discontinuities across children's home, school, and community contexts.

Implications for Educators

Create and support sustainable, meaningful, and congruent daily routines and activities for children, in order to promote their positive development and well-being. This implies that teachers and service providers should develop greater awareness of cultural continuities and discontinuities among children's multiple environments. It also suggests that it could be useful to think of the school and classroom as a cultural activity in itself. Classroom life is a small-scale community that is important for children, and has a set of scripts, beliefs, and practices. Its activities can be analyzed just like nonschool activities. Change in classroom communities and activities, including changing how teachers teach, can be difficult, and one reason for this is that daily routines have their own local rules and logics that have to be taken into account (Gallimore, 1996).

Become familiar with children's daily home lives—how their day is organized, with whom and where they spend time, and how this time is spent. Children bring their prior scripts and expectations into the classroom, as well as learn new ones. Teachers and service providers can be cognizant of the continuity and discontinuity that exists among family, community, and school values and expectations. By developing awareness of potential cultural conflicts between home and school, teachers and service providers can consider how they may affect children's school and achievement-related behaviors. They can then create plans to address these challenges by selectively changing some classroom activities to produce a better fit.

Ideally, children will go to the same classroom every day and can expect a fairly predictable mix of activities—reading, writing, experimenting, and so forth. However, when schools are overcrowded, unpredictable classroom arrangements can make sustainable routines difficult (e.g., rotating classrooms, trailers, schedule changes).

Provide daily routines that are congruent, in which there is a balance between each individual child and the class as a whole. This can be achieved through small-group work, whole-class instruction, and utilizing parent volunteers for one-on-one work with children who need additional assistance.

Ensure that daily practices and values are meaningful to children and their families. This might be achieved through classroom management practices wherein the values of sharing, respect for property of others, taking turns, and following teacher instructions can be encouraged.

Be aware of how culture may shape parental expectations of children as they get older. A family may, for example, emphasize a child's contributions to the household (e.g., child care, income, household chores) more than the child's spending time with friends.

Develop greater awareness of how one's own practices and expectations of children (at the individual and institutional level) reflect one's own cultural background. For example, classrooms can emphasize individual competition or group cooperation to varying degrees, which reflect teachers' and schools' conventional practices.

Ethnic and Racial Diversity

by Cynthia García Coll and Celina Chatman

Parenting is a very rewarding yet often challenging life task. Parents—whether biologically or otherwise appointed—are typically the primary caregivers of children from infancy into late adolescence. Parents are responsible for fulfilling children's basic needs, such as food and shelter, as well as shaping psychosocial attributes, such as personality characteristics and beliefs and values. Moreover, as children mature and begin to interact more frequently with institutions beyond the family, parents must consider these other socializing agents in ensuring their children's continued well-being and positive development (see Social Executive Functioning, Chapter 3). Ideally, such activities contribute to children's development into independent, well-functioning adults. These processes can be compromised in family situations where cultural and structural obstacles prevail.

Theoretical Issues

Ecocultural theories in child development describe children's development as occurring within a dynamic system of daily routines that are embedded, simultaneously, in several interacting contexts (see Ecocultural Understanding, this chapter). These social and cultural contexts include the physical environment as well as the outlets available within the community for families and children to carry out their various roles. Thus, parents' socialization of children can be constrained or facilitated by schools and other community contexts to the extent that there is congruence between the beliefs, values, and behaviors reinforced within each. Similarly, theories in developmental psychology posit that community contexts such as neighborhoods and schools, as well as the cultural predispositions shared among the mainstream, interact with family demographics and can constrain or facilitate parents' influences on children (Bronfenbrenner, 1989).

In their integrative model for studying developmental competencies among ethnic minority children (see Figure 7.1), García Coll and colleagues argue that researchers must consider both those sources of variation uniquely salient to populations of color and more generalized sources of variation (García Coll et al., 1996). They posit that social position factors—or demographic markers used to stratify populations within a society—predispose children to particular developmental pathways, as mediated through social disadvantage mechanisms such as racism and discrimination. The resulting spatial and social segregation, in turn, subjects children to promoting or inhibiting environments, including schools and neighborhoods. The unique set of goals, values, and attitudes that is created in response to these environments—or the adaptive culture—shapes children's experiences and ultimately requires a specific set of competencies that may differ from those required for mainstream notions of success. In the following section, we describe in greater detail some of the specific mechanisms that can create disadvantages, as explained in this model.

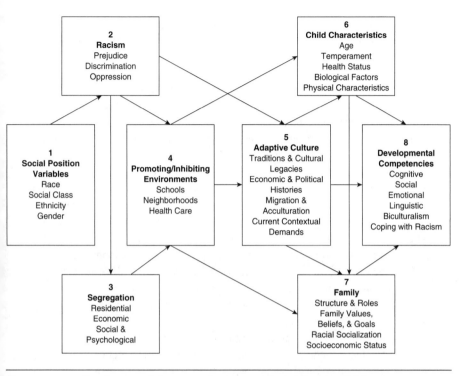

Figure 7.1   Developmental Competencies Among Ethnic Minority Children

SOURCE: Reprinted with permission from García Coll, C. T., Lamberty, G., Jenkins, R., McAdoo, H. P., Crnic, K., Wasik, B. H., et al. (1996). An integrative model for the study of developmental competencies in minority children. *Child Development, 67*(5), 1891–1914.

Cultural Considerations in the Development of Ethnic and Racial Minority Children

Despite the lack of attention to culture, historically, in theories regarding children's development, many cultural processes play a significant role in children's development across contexts. **Culture** is an amorphous concept, but there remains some consensus across social science disciplines such as anthropology, sociology, and psychology that it refers, broadly, to a set of values, norms, beliefs, and symbols that define what is acceptable to a given society, are shared by and transmitted across members of that society, and dictate behavioral transactions within that society (e.g., Goodenough, 2003; Keesing, 1974; Peterson, 1979; Phinney, 1996) Here we focus on two specific cultural processes: cultural mismatch and acculturation. Although there is considerable overlap between these concepts, each plays a distinctive role in children's development.

Cultural mismatch. **Cultural mismatch** occurs when parents' (and eventually children's) beliefs and values conflict with those held by other socializing agents, such as teachers and other school personnel. These conflicts range in scope from beliefs about how child development occurs to beliefs and values about what aspects of a child's development warrant special attention and even intervention (García Coll, Meyer, & Brillon, 1995). In such circumstances, parents may teach children behaviors and attitudes that may be adaptive in their home or neighborhood environment but not functional within the school (García Coll & Magnuson, 2000). For example, in some countries it is not acceptable to question elders or persons with authority, such as teachers, a practice that is encouraged in many interactive learning approaches currently endorsed in the United States. Likewise, within school contexts children may learn behaviors and attitudes that may be disruptive within the family. For example, a child who speaks a language other than English at home may have difficulty making friends in the neighborhood and at school; loss of the home language in favor of English, however, may strain the child's communication with family members who are not proficient in English. This example illustrates conflicts that can arise between children and parents when there is a cultural mismatch between the family and, for example, the school.

In some instances cultural traditions upheld by the family are not only rewarded outside of the family system, they are explicitly sanctioned by mainstream institutions. For example, in the early 1990s, a task force made up of parents, scholars, and various school personnel from throughout an Oakland, California, school district noted that African American students whose speech was based in African Language Systems (more colloquially and controversially referred to as Ebonics) were stigmatized and otherwise negatively perceived by teachers and school personnel (this argument was but one point included within a broader context of improving schooling for African American children). Some scholars, parents, and educators believed that these biased perceptions lowered teachers' expectations of students who did not use standard English (even if they were capable), and perhaps contributed to their under-achievement.

The concept of cultural mismatch is also apparent in family involvement in schools. For example, in a recent study we found that the relatively low involvement of Cambodian immigrant families as compared to those from Portugal and the Dominican Republic can be explained in part by cultural considerations (García Coll et al., 2002). Specifically, Cambodian families traditionally have viewed school as the domain of teachers (in traditional Cambodia, monks serve as teachers). Many Cambodian parents believe parental involvement in schools to be inappropriate and disrespectful. In the United States, however, some forms of parental involvement in schools are not only rewarded but are expected and are predictive of positive academic achievement (e.g., Hara & Burke, 1998; Lopez, Sanchez, & Hamilton, 2000). For this reason, school success among children of traditionally oriented Cambodian parents may be compromised to the extent that these parents do not engage in the forms of involvement that are linked to student achievement. Importantly, however, we also see situations in which positive academic outcomes are facilitated by the families' other achievement-related dispositions, such as valuing education highly.

Research on minority family involvement has documented this cultural chasm between parents and schools, but also revealed that family educational involvement goes beyond participation in school activities (Collignon, Men, & Tan, 2001; Delgado Gaitán, 1992, 1994; Huss-Keeler, 1997; Lawrence-Lightfoot, 1978; Moll & Greenberg, 1992). For example, many ethnic and racial minority parents hold high aspirations for their children's academic and vocational achievements and consistently convey this to their children (Huss-Keeler, 1997). Although studies have indeed documented lower levels of parental involvement among parents with various limited resources (e.g., income, education, psychological adjustment), these findings were also limited to traditional notions of involvement (e.g., attending parent-teacher conferences, P.T.A. meetings, and participation in school-sponsored activities; Griffith, 1998). Examples of other forms of family educational involvement include the communication of positive attitudes toward schooling and achievement and obtaining homework assistance for children from members of an extended family network.

Acculturation. In the preceding Oakland example, cultural mismatch gave rise to issues of acculturation as well. **Acculturation** refers to a process whereby individuals, families, or whole communities adopt the practices, attitudes, and beliefs of a culture that is different from their own. The parents in Oakland experienced pressure (real or perceived) to negotiate a balance between the family culture and the push for their children's acculturation into the mainstream (e.g., Boykin & Toms, 1985; Harrison, Wilson, Pine, Chan, & Buriel, 1990). Acculturation provides one way of examining individual differences as a moderator of cultural influences on development. Levels of acculturation vary greatly, even within families (as illustrated in the preceding example of the child who abandons the family's home language in favor of English). To the extent that acculturation levels are high, cultural mismatch will be less likely to play a role in children's development; however, highly acculturated individuals who are disconnected with their family's culture can also be at risk. Biculturalism—developing competencies in both cultures and being able to determine for which contexts and situations they are most appropriate (or accepted)—has been shown to lead to more favorable developmental outcomes (e.g., LaFramboise, Coleman, & Gerton, 1993).

Despite acculturative pressures and instances of cultural mismatch, culture as it is enacted within families can often be a resource in children's development. By most definitions within the social sciences, culture is bound to contexts, as it represents the set of dispositions accepted by a self-defined group of people as being most adaptable to their given environments (Goodenough, 2003; Keesing, 1974). Thus, parents who are acting in their children's best interests are likely working to develop their children's competence within the multiple contexts in which they experience everyday life, including home, school, neighborhood, community, and society at large. To the extent that parents are successful in this goal, the children will likely be successful within those contexts. Moreover, instrumental competencies—those basic, universal skills that facilitate overall functioning within any context, such as cognitive and socioemotional skills, are valued across many cultures (García Coll & Magnuson, 2000). To the extent that these universal developmental skills are valued within a given culture, the teachings and practices of that culture are likely to be a developmental resource. For example, being able to solve problems is a universal skill that is likely valued among most cultures and is linked to many positive outcomes.

Minority Status and Social Disadvantage

Besides instances of cultural mismatch, ethnic and racial minority families must also deal with more **structural barriers to resources**, both objective and perceived. For example, because such groups are overrepresented among the socioeconomic strata below the poverty level, ethnic and racial minority parents are more likely to experience economic strain and have limited access to resources (McLoyd, 1990; Ogbu, 1981). Even in the absence of such strain, such as among more socioeconomically advantaged families, ethnic and racial minority parents must consider other forms of **oppression** such as unfair treatment (discrimination), unfounded negative attitudes (prejudice), and unfavorable affective dispositions (racism) based on their racial or ethnic group membership (García Coll et al., 1996). These issues present additional domains of life for which ethnic and racial minority parents must prepare their children. Moreover, limited financial and psychosocial resources (such as psychological adjustment) have been linked to lower levels of traditional forms of parental involvement (e.g., parent-teacher conferences, P.T.A.) among ethnic and racial minority families (Ascher, 1988).

Minority status, by definition, relegates families and children to disadvantaged social positions. The structural barriers and social biases just described derive from these social positions and require families to develop unique coping skills in order to protect themselves and their children from negative outcomes. But even if families become competent in their coping capacity, it remains that they must deal with stressors not experienced by families who are in more advantaged social positions. Thus, social position for ethnic and racial minority families can put them at risk for compromised well-being, including children's educational outcomes (García Coll et al., 1996).

Boykins's and Tom's (1985) **Triple Quandary Theory** of African American parental socialization captures the complex social and cultural dilemma faced by ethnic and racial minority families. Although the theory is specific to African Americans, it is logically applicable to other racial and ethnic minority groups. The theory posits that African American families must prepare their children in three general domains in order to ensure their successful development. First, they must socialize their children in terms of the cultural traditions, beliefs, and values held by African Americans as a group. Second, they must socialize their children in terms of the traditions, beliefs, and values that are rewarded by the mainstream American institutions to ensure their success within those institutions. And third, they must prepare their children for potential encounters with stereotypes, racism, discrimination, and other like biases. This third quandary is particularly salient for African Americans, given this group's unique history of slavery in the United States. Socialization within this triple quandary can be a formidable task for a family system already coping with many sources of economic and social disadvantage, such as living in crime-ridden neighborhoods, attending schools with lower resources, and suffering many financial strains.

Conclusion

Cultural differences can heavily impact children's development. When cultural conflicts between families and schools persist, the rich ethnic backgrounds of minority students can create obstacles instead of resources for development. Language differences, diverging views on parenting practices, and acculturation all potentially lead to uncomfortable inconsistencies for the children caught between cultures. Unresolved cultural conflicts and a lack of support or understanding from educators often restrict family involvement.

Implications for Educators

Understand the cultural, structural, economic, and historical bases of family involvement. Educators must consider both cultural and structural issues in addressing low levels of traditional parental involvement among some ethnic and racial minority families. Rather than inferring that minority parents are simply uninterested in their children's achievement, teachers and other school personnel should seek to understand the bases of parents' beliefs about their children's school experiences and the many barriers to resources and knowledge experienced by families (García Coll et al., 2002). All parents share educators' general goals of seeing children succeed educationally, but their daily demands or their lack of know-how may get in the way of translating these values into routines that are supportive of the development of school-specific skills. This basic assumption is prerequisite to understanding educational involvement among ethnic and racial minority families. Otherwise, any efforts to increase involvement among these families and in training school personnel in attempts to involve them will likely be misguided and misinformed.

Support family involvement beyond the school grounds. Likewise, educators must recognize and support forms of family involvement likely to occur among minority families outside of the school. In one study, Mexican-descent parents in California perceived their primary obligation in their children's educational experiences to be to instill in them a moral foundation. As long as their children were respectable and honest, they believed, they would be rewarded in school and would henceforth be successful academically (Cooper, Dominguez, & Rosas, in press). These types of beliefs, together with the valuing of academic achievement, led parents to provide supports to their children in a variety of ways, short of their actual presence in and interaction with the school institution. For example, children reported being frequently reminded by their parents of the importance of school success and excused from their chores and other responsibilities so that they could complete homework and studying assignments. Educators should be aware of and actively encourage families in resolving family-school conflicts in such a way as to facilitate student achievement and maintain a functional routine within the family's household.

Attend to minority family socialization processes. Racial and ethnic minority parents have the triple quandary of socializing their children in at least two cultural systems (the family's ethnic culture and the mainstream) and preparing them to deal with racism and other biases. Depending on the specific strategies employed by parents in these domains, ethnic and racial minority children can be equipped with ample resources for buffering against both cultural mismatch and social devaluation. Schools' attention to and understanding of these domains of socialization would likely facilitate family educational involvement. For example, psychologist Beverly Tatum (1997) recommends that schools provide training to encourage and facilitate open dialogue on race and ethnicity among students, families, and personnel, especially discussions about prejudice and discrimination. Putting the issues on the table (by people who are knowledgeable and skilled to do this work), she argues, allows people to share their beliefs and even their fears as they pertain to race and ethnicity, and consequently leads to opportunities for clarifying and correcting previously unaddressed misconceptions.

8

The Cases

In Chapter 7 and in the introduction to Section 4, we have tried to capture the complexity of processes occurring at the level of the macrosystem. The macrosystem might be represented as the forest containing the trees, the bounds within which the function of the trees at the individual level is defined and maintained. That is, children's and families' existence is not independent of the larger structural and cultural foundations on which it is formulated. What happens in our everyday lives—what we see, learn, think, and do—in large part depends on when and where our lives take place.

In Chapter 8, we have included three teaching cases for which macrosystem issues have a salient role in the everyday experiences of young school children and their families. In "What Words Don't Say," we confront overlapping issues of racism and classism, and we see how these issues can directly affect children's experiences at school and perhaps their academic future. In "Raising Children Alone," we witness how history and not personal experience can shape parents' distrust in institutions, which in turn can be seriously damaging to children's academic motivation and engagement in school. We see, also, how conditions such as poverty and reliance on public assistance can contribute to the creation of subcultural scripts for family routines, many of which are not adaptive to children's educational demands. Finally, in "Learning in the Shadow of Violence," issues of immigration, acculturation, and a family's escape from a war-torn country to a heavy-crime neighborhood all come into play in a child's educational aspirations and experiences. Considerations of these and other macrosystem processes may prove useful in providing deeper insights to the cases that follow, as well as to situations not covered in this volume.

Case 10: What Words Don't Say

Talking About Racism[1]

by Ann Barger Hannum

Characters:

Martin, first grader

Lorreen, Martin's mother

Rhona, Martin's grandmother

Joan, Martin's teacher

Shawn, Martin's friend

As you read this case, consider applying the following theoretical lenses to your analysis:

- Ecocultural Understanding: What are the different ecocultural contexts that influence Martin's identity development? What are the sources of continuity and discontinuity within and across these contexts?
- Racial and Ethnic Minority Parenting: How can the school and community maintain and reaffirm Martin's interests in African American and Native American culture?
- Developmental-Contextual: How does Martin's well-being drive Lorreen's life choices and affect her sense of efficacy as a parent?

MARTIN'S SITUATION

Martin slumped off the school bus, barely glancing at his mother, Lorreen, who was waiting with his grandmother on the corner for him. "Hey, honey, what's the matter? Did you have a bad day?"

"Naw, nothin's the matter," Martin responded flatly and walked on.

Lorreen shared a concerned look with her mother, Rhona, about Martin's despondent attitude. As they walked toward the house, Martin asked, without looking at them, "Mom, what happens if someone says you did something that you didn't do? Like if someone says you took something, but you didn't take it?"

"Well, you tell the person that you didn't take it and talk about what happened. Sometimes it's just a misunderstanding. Why? Did someone say you took something that didn't belong to you?"

Martin started to get agitated. "Yeah, at lunchtime. Johnny and Mack and Jose said I stole Steven's watch, but Steven gave it to me! I told 'em so, but they said I stole it because I come from a bad neighborhood, and we don't have any money!" "Honey, that's awful! When did Steven give you the watch?" "He gave it to me last week. He's my friend, and he gave me a present! Steven told them he gave it to me, too," Martin answered. "But they just said Steven was stupid. Are we poor, Mom?" Martin looked up at his mother.

"Honey, we have a good life and everything we need," Lorreen assured Martin. "I know you always tell the truth, and I'm glad that you told those boys what happened. It's good that Steven stuck up for you. You stick with boys that are nice to you and don't pay any mind to those other kids."

Martin's mood lightened somewhat, and he smiled a little as they walked into the house. But Lorreen remained troubled, and her thoughts drifted to other worries about Martin.

LORREEN AND RHONA, MARTIN'S MOTHER AND GRANDMOTHER

As Martin loped ahead toward home, Lorreen's gait slowed to match her mother's. "Ma, I'm worried about the problems Martin's been having with these kids at school. His grades are so good, but he's been misbehaving a lot in class." "Oh, he is *so* smart. Why's he acting out?" asked Rhona.

"I think it's this thing about friends," Lorreen explained. "Mrs. Taylor and I have talked on the phone about the fact that Martin's hanging out with Shawn in school again—you know, his friend from the old neighborhood. She says that Martin looks up to Shawn, and he's a troublemaker, so we're working on a way to separate them as much as possible.

"She sends home notes every few weeks saying how well he's doing. And even in our last few conversations, she kept telling me that Martin was a great student. But she's basically just worried that Shawn's a bad influence on him.

"But this business today about boys in school accusing him of stealing and being poor makes me think there's a lot more going on at that school than Mrs. Taylor is saying. Besides, I doubt she knows about what's gone on with all his friends since we've moved."

"You mean because he doesn't see his friends from the old neighborhood as much? What about his making new friends?" Rhona interjected.

Martin still attended the same school but had left good friends in their neighborhood behind when they moved. "Well, he definitely misses his old friends," Lorreen agreed. "I think that's partly why he's started hanging out with Shawn in school. His other old friends come over to the house sometimes but make fun of him right to his face. They criticize his clothes. They tease him about his interest in African American and Native American heritage. They tease him about his darker skin color. But he still wants to hang out with them, I guess because otherwise he doesn't get to spend much time with kids his own age. But you know it bugs me. Not to mention all their street talk and him trying to copy it.

"On top of that he doesn't get invited to any of the other kids' houses in the new neighborhood. His little Vietnamese friend moved away. And I won't let Martin have anything to do with these two White kids down the block. They're rough and talk back to their mothers. I wouldn't be surprised if they end up in jail some day.

"And he's having trouble finding other new friends in the neighborhood. When we first moved here, things got racial. A few boys told Martin that their parents wouldn't let him come over because he was Black, even though the boys really liked each other. Martin just took it in stride because he wanted to stay friends with them."

Lorreen also recalled one of their new neighbors using the most hated of all racist words. "I was outraged. I didn't lose my temper, but I set her straight that no one was going to make any racist comments about me or my family. I haven't heard anything like that since."

Lorreen admitted to her mother that the move had affected Martin, that he missed his old neighborhood and wished he could have both Black and White friends. Lorreen apologized to her mother, "I'm sorry I didn't mention this before, but I wanted to focus on the good things that were happening and not think about anything negative. Plus, Martin and I talked about the bad things that people say and do to each other and about fighting racism. He knows how I feel about dignity and fairness and what it means to succeed in a competitive world. I think our talks have helped."

Rhona spoke lovingly to her daughter: "I know how much you love your new home and fixin' it up and makin' it look good. You should be proud of yourself. I'm always telling my friends how strong and smart my grandson is and what a good mother you are."

Lorreen surveyed the small, well-kept yards in their new neighborhood and mentally compared them to the sea of broken asphalt surrounding the public housing complex they had lived in the year before. "It's true, Ma. Each flower and tree reminds me of things growing and the possibilities that are ahead of us. I never thought we'd ever *really* be able to move. Remember how I used to worry about Martin day and night? I thought it was just a matter of time before I lost him to gangs. I always prayed we'd be able to move someplace safer. And now, for the first time, I really believe Martin has a chance for a good future."

Lorreen had held several jobs at once to save enough money to move from the public housing where Martin had spent his first five years of life. Ray, her fiancé, had supported her efforts and shared the excitement of their new home with them. Lorreen felt lucky to have Ray in her life and living with them, and to have her mother and other relatives so close by now. They all spent a great deal of time together, and Martin enjoyed playing with both his younger and older cousins. Even though he and his cousins were close, he still wanted to play with other kids in the new neighborhood.

Lorreen reassured herself out loud, "I know the move was the right thing for Martin, even though things haven't been perfect."

"Even so, you ought to talk to his teacher," Rhona countered.

JOAN, MARTIN'S FIRST-GRADE TEACHER

Joan put the finishing touches on her mid-year progress report to Martin's mother. She wrote that Martin's reading had improved since the weekly meetings with his tutor had begun. Joan liked Lorreen and wanted her to know what a good reader Martin was becoming. Joan tried to stay in touch with parents as much as possible, even through short notes home, to help involve them in their children's schooling, which helped ensure greater success in school. Joan had taught first and second grades at Hanford for four years and had enjoyed the mix of the students and families (see Table 8.1). Like all of the other teachers and administrators, she was White, but she felt that she communicated well with students of all ethnic and racial backgrounds.

Lorreen had made a strong impression on Joan from the start. Eventually Lorreen had opened up to Joan about having just finished her high school diploma as a single mother. Joan knew of Lorreen's promotion to assistant manager of a beauty supply company and of her hopes of going to college one day. "My grandmother, she always tried to instill in us, get your education, do this and that, and don't have any kids when you're young . . . don't just sit on welfare—my grandmother didn't believe in that," she had told Joan.

Besides, Joan appreciated Lorreen's concern about her son's schoolwork, a commitment that Joan didn't sense from all of her students' parents. And Lorreen had stressed that Martin show respect toward his teachers and family members. She also

Table 8.1   Hanford Elementary School

Location	Northeastern city, population over 250,000
Grades served	K–3
Enrollment	$N = 303$
• Caucasian	73%
• African American	26%
• Other	1%
Students eligible for free and reduced-priced lunch	34%
Students performing at least one year below grade level in reading	26–50%
Students performing at least one year below grade level in mathematics	26–50%
School-based services	Family counseling and support, health care, links to public assistance

clearly supported Martin at home with his homework. They'd even bought a computer for him to practice spelling and reading on. It was true that Lorreen hadn't made it to any school-wide events such as the P.T.A., which Joan often attended, but maybe she was just too busy with work. Otherwise, Lorreen seemed to live up to her belief that "You can't ever be TOO involved in your kid's school-work." Even Martin seemed to share this involvement ethic, by helping his younger cousins with their school work.

Lorreen struck Joan as a very serious and success-oriented person, which she seemed to convey to Martin. "I always tell Martin," Lorreen had said, "that being successful is trying new things, even if they're hard, and finishing things, even if you don't always do well, because one day you might do well. I always remind him about Michael Jordan, who wasn't successful at first, but he kept at it. Martin has to learn that determination is an important part of success."

Martin had a lot of his mother's determination; somewhat small for his age, he still took on all of the bigger kids in outdoor games. Joan also really liked how bright, engaging, and enthusiastic he had always been in class.

Despite Martin's strong academic performance, Joan had recently started to worry about his acting out in class. She attributed this to his spending more time with Shawn, another African American boy, who seemed to have a lot of influence on him. Shawn was one of several African American boys in school who expressed a lot of anger and got in frequent fights. She viewed their behavior as a product of their always having to defend themselves in the tough public housing neighborhood where they lived. Martin seemed different to her, though; he lived in a better neighborhood and obviously came from a strong, concerned family.

Joan had called Lorreen numerous times to talk about Martin's behavior and felt the two of them could speak frankly about Martin. They agreed that Martin's friendship with Shawn encouraged his acting out, and that Joan should try to separate the two boys as much as possible.

Joan had also learned about the incident when a few boys had taunted Martin about stealing a watch from his friend, Steven. She had spoken with the boys, who explained that Steven's grandmother had said Martin had stolen the watch. Joan figured that Steven's grandmother must have told other parents, because several boys knew about it, had concluded that Martin was too poor to buy his own watch, and had confronted Martin in school. From what Joan could tell, however, the problem had been resolved when Steven corroborated that the watch had been a gift to Martin. She liked to think that her constant encouragement of students to negotiate peaceful solutions to quarrels was paying off. Plus, her efforts to separate Martin and Shawn seemed to be working fairly well.

THE MEETING

Despite feeling things were improving, here Joan sat in a meeting with Lorreen one week later, presumably to discuss that same watch incident. In the back of her mind, though, Joan worried that it might be something more serious. She and Lorreen spoke frequently on the phone, but neither had ever had reason to call a meeting. Joan hoped it wasn't about the boys calling Martin poor, because she hardly knew how to address that one on her own.

Lorreen sat across the child-sized reading table from Joan, who looked just as uncomfortable about broaching the recent peer incident as Lorreen felt, and who probably didn't know all of what Martin had gone through in the past few months. Lorreen thought about the fact that, like all of the teachers and administrators, Joan was White. And for the same reason Lorreen avoided the P.T.A. meetings, she now found herself silent. She just wasn't sure they'd take a young Black woman seriously. And yet here she was, heeding her own mother's advice to meet with the teacher. Something at the school had to change, for Martin's sake.

DISCUSSION QUESTIONS[2]

Major Issues

The purpose of this case is for educators to consider the intentional and unintentional messages that communicate to children how they are to perceive, process, and respond to discrimination, prejudice, and other barriers based on race, class, and gender. Educators will also think about complex home-school relations and responsibilities relating to race and class. The case is designed to help educators gain an ecological understanding of the child, including the following:

- How the child makes sense of race and class in multiple contexts
- What different ecological contexts shape the child's development and how
- How families and schools can dialogue about sensitive issues

Describing the Situation

- Why is Martin upset at the beginning of this case? What happened to him? How does his mother, Lorreen, respond to him?
- Which players and events in the home, school, and neighborhood provide race-related messages to Martin, and what are those messages? Read carefully for both tacit and explicit messages.
- How is Lorreen engaged in Martin's education? What are the barriers to her involvement? How might the community and workplace provide her further support?

Exploring Contributing Factors

- Consider Martin's past, recent-past, and present communities. What are the subtle messages he receives from each of his neighborhoods?
- How has Martin's recent move affected his friendships? How do Lorreen and Joan think that his friendships influence his academic achievement?
- How did Joan handle the stolen watch incident? What message does this send to the children in her class and their families?

- What are Joan's perceptions of the community she teaches in and the families of the children she teaches? How do these perceptions affect her family involvement practices and relationship with Lorreen?
- How well is Martin managing the various messages about who he is? What impact does this have on his school behavior? On his identity?

Articulating Possible Next Steps

- How does the title of the case relate to the last scene between mother and teacher?
- Why is Joan uncomfortable? Why does Lorreen feel disempowered? How might these feelings be ameliorated?
- What should happen in the meeting? How might Lorreen begin? How might Joan begin?
- What is the responsibility of the school or the larger community in this situation?
- What are some potential solutions to this problem on a larger scale? Is teaching tolerance or celebration of differences a useful approach?

Replaying the Case

- What really happened to Martin? What roles do race and class play in this case? In what ways is Martin a victim of prejudice and stereotyping?
- How might Joan have handled the stolen watch incident differently? Should she have called Steven's family, the other boys' parents, and Lorreen into school for a discussion? Why or why not? If she had called a larger meeting about the incident, what might she have said? How would it have changed Martin's and Lorreen's reactions?

Looking at the Bigger Picture

- How do age and developmental level affect children's racial socialization? How might Martin's and others' responses in this situation have been different if he were younger or older?
- How can educators belonging to the racial majority communicate effectively and respectfully with racial minority families?

RECOMMENDED READING

Jarrett, R. L. (1999). Successful parenting in high-risk neighborhoods. *Future of Children, 9*(2). Available online at: http://www.futureofchildren.org /usr_doc/v019n02Art4 done.pdf

Lareau, A., & Horvat, E. M. (1999). Moments of social inclusion and exclusion: Race, class, and cultural capital in family-school relationships. *Sociology of Education, 72,* 37–53.

Case 11: Raising Children Alone

Poverty, Welfare Reform, and Family Involvement

by Eboni C. Howard

Characters:

Aiesha, third grader

Ms. Park, Aiesha's teacher

Tamara, Aiesha's big sister

Samantha, Aiesha's mother

Shaun and Dylan, Aiesha's brothers

As you read this case, consider applying the following theoretical lenses to your analysis:

- Racial and Ethnic Minority Parenting: What kinds of structural and social disadvantages must Samantha deal with? How might these be mediating Aiesha's developmental pathway?
- Ecocultural Understanding: How do Samantha's parenting strategies and Aiesha's behavior at home and school reflect their valorized cultural and community goals?
- Family Support: In what ways does the teacher convey a strengths- or deficit-based view of Aiesha and her family to her mother, Samantha?

INTRODUCING AIESHA

At the end of the day, Ms. Park passed out permission slips for the upcoming field trip to her third-grade students. She took an extra second to lean over and quietly whisper into Aiesha's ear, "Now, don't forget to get this signed and turned in on Monday, okay? It's very important that you do."

Thrilled by the thought of the field trip, Aiesha responded with a bright smile, "I promise, Ms. Park."

AIESHA

Aiesha ran out to the school bus, eagerly telling her older sister, Tamara, about the school trip. Aiesha and Tamara, ages 9 and 12, lived with their mother and two brothers, Shaun and Dylan, ages 6 and 2, in a middle-class suburb just outside of Milwaukee, Wisconsin. On the ride home, Aiesha passed several of the places her mother had worked in the past year: a dry cleaner, a video store, a fast-food restaurant, a gas station, and the mall.

The bus turned into Aiesha's mixed-income apartment complex, which her mother described as, "a few apartment buildings that are designated for low-income families and all the rest are for rich White people." Staring out the bus window, Aiesha recalled the time she and her sister discovered a neighborhood party near the complex's central pond—with food, a petting zoo, face painting, and games. She painfully remembered being turned away because the party was only for tenants living in designated buildings, which did not include the low-income buildings. That's when Aiesha noticed that all the families enjoying the picnic festivities were White.

Aiesha couldn't help noticing that her building looked run down, with peeling paint, burnt-out lights, and broken screen doors, unlike the "rich" buildings where most of the White people lived. Aiesha's mother always said, "Whites, no matter what type of life they have, always have some sort of advantage over us."

SAMANTHA, AIESHA'S MOTHER

Samantha was a 25-year-old African American single mother who lived alone with her four children. Samantha had never been married, did not currently have a boyfriend, and her children's fathers (each child had a different father) were absent from their lives. She had no family she could turn to for help; her mother lived in another state, one brother was illiterate and in prison for selling drugs, and the other brother was unemployed and homeless.

Samantha stopped her full-time dependence on the welfare system almost two years ago in hopes of earning more money and more meaningful work than she felt Wisconsin's Temporary Assistance for Needy Families (TANF) program could provide. Since then, she had worked at several part-time, low-wage service jobs, often being fired or laid off due to conflict between work and parenting obligations. Despite a great amount of effort and determination, Samantha still depended on various formal support services such as the Special Supplemental Nutrition Program for Women, Infants, and Children (WIC), the Food Stamp program, Medicaid, a subsidized housing grant, and a TANF cash grant.

Samantha's short hair was not styled, and she regularly tried to smooth it down with her dry hands. She was in desperate need of a touch-up and a trim, but did not have the energy or the $15 to buy the needed supplies. Samantha thought, "I know I look a mess, and that's how people look at me. But I put all my money and time toward making sure my kids look together when they leave this house. I always take care of the bills first. Nobody can say that my children don't come first.

"I also know that 'real work' can get me and my children into better situations, but I just don't have the time or energy to get those jobs. And the jobs I do get just add stress and don't add any money. If I had some help, I probably could get far in life. But right now I can't see past getting what I need to survive today."

Recently, a medical diagnosis of clinical depression exempted Samantha from mandated work requirements for her TANF grant of $674 a month. "I've been depressed my whole life, but I'm glad someone finally noticed. The welfare check is something, but not much. Doesn't cover the real cost of living, you know. Welfare can go on forever, but people will still be poor."

THE CHILDREN'S FATHERS

None of the children's fathers provided Samantha with support. Samantha was 13 years old when she was coerced into sex by Tamara's father (who was 17 years old at the time). She had not had contact with him since Tamara was an infant. Aiesha's father, who was in college and engaged to Samantha at the time, was now serving a life-term in prison. Unbeknownst to Samantha until after she became pregnant with his child, Shaun's father was married. Dylan's father broke up with Samantha when he found out she was pregnant, and had ignored Samantha since Dylan's birth. "I don't get why the government don't get after the fathers like they get after the mothers. If I could get a break just for one afternoon a week, I could get things done and feel less stressed. Having a man or a father around is not just about money. They could just help by being there.

"I admit that I had bad judgment to have sex with these men, and now I am reaping what I sow. You know, these men also need to reap what they sow, it wasn't just me. I thought they cared, I thought I was doing different, but I followed the same path as my mother, who struggled to raise me and my brothers on welfare alone.

"But I do not want the same thing for my children. My mother never talked to me about sex or boys. I talk to the girls so they know and won't find themselves in the same situation. I've seen Aiesha try to act grown, doing all those nasty dance moves and flirting with boys. I've beaten her for it, and then she'll act right. But I don't know how to make sure that she will do good with all my energy focused on daily survival.

"I also try to keep the girls busy and involved in school and sports activities so they won't have time for boys. But you know, school trips, sports teams, the zoo, and even the school band cost money. I hope that I can at least get them into the YMCA next summer, but that will cost $30 a child for every month plus the cost of lunch and special clothes."

THE CHILDREN

Samantha believed that her high stress level and feelings of helplessness negatively influenced her children, especially Aiesha and Shaun, who had been starting to experience more behavior problems. Samantha said, "I know this is not good to say, but I have really started to hate my children, and I don't enjoy being at home with them like I used to, before trying to work full-time."

Samantha explained, "I don't want to be bothered by a messy house, a baby who refuses to wear his diapers, a son who doesn't listen to me, two daughters who fight all the time, and one, Aiesha, who always has to sass back! I'm so exhausted by the end of the day that I usually have just enough energy to sit on the couch holding a wooden spoon ready to whip any child of mine who gets out of line."

Samantha has attempted without success to find relatives willing to keep her children for a weekend so she can get a break.

"I love my children, and I want them to be successful. But say Aiesha's teacher calls to talk about her work in class. I care, but then again, sometimes I really don't. It's just so hard to keep concerned all the time, because they really drive me nuts. I have to yell at Aiesha constantly to get her stuff together for school, pick up her clothes, and wash out her cups. And if she gets an attitude, she'll leave things on purpose just to piss me off. Aiesha is old enough to know better. I don't have enough energy to go behind her all day, and she don't have enough respect to take care of her things."

Samantha states clearly, "The only person my children have is a stressed-out, overworked, exhausted mother, and I deeply believe, no, I know, that's not enough for them, so they've just gone crazy."

AIESHA'S LIFE AT HOME

Slumped on the living room couch, Samantha grabbed Shaun's leaping body and forced him to stop his trampoline act and sit down. Holding a wooden spoon in her hand, Samantha yelled at Aiesha.

"Get off that computer, pick your stuff up right now, and get to your home-work. Don't make me have to tell you again."

Aiesha turned to her mom, rolled her eyes, and leisurely started to collect her belongings off the floor and furniture. "I'm hungry," Aiesha whined.

"Y'all get your homework out first, then you'll eat."

Samantha's refrigerator was almost empty. Her constant worry about feeding her children was a major reason Samantha hated it when they missed school or when school closed—she knew they would at least get a good breakfast and lunch at school.

Tamara already had her school binder out, which she had neatly organized by class subject. She sat down on the couch to show Samantha her vocabulary words. Meanwhile Aiesha dumped the entire contents of her backpack on the floor to search for her homework in the jumbled mess of papers. She found her English homework and carelessly started filling in the blanks with words. Samantha tenderly asked Aiesha what she had to do. Aiesha hesitantly handed her mother the paper. Samantha assumed that Aiesha was either not reading the sentences, or did not know what the words meant, because many of the answers were incorrect. Samantha began to explain to Aiesha that some of the words were wrong to help her get the right answer. Aiesha abruptly grabbed the paper back, shrugged off her mother's comments, and continued filling in the blanks, ignoring her mother's direction.

Hungry and distracted by Dylan riding his big wheel bike around the living room and deliberately over her school papers, Aiesha stopped all attempts to do her homework and jumped back on the computer. Samantha asked her if she had any other work due on Monday. Aiesha did not respond. "I'm talking to you Aiesha, or would you rather be talking to this spoon?!"

Aiesha turned with a sour look on her face and responded that she did not have anything else. She started to pick up the papers from her backpack to confirm this when her mother instructed her to start dinner.

"Why do I have to cook every day?!" Aiesha whined.

"Because that is your responsibility to the house. You should be thankful there is a little something to cook, so get your self at it and don't make me have to say anything else to you about it!"

Aiesha stomped up the stairs to the kitchen, while Samantha wondered why Aiesha had to be so stubborn and negative all the time.

Samantha believed the only way to get her daughter to act right was to beat her. Samantha explained that all children should be whipped if they act up, because "a smack makes kids behave better and learn how to treat adults with respect."

Aiesha agreed with her mom's opinion. She said, "I think I do need a whooping or at least a threat of one to help me behave. I guess I'm just bad like that. I know it's partly our fault that mom is so tired and stressed out all the time. We get on her nerves by fighting and picking on each other. I think it was better when mom was just home or in school, not trying to get a job all the time."

AIESHA'S LIFE AT SCHOOL

Up until this year, Aiesha did well in school. However, by the third grade, when Samantha's own stress level had peaked, Aiesha was failing writing and reading, and performing poorly in other subjects as well.

Ms. Park, Aiesha's teacher, was 25 years old, Polish American, and had been teaching the third grade for three years. She was single and did not have any children of her own. Ms. Park tried to talk to Samantha a few times about Aiesha's missing homework, declining grades, and lack of organization. She wanted to ensure an established routine of completing assignments in and outside of the classroom.

Samantha recalled these conversations with contempt.

"Aiesha's confused!? Unorganized? Okay, you try to be organized in a household with three other kids, little food, and a stressed-out mother that has no stable work or income. She may be a little confused. But at her age, she doesn't have enough to worry about to be that confused. School and helping me out at home, that's all she has to do!

"I told Ms. Park that Aiesha's problem is attitude. The girl needs to learn how to respect adults, or she is going to get herself in trouble. That is what the wooden spoon is for, to make the girl act right. I had to explain to Ms. Park that a lot of children don't have any respect for teachers, and if teachers could whack them across the butt, that would change.

"Now, I did make it very clear that a parent or a teacher shouldn't abuse or harm a child in any way, but a little red bottom won't hurt anything. I remember when I was a child, the teachers used to hit kids that got out of line with a wood paddle across the butt."

Samantha deeply believed that most teachers don't really care about poor black kids. They don't understand blacks, being poor, or the challenges of being a parent. Samantha explained, "Teachers learn all this stuff in school, but they don't have the common sense to figure out ways to help kids 'cause they don't know what the kids or their parents have to go through. And most of them are not even parents themselves.

"I don't think teachers really want these kids to succeed 'cause they don't put the effort in. I mean how you going to let a nine-year-old just sit in the class and not *make* her do something? I make her do something at home; they should make her do something at school. They're the teachers, they're the ones who are supposed to know how to do this."

Samantha believed that parent-teacher conferences were a waste of her time. School meetings were hard to schedule because of her work hours, then the teachers did not listen to her, or always asked about the father of the kids or other "influential adults in their lives." Samantha said, "When they ask that question, I just roll my eyes."

BACK TO SCHOOL ON MONDAY

As Samantha quickly walked her daughters to the bus stop on Monday morning, Aiesha turned to her mom with wide eyes and screamed, "Oh no, I forgot the slip!"

This was the first Samantha had heard about a slip for school. She said to Aiesha, "Well, you can't get it now because the bus will be coming."

"I have to go back to the house and get it so you can sign it. I promised to turn it in today!" Aiesha responded in a panic.

"Well, you can't miss this bus, because I can't drive you. I don't have enough money to get more gas," explained a frustrated Samantha.

Aiesha angrily screamed, "I'm getting it, whether you like it or not," and ran off toward the house. Tamara boarded the bus alone, while Samantha took off after Aiesha just in time to have the front door of the house slammed in her face. Seething with anger, Samantha opened the door, grabbed Aiesha and wrestled her down to the floor. Sitting her thin frame down on Aiesha's petite body, Samantha started to hit her with her bare, open hand. When Samantha finished, Aiesha laughed in her mother's face and ran out of the door screaming with devilish delight. Samantha sat dumbfounded, shocked at her daughter's disrespectful behavior.

Later that morning, Aiesha returned to the house on her best behavior. Without being asked, Aiesha cleaned the kitchen, started the laundry, and changed Dylan's diapers. Samantha decided to use the last of her gas to drive Aiesha to school so she could be there for lunch.

As Aiesha walked into the classroom, Ms. Park noticed that she looked tired, distracted, and a little unkempt. Aiesha calmly handed Ms. Park the unsigned permission slip, and took her seat at the back of the classroom. Ms. Park looked at the bare signature line and wondered what she should do next to get the slip signed.

DISCUSSION QUESTIONS

Major Issues

The purpose of this case is for educators to consider the stresses and challenges of single-parent families living in poverty and isolation. In particular, the case is designed to help educators understand the following:

- Economic and racial disparities and how they intersect with children's daily routines, family relationships, parent-teacher interactions, and children's school performance
- How to problem solve divergent beliefs and practices about child discipline
- Children's influence on parental well-being

Describing the Situation

- What challenges does Samantha face as a single parent? Consider challenges posed by each system described in Bronfenbrenner's ecological model.
- Describe how Samantha's children affect her well-being.
- Describe Ms. Park, Aiesha, and Samantha's different interpretations of Aiesha's school difficulties. To what do they attribute her poor school performance?

Exploring Contributing Factors

- What are Aiesha's strengths and struggles when it comes to self-regulation? In which situations and domains does she demonstrate good self-regulation? Poor self-regulation? How do her self-regulation skills affect her in school and at home?
- What strengths does Samantha bring to the family? How do the challenges she contends with affect her psychological resources, ability to manage her children's lives, and more specifically, her involvement in Aiesha's education?

Articulating Possible Next Steps

- How should Ms. Park proceed now that Aiesha has returned the unsigned permission slip?
- What resources could the school and/or Ms. Park provide Aiesha and her family to support her academic performance?
- What courses of action could Ms. Park undertake to increase the salience of shared goals between herself and Aiesha's mother?
- What are some strategies and/or resources Samantha could use to help Aiesha become more organized in doing her homework? How could Ms. Park support this effort?

Replaying the Case

- What, if anything, could Ms. Park have done differently in the story? For example, how else could she have conveyed her concern to Samantha about Aiesha's school work? Consider how Samantha's attitudes might shift as a result of different courses of action on the part of the teacher.
- Consider the incident when Aiesha forgets her permission slip. Explain how the family's economic and social resources contribute to her subsequent interactions with her mother. How might the outcome have been different had the family's finances or support networks been less precarious?

Looking at the Bigger Picture

- How can schools and educators best support families and children that are struggling with economic stress and a dearth of social support?
- What types of misinterpretations occur when educators and families discuss children's school problems? Can the cultural use and understanding of language contribute to the misinterpretations? For example, consider the vocabulary Samantha used to describe her practices about child discipline. How can different perspectives of the problem be addressed, minimized, or rectified?

RECOMMENDED READING

Bloom, L. R. (2001). "I'm poor, I'm single, I'm a mom, and I deserve respect": Advocating in schools as/with mothers in poverty. *Educational Studies, 32*(3), 300–316.

Chin, M. M., & Newman, K. S. (2002). *High stakes: Time poverty, testing, and the children of the working poor.* New York: Foundation for Child Development.

Weiss, H., Mayer, E., Kreider, H., Vaughan, P., Dearing, E., Hencke, R., et al. (2003). Making it work: Low-income working mothers' involvement in their children's education. *American Educational Research Journal, 40*(4), 879–901.

Case 12: Learning in the Shadow of Violence

Community, Culture, and Family Involvement

by Cynthia García Coll

Characters:

Thandi, fourth grader

Sak, Thandi's father

Maryna, Thandi's mother

Alice, Rosewood Elementary School principal

Seyha, community member

From the middle of 1975 until 1978, the Khmer Rouge regime controlled Cambodia. During this period, one to three million Cambodians out of a population of seven million died in torturous conditions and work camps. Many who escaped the modern-day holocaust fled to refugee camps and from there resettled in the United States to rebuild their lives.

PERSPECTIVES ON THANDI

Thandi stood silently behind her father as he looked over her math homework. He checked to make sure that she had completed the assignment, although he knew he was unable to help her answer the questions. Thandi, who was nine years old and in the fourth grade, enjoyed this time with her father immensely.

When he finished looking over her assignment, he turned to her and kissed her forehead. "I am very proud of you," he said in Khmer. "You will go to a great college when you get older."

She smiled shyly and walked to the kitchen to help her mother and sister–in-law put away the dishes. She loved her father very much and did not want to tell him that she was failing math. In fact, she was doing very poorly in school. On her last report card, she received three B's (art, gym, music), one C (English), and two D's (math and social studies). "There's no way I'll ever go to college," she thought.

As you read this case, consider applying the following theoretical lenses to your analysis:

- Ecocultural Understanding: How does violence as an ecocultural context affect Thandi's daily routine and well-being? How do various relationships shape Thandi's cultural knowledge and activities?
- Ethnic and Racial Minority Parenting: Where are there points of cultural mismatch in this case? How is Thandi's socialization constrained or facilitated by the school and community context?
- Community Support: What resources can Thandi and her parents draw from in the community to ensure her safety and support her school learning?

THANDI

The youngest daughter of Cambodian refugees, Thandi Hong lives in the small house her parents have owned in a small Northeastern U.S. city for the past 16 years. She lives with seven of her relatives: her mother and father, her second-oldest brother, his wife and five-year-old child, and her two older sisters, who are

17 and 13, respectively. Her oldest brother, Arun, 24, is currently serving time in jail for gang-related violence. Thandi Hong is one of the most acculturated members of her family. She doesn't speak Khmer well but is able to understand her parents' conversations. She watches some Asian films and eats Cambodian food.

"I am a girl because God made me one. I am Cambodian because my parents were born in Cambodia. I am Cambodian American because I was born here, go to school, talk English, and come back home and listen to Khmer."

Thandi sees many differences between her home and school life.

"When you come home from school, everything changes. You have to be really quiet and really sensitive to things, be a good girl. You can't go out or make phone calls. That's frustrating. Some kids think that their parents are low people because they don't speak English well, or they don't read and write. I think my parents aren't low at all. But they don't really know what it's like to be a kid in the United States either. They think I'm totally like an American."

Thandi sees the importance of working hard in school and going to college. However, her positive school attitude is not reflected in her performance.

"I really want to go to college when I get older. I'm trying really hard, and I'm really serious, but I'm scared because my grades aren't so good. The homework is getting really tough, and my dad tries to help, but I know it's hard for him too.

"I get a lot of help from other adults in my life. Like my teachers are all okay, my parents, and my older brothers and sisters are great too. But when things get really hard, I have to answer the questions myself. I really have to rely on myself when challenges come up. That's not just school work but everything really. Sometimes I'll go to my friends, but mostly, myself."

Thandi is popular among her friends and very in tune with the social groups that exist in her elementary school.

"Jenny is my best friend. She speaks Khmer better than I do, but we talk to each other in English mostly, unless we don't want someone to understand what we're saying. We're not in with the cool kids—like we don't wear short skirts and tank tops—but I think people want to be our friends. At lunchtime, Jenny and I usually sit with some other Cambodian girls and boys and whoever else wants to sit with us.

"Sometimes, though, I do get a little sad. I don't get to do a lot of stuff outside of school. My dad says it's too dangerous. He's sort of right. I'm scared that I might get shot at. Last year, in a drive-by shooting, one of the bullets hit our house. The gun was so loud. I'd never heard a gun go off before. My dad went to the door yelling. I was scared he might get shot too. Arun went to jail for being in a gang, and I'm scared that that sort of thing could happen to me. Sometimes at night I hear a loud noise, and I'm just so scared that something bad has happened, and I don't want to go back to sleep.

"But I also feel like I miss out on things. For example, a lot of my friends are in after school programs. At three o'clock, they go down to the school gym and spend a few hours doing homework and getting tutored and then get to play sports like basketball and softball. That sounds really neat, but when I asked my dad if I could do it, he just said I couldn't and that it was better I be safe. I know he's right. I would never want anything bad to happen to me or my family."

SAK, THANDI'S FATHER (TRANSLATED FROM KHMER)

"A few years ago, my oldest daughter came home after school one day very upset. She had seen the movie called *The Killing Fields* in her history class. She asked me if this is where we were from. I told her it was, and she began to cry. The teacher asked her to interview me. I think this was a very good idea.

"I told her what life was like when I was her age. The war started in 1968 in our village, so we started running from place to place when I was only nine years old. That is the age Thandi is now. In 1975, when the Khmer Rouge came to power, I was 16 years old. I lived almost three years in an internment camp in the fields harvesting rice. I worked from dawn to midnight with no food. There were times I was so hungry I thought I would die. After Pol Pot's decline I was able to escape to a refugee camp where I met Maryna, and we decided to get married. In 1982, we came to the United States as refugees with our two young children. I soon began working the night shift at a nearby factory, and Maryna cleaned houses during the day. One of the women she cleaned for suggested we invest and buy property, and I am proud that we have owned our own home for 16 years now. We have a good income. We make more than $60,000 a year, which is a lot more than most of the other Cambodian families in this area.

"I am proud of what we have accomplished here, but I miss Cambodia, our home. The Cambodian government is still unstable, but the killing has stopped. Once Thandi is fine on her own, I might return to Cambodia. I do not like the neighborhood we live in. The violence is too great. I have seen violence in my life. I have seen many people die. I still have nightmares about what I have seen. It makes me very sad that it continues here. Our house was shot at last year by a gang. I was very angry. I was a soldier in Cambodia, and I have killed many people, but I live in the United States under a law that I really respect. But I swear vengeance if any of my children are killed. I will not allow that to happen."

Sak was adamant his children not be exposed to violence the way he was. When his older son Arun was sent to jail, Sak began to learn more about his son's gang participation. He had been unaware that the changes that were occurring in his child such as his change in dress and selection of friends were signs of gang affiliation. He assumed all of these things were a normal part of being an American adolescent.

The father and son talked one afternoon at the prison. Arun explained how he always had the feeling of being an outsider, throughout his elementary and middle school career. He was always at the bottom of the class and had few friends. He couldn't negotiate his identity between the Cambodian and American cultures. He was confused. When he began his involvement with one of the Cambodian gangs in the area, he couldn't stand the violence, but loved the opportunities the group offered him. As Sak listened to his son, he was struck by the bitter irony of a history of violence perpetuating itself in the next generation. Sak vowed to protect his other children from the same fate by any means possible.

"I worry about the safety of my children and the potential for them to be in gangs. I make sure that none of the others turn out like Arun and go to jail. I tell Thandi all the time not to get involved in gangs. I try to control my family so they don't get in trouble. I have rules in our home regarding who Thandi and her sisters can be friends with and when and where they can spend their time. When they are not in school, I like for them to be at home where I can watch over them and nothing bad can happen.

"I have high expectations for Thandi. She is my youngest child, and I want her to finish college. The U.S. school system is the best. I want all my children to learn to follow the rules and study hard in school. Although I am not able to teach her that much math, I make sure I check her homework every night to ensure that she has finished the assignments. Her mother and I support Thandi with everything she needs."

MARYNA, THANDI'S MOTHER (TRANSLATED FROM KHMER)

"Sak and I have struggled to provide the best for our family here in the United States. I know he is still very much frightened and upset by the things that happened to us in Cambodia. It doesn't help that we then come here and are still surrounded by violence. We try to tell Thandi about her culture, but it is hard. I sometimes don't know how strong or good Thandi feels about being Cambodian. She acts between Cambodian and American. I worry that if she ever goes back to Cambodia, she will not be able to speak to her grandparents. I really believe in traditional Khmer values, but I don't see that Thandi has developed any of them.

"I like that she speaks good English. In America, education is the key. She will have a better life because of good schooling. I learned this from her older sisters going through the schools. Here in America, schools are different than they were when I was a girl in Cambodia.

"In Cambodia, we respect and regard the teacher just like second parents. 'Good kids' will prosper anywhere but it's the teachers who are best equipped to guide children's academic and moral development. In Cambodia, once children were registered in schools, everything was taken care of by the teachers. My own parents had no right to interfere in the system regarding my own education. To do so would have been inappropriate and disrespectful.

"I know it's different here, but I don't exactly know how the school works or how to teach my child. My English is not so good, and I work long hours so I don't really have time to go see any of the teachers. I think Thandi as she gets older is getting better at doing things on her own. She's so much more serious and motivated about her work, and I really support that."

THANDI'S COMMUNITY: ALICE, PRINCIPAL

"Here at Rosewood Elementary we have a really diverse student population, and we do a good job reaching out to the families. We have multicultural classroom climates and teachers with a variety of teaching styles. Our school has a range and distribution of ethnic and language groups, and our bulletin boards, curricula, and school rituals all reflect the multicultural content.

"At the beginning of the school year, we have the parents of children in the younger grades fill out a home survey of languages spoken in the home. We use this information to identify children for language testing and classroom placement. We've got a lot of Southeast Asian kids and they go into ESL classes while the Spanish-speaking children we place in the bilingual track. The survey also lets us know the school's ethnic profile; for example, how many English-speaking kids we have, how many Hispanic, how many Asian.

"The teachers and I do notice, however, that a lot of the parents in our school are hard to reach and don't know how to be involved in children's academic lives. Few of the parents come to P.T.A. meetings or parent-teacher conferences. Parents don't even really check their kids' homework and things like that. If they say they value education so much, and we have translators for them, why don't they get more involved with school and with their kids' education?

"Another thing we do well here is linking to the community. We have a number of extended-day programs in both the morning and evening. Many of our teachers are involved in the afterschool programs and help design the curricula. It's also contributed to a decrease in the community violence. There are a lot of problems with gangs in the nearby neighborhoods, but ever since our kids have had a safe place to hang out after school we see them channeling their energies constructively. We even have some school-based therapy groups for children who have witnessed violence. Children do better when they are keeping themselves busy with activities in their free time, such as sports, library, Boys and Girls clubs, and community centers and temples. Unfortunately, I don't see a lot of the Southeast Asians involved in these sort of things. It's mostly the Latino kids."

SEYHA, COMMUNITY MEMBER

"My parents relocated to the United States in 1980, I went to university and have been working at Global Society for eight years now. The mission of our organization is to create links between the community, the nearby Buddhist temple, the families, and the schools. The Buddhist temple is a site for local worship and observance of important holidays, especially the New Year. We also hold different programs such as weekend classes and instruction in Khmer language, writing, and culture there. In addition, we help promote community festivities adorned with traditional dance and music.

"A major problem for us, however, has been that there are no other community organizations. Other immigrant groups have newspapers, active organizations, and groups that help everyone in their community. For us, it has been difficult to reach parents and help them acculturate to U.S. systems because of the severe lack of local media. There are no local TV or radio stations or newspapers in Khmer: We communicate largely through word of mouth and flyers posted in Asian groceries and businesses.

"One of our biggest issues we've been trying to tackle is that our community and schools don't seem to understand each other. I see that teachers in our schools use the term 'Southeast Asian' to refer to students' ethnicity but they do not know who is Cambodian, Hmong, Vietnamese, or Laotian, which is critical information for sending translated notices home to parents. Part of my job is to help translate school information to Khmer. Yet, even when notices do get translated, a problem that remains is that many Cambodian parents don't read—even in their own language. The Khmer Rouge killed off much of the educated class in Cambodia, so a lot of the immigrants who survived and made it to the United States were immigrants from the highlands with agricultural backgrounds and little formal education.

"Even when this is not the case, parents often throw out anything that comes in writing because in Cambodia when you signed papers, people would take away your house and land. I see in parents the burden of recent memories of life under Pol Pot when meetings in schools were places of punishment and educated people were killed. Schools were used for jails, torture, and mass killings. In turn, families don't want to go to schools. The trauma of that experience has led to a serious lack of trust in people and institutions. Local adults often have physical and emotional scars such as depression, post-traumatic stress syndrome, and mutual suspicion, which makes it difficult for some parents to become more engaged in community activities and their children's schooling.

"We have plans next summer to develop a community program in conjunction with the school that weaves together Cambodian, Vietnamese, Hmong, and Laotian families and children in an eight-week summer academy. I hope that this program might become a support for families in our community, but I'm so worried that we won't get anyone to participate in it."

DISCUSSION QUESTIONS

Major Issues

The purpose of this case is to consider the role of community and cultural contexts in children's school experiences. The case is designed to help educators understand the following:

- The impact of the community context on student academic socialization and performance.
- The role of community and community-based organizations, such as ethnic organizations and afterschool programs, in linking home and school.
- How schools can better communicate with families and understand families' cultural and immigration experiences.

Describing the Situation

- What is the central dilemma in this case?
- Describe the community in which Thandi lives and goes to school.
- What does Alice understand about the cultural diversity of her school and community? How does she come to understand it?
- How has Thandi's family been successful since their immigration to the United States?
- How has Seyha been successful in her outreach efforts? What are some problems she faces?

Exploring Contributing Factors

- How does the violence in Thandi's community affect her life? Her academic and social experiences in school?
- In what ways does community violence influence Sak's parenting and educational involvement practices?
- How does community violence intersect with Sak and Maryna's experiences as Cambodian refugees?
- Who does Thandi rely on when challenges come up? Why?
- What are Maryna's beliefs about the role of families in the school? How does this compare and contrast with the ideas Alice has?
- How does Alice make sense of the lack of family participation in activities at her school?

Articulating Possible Next Steps

- How can school personnel connect with Thandi, her family, and her community to improve her school performance?
- How can the school leverage existing community resources?
- Are there things the school should and can do to decrease the level of violence in the community?

Replaying the Case

- What types of community-bridging strategies are available to Thandi's parents? What would enable Thandi to use them? Consider what the principal and Global Society might do differently.
- What might any of the key players in the case have done to address issues of cultural mismatch, and how might this have altered Thandi's situation?
- In your home community, what is the largest immigrant population? How much do you know about them? Who would you like to talk with to learn more about them?

Looking at the Bigger Picture

- What roles might ethnic identity and family cultural beliefs play in shaping children's relationships with their parents, their school, and their friends?
- How might gang violence influence the executive functioning role of families?
- How do parents' cultural beliefs and life experiences shape their relationships with schools?

RECOMMENDED READING

Garbarino, J., Kostelny, K., & Barry, F. (1997). Value transmission in an ecological context: The high-risk neighborhood. In J. E. Grusec & L. Kuczynski (Eds.),

Parenting and children's internalization of values: A handbook of contemporary theory (pp. 307–332). New York: Wiley.

Te, B., Cordova, J. M., Walker-Moffat, W., & First, J. (1997). *Unfamiliar partners: Asian parents and U.S. public schools.* Boston: National Coalition of Advocates for Students.

Notes

1. An earlier version of this case was originally published on the Family Involvement Network of Educators, Harvard Family Research Project, Web site: http://www.gse.harvard.edu/hfrp/projects/fine/resources/teaching-case/words.html

2. We would like to thank Deborah Johnson for contributing to an earlier version of these discussion questions.

References for Introduction

Bronfenbrenner, U. (1989). Ecological systems theory. In R. Vasta (Ed.), *Six theories of child development: Revised formulations and current issues* (pp. 185–246). Greenwich, CT: JAI Press.

Goodenough, W. H. (2003). In pursuit of culture. *Annual Review of Anthropology, 32,* 1–12.

Keesing, R. M. (1974). Theories of culture. *Annual Reviews,* 73–97.

Peterson, R. A. (1979). Revitalizing the culture concept. *Annual Reviews,* 137–165.

Phinney, J. S. (1996). When we talk about American ethnic groups, what do we mean? *American Psychologist, 51*(9), 918–927.

References for Weisner

Bornstein, M. H., Davidson, L., Keyes, C. L. M., & Moore, K. (Eds.). (1993). *Well-being: Positive development across the life course.* Mahwah, NJ: Erlbaum.

D'Andrade, R. (1992). Schemas and motivation. In R. D'Andrade & C. Strauss (Eds.), *Human motives and cultural models* (pp. 23–45). New York: Cambridge University Press.

Gallimore, R. G. (1996). Classrooms are just another cultural activity. In D. L. Speece & B. K. Keogh (Eds.), *Research on classroom ecologies: Implications for inclusion of children with learning disabilities* (pp. 229–250). Mahwah, NJ: Erlbaum.

Nuckolls, C. (Ed.). (1993). *Siblings in South Asia: Brothers and sisters in cultural context.* New York: Guilford Press.

Shore, B. (1996). *Culture in mind: Cognition, culture and the problem of meaning.* New York: Oxford University Press.

Tharp, R. G., & Gallimore, R. (1988). *Rousing minds to life: Teaching, learning and schooling in social context.* Cambridge, UK: Cambridge University Press.

Weisner, T. S. (1984). A cross-cultural perspective: Ecocultural niches of middle childhood. In A. Collins (Ed.), *The elementary school years: Understanding development during middle childhood* (pp. 335–369). Washington, DC: National Academy Press.

Weisner, T. S. (1996). The five to seven transition as an ecocultural project. In A. J. Sameroff & M. M. Haith (Eds.), *The five to seven year shift: The age of reason and responsibility* (pp. 295–326). Chicago: University of Chicago Press.

Weisner, T. S. (1998). Human development, child well-being, and the cultural project of development. In D. Sharma & K. Fischer (Eds.), *New directions for child and adolescent development: No. 81. Socioemotional development across cultures* (pp. 69–85). San Francisco: Jossey-Bass.

Weisner, T. S. (2002). Ecocultural understanding of children's developmental pathways. *Human Development, 45*(4), 275–281.

Weisner, T. S. (Ed.). (2005). *Discovering successful pathways in children's development: New methods in the study of childhood and family life.* Chicago: University of Chicago Press.

References for García Coll and Chatman

Ascher, C. (1988). Improving the school-home connection for poor and minority urban students. *Urban Review 20*(2), 109–123.

Boykin, A. W., & Toms, F. D. (1985). Black child socialization: A conceptual framework. In H. P. McAdoo & J. L. McAdoo (Eds.), *Black children.* Beverly Hills, CA: Sage.

Bronfenbrenner, U. (1989). Ecological systems theory. In R. Vasta (Ed.), *Six theories of child development: Revised formulations and current issues* (pp. 185–246). Greenwich, CT: JAI Press.

Collignon, F. F., Men, M., & Tan, S. (2001). Finding ways in: Community-based perspectives on Southeast Asian family involvement with schools in a New England state. *Journal of Education for Students Placed at Risk, 6*(1–2), 27–44.

Cooper, C. R., Dominguez, E., & Rosas, S. (in press). Soledad's dream: How immigrant children bridge their multiple worlds and build pathways to college. In C. R. Cooper, C. García Coll, W. T. Bartko, H. M. Davis, & C. M. Chatman (Eds.), *Developmental pathways through middle childhood: Rethinking contexts and diversity as resource.* (pp. 235–260). Mahwah, NJ: Erlbaum.

Delgado-Gaitan, C. (1992). School matters in the Mexican-American home: Socializing children to education. *American Educational Research Journal, 29*(3), 495–513.

García Coll, C. T., Akiba, D., Palacios, N., Bailey, B., Silver, R., DiMartino, L. et al. (2002). Parental involvement in children's education: Lessons from three immigrant groups. *Parenting: Science and Practice, 2*(3), 303–324.

García Coll, C. T., Lamberty, G., Jenkins, G., McAdoo, H. P., Crnic, K., Wasik, B. H. et al. (1996). An integrative model for the study of developmental competencies in minority children. *Child Development, 67*(5), 1891–1914.

García Coll, C. T., & Magnuson, K. (2000). Cultural differences as sources of developmental vulnerabilities and resources: A view from developmental research. In S. J. Meisels & J. P. Shonkoff (Eds.), *Handbook of Early Childhood Intervention* (pp. 94–111). Cambridge, UK: Cambridge University Press.

García Coll, C. T., Meyer, E. C., & Brillon, L. (1995). Ethnic and minority parenting. In M. H. Bornstein (Ed.), *Handbook of parenting* (pp. 189–209). Mahwah, NJ: Erlbaum.

Goodenough, W. H. (2003). In pursuit of culture. *Annual Review of Anthropology, 32,* 1–12.

Griffith, J. (1998). The relation of school structure and social environment to parent involvement in elementary schools. *The Elementary School Journal, 99*(1), 53–80.

Hara, S. R., & Burke, D. J. (1998). Parent involvement: The key to improved student achievement. *School Community Journal, 8*(2), 9–19.

Harrison, A. O., Wilson, M. N., Pine, C. J., Chan, S. Q., & Buriel, R. (1990). Family ecologies of ethnic minority children. *Child Development, 61,* 347–362.

Huss-Keeler, R. L. (1997). Teacher perception of ethnic and linguistic minority parental involvement and its relationships to children's language and literacy learning: A case study. *Teaching and Teacher Education, 13*(2), 171–182.

Keesing, R. M. (1974). Theories of culture. *Annual Reviews,* 73–97.

LaFramboise, T., Coleman, H. L. K., & Gerton, J. (1993). Psychological impact of biculturalism: Evidence and theory. *Psychological Bulletin, 114*(3), 395–412.

Lawrence-Lightfoot, S. (1978). *Worlds apart: Relationships between families and schools.* New York: Basic Books.

Lopez, L. C., Sanchez, V. V., & Hamilton, M. (2000). Immigrant and native-born Mexican-American parents' involvement in a public school: A preliminary study. *Psychological Reports, 86,* 521–525.

McLoyd, V. C. (1990). The impact of economic hardship on black families and children: Psychological distress, parenting, and socio-emotional development. *Child Development, 61,* 311–346.

Moll, L. C., & Greenberg, J. B. (1992). Creating zones of possibilities: Combining social contexts for instruction. In L. C. Moll (Ed.), *Vygotsky and education: Instructional implications and applications of sociohistorical psychology* (pp. 319–348). New York: Cambridge University Press.

Ogbu, J. (1981). Origins of human competence: A cultural-ecological perspective. *Child Development, 52*(2), 413–429.

Peterson, R. A. (1979). Revitalizing the culture concept. *Annual Reviews, 5,* 137–165.

Phinney, J. S. (1996). When we talk about American ethnic groups, what do we mean? *American Psychologist, 51*(9), 918–927.

Tatum, B. D. (1997). *Why are all the black kids sitting together in the cafeteria? And other conversations about race: A psychologist explains the development of racial identity.* New York: Basic Books.

Index

About the Editors

Heather B. Weiss is founder/director of Harvard Family Research Project (HFRP; www.hfrp.org) and a senior research associate/instructor at the Harvard Graduate School of Education. Founded in 1983, HFRP's mission is to improve practice, intervention and policy supporting children's successful development from birth to adulthood. Toward this mission, Dr. Weiss and colleagues conduct, synthesize, and disseminate research and evaluation information; develop professional and organizational learning tools; support evaluation, continuous improvement and accountability; and spark innovation. Key activities include publication of *The Evaluation Exchange*, a quarterly review of recent advances in evaluation and practice in child and family policy; establishment of a national database of out-of-school time and youth program evaluations to inform policy and practice; creation of the national Family Involvement Network of Educators (FINE), consisting of over 4,000 professionals to whom HFRP provides a breadth of informational services; and development of the Home Visit Forum, a group of national home visit programs working together in their utilization of evaluation to improve services.

Dr. Weiss writes and speaks about child and family policy and programs, serves on advisory boards for several public and private organizations, and provides consultation on strategic grant-making and evaluation to numerous foundations. Publications include articles and papers on family involvement in children's development, measuring and encouraging youth participation in after-school and youth programs, and the use of data and evaluation in democracies. She received her Ed.D. in education and social policy from Harvard University.

Holly Kreider is a project manager and research associate at Harvard Family Research Project. Dr. Kreider leads family involvement research on the School Transition Study, a longitudinal, mixed-method study of low-income children's successful development through middle childhood. She also co-founded the Family Involvement Network of Educators (FINE), which makes research findings on family-school-community partnerships accessible and applicable to education professionals nationwide. Her research interests include the processes and outcomes of family involvement for the development of children and youth, particularly underserved low-income children; qualitative and mixed methodologies in social science research; and innovative pedagogy in higher education, including the case method. She also serves as an instructor at the Harvard Graduate School of Education, co-teaching a module on Family-School Partnerships. Prior to joining HFRP, she worked as an evaluation consultant to public schools and residential treatment facilities and as a counselor with children, youth and families. Publications include *New Skills for New Schools: Preparing teachers in family involvement* and *Making it work: Low-income working mothers' involvement in their children's education.* Dr. Kreider received her Ed.D. in Human Development and Psychology from Harvard University.

M. Elena Lopez serves on the senior management team of the Harvard Family Research Project. Her research interests focus on the relationships of families, schools and communities in children's education. She has also evaluated public and philanthropic initiatives to improve the well-being of children and families. As a co-founder of the Family Involvement Network of Educators, Dr. Lopez seeks to improve the connections between research and practice and to advance educator preparation in family involvement in education. Her other professional experiences include lecturing at the Harvard Graduate School of Education, providing technical assistance on capacity building for family involvement, and serving on national advisory and governing boards. Publications include *Paths to School Readiness, Early Childhood Reform in Seven Communities,* and *Family Centered Child Care.* She received her Ph.D. in Anthropology from Harvard University.

Celina M. Chatman is associate director for the Center for Human Potential and Public Policy (CHPPP), a research center at the University of Chicago's Harris Graduate School of Public Policy Studies. Under the direction of Harris School Professor and developmental psychologist C. Cybele Raver, CHPPP endeavors to both conduct and bring the highest quality research to bear on local and national policy affecting children, youth and families. Before joining CHPPP, Dr. Chatman was a Senior Research Associate at the University of Michigan's Gender and Achievement Research Program, where she conducted quantitative and qualitative analyses of data on identity and achievement motivation among adolescents, with emphasis on race and ethnicity. She also served as science writer for the MacArthur Foundation's research Network on Successful Pathways through Middle Childhood. She received her Ph.D. in social psychology from Rutgers University.

About the Contributors

Margarita Azmitia is a professor of psychology at the University of California at Santa Cruz. She researches the role of family, peers, and schools in how ethnically and socio-economically diverse adolescents manage school and life transitions.

Phyllis C. Blumenfeld is a professor of education at The University of Michigan. She teaches in the Combined Program in Education and Psychology. Her research focuses on how teacher behavior and classroom tasks influence student motivation.

Margaret Caspe is a consultant to the Harvard Family Research Project at the Harvard Graduate School of Education. She investigates relationships between families and schools and connections to children's language and literacy development.

Gabriela Chavira is an assistant professor of psychology at California State University Northridge. She conducts research on the role of family involvement in the academic achievement and identity development of low-income ethnic minority youth.

Pamela E. Davis-Kean is an assistant research scientist at the University of Michigan. Her research focuses on the impact of parents' education attainment on children and the role that families, schools, and significant figures play in the development of children.

Cynthia García Coll is the Charles Pitts Robinson and John Palmer Barstow Professor of Education, Psychology and Pediatrics at Brown University. Her work focuses on the sociocultural and biological influences on child development with particular emphasis on at-risk and minority populations.

Catherine Cooper is a professor of psychology and education at University of California, Santa Cruz. She researches how youth forge their personal identities by coordinating cultural and family traditions with worlds of schools, peers, and communities. She builds university-community partnerships to strengthen diversity from preschool through college.

Elizabeth Domínguez is director of the Cabrillo Advancement Program of Cabrillo Community College in Aptos, California. The program works with families, schools, and youth to provide academic support and scholarship to increase the numbers of low-income students in local schools who graduate and attend college.

Jacquelynne S. Eccles is the Wilbert McKeachie Collegiate Professor of Psychology at the University of Michigan. Her research focuses on the role schools, families, neighborhoods, and ethnicity play in the ontogeny of belief and motivational systems in children.

Ann Barger Hannum was an instructor and administrator at the University of Arizona for many years and then spent over 10 years at Harvard in academic project management and communications. She is now a writer and consultant to nonprofit organizations in Boston.

Penny Hauser-Cram is a professor of Applied Developmental Psychology at the Lynch School of Education at Boston College. She conducts longitudinal research on children with disabilities and children living in poverty. Her research focuses on how the family and educational systems support children's development and learning.

Erica Holt earned a master's degree in developmental psychology from the University of California at Santa Cruz and is an adjunct instructor at Germanna Community College in Fredericksburg, Virginia.

Eboni C. Howard is a senior researcher/research associate at Chapin Hall Center for Children and an Instructor at the School of Social Service Administration at the University of Chicago. Her work includes applied and evaluative research that considers the influence of social programs, poverty, ethnicity, and social support on the well-being of families and children.

Marty Wyngaarden Krauss is Provost and Senior Vice President for Academic Affairs at Brandeis University. Her research focuses on the social and familial consequences of developmental disabilities.

Ellen Mayer is a research associate at the Harvard Family Research Project at the Harvard Graduate School of Education. She conducts research in family educational involvement and develops research-based practitioner tools, including children's storybooks with family involvement content.

Dolores Mena is a doctoral student in developmental psychology at the University of California, Santa Cruz. Her research focuses on low-income and ethnic minority students' educational and career pathways and parental educational involvement practices.

Jennifer Romich is an assistant professor in the School of Social Work at the University of Washington. Her research focuses on resources and families, with an emphasis on the policies affecting low-income working families.

Aline Sayer is an associate professor of Psychology at the University of Massachusetts at Amherst. She is a quantitative social scientist with particular interests in multilevel models, structural equation models, and longitudinal data analysis.

Jack P. Shonkoff is Dean of The Heller School for Social Policy and Management, and Samuel F. and Rose B. Gingold Professor of Human Development and Social Policy at Brandeis University. He currently chairs the National Scientific Council on the Developing Child, which is designed to address the gaps among early childhood science, policy, and practice.

Jennifer Simmelink holds a master's degree in social work and is a research assistant with Jennifer Romich in the School of Social Work at the University of Washington. She is also a Chemical Dependency Counselor at Evergreen Treatment Services in Seattle.

Deborah J. Stipek is the James Quillen Dean and Professor of Education at Stanford University. Her scholarship concerns instructional effects on children's achievement motivation, early childhood education, elementary education and school reform.

Barrie Thorne is a professor of sociology and women's studies at the University of California, Berkeley. She is the author of *Gender Play: Girls and Boys in School* (1993) and is currently writing an ethnography about kids growing up in a mixed-income, ethnically diverse area of California.

Margaret (Peggy) Vaughan is a doctoral candidate in the Eliot-Pearson Department of Child Development at Tufts University. Her research interests include early intervention, childhood disability, and foster care.

Carole Upshur is a professor in the Department of Family Medicine and Community Health at University of Massachusetts Medical School. She is a licensed psychologist and conducts research in the areas of adult and child development and disability, health access and disparities, and integration of primary care and behavioral health.

Marji Erickson Warfield is a scientist and interim director of the Starr Center for Mental Retardation in the Heller School for Social Policy and Management at Brandeis University. She conducts longitudinal research on children with disabilities and their families and evaluates early intervention and support programs.

Thomas S. Weisner is a professor of anthropology in the Department of Psychiatry (Neuropsychiatric Institute, Center for Culture and Health), and the Department of Anthropology, at UCLA. His research is in culture and human development, family adaptation and children at risk.